Sport and Exercise Psychology

Active Learning in Sport – titles in the series

Coaching Science	ISBN 978 1 84445 165 4
Critical Thinking for Sports Students	ISBN 978 1 84445 457 0
Personal Training	ISBN 978 1 84445 163 0
Research Methods in Sport	ISBN 978 1 84445 261 3
Sport and Exercise Science	ISBN 978 1 84445 187 6
Sport in the UK	ISBN 978 1 84445 383 2
Sport Management	ISBN 978 1 84445 263 7
Sport Marketing	ISBN 978 0 85725 090 2
Sport Sociology (second edition)	ISBN 978 1 84445 464 8
Sport Studies	ISBN 978 1 84445 186 9

To order, please contact our distributor: BEBC Distribution, Albion Close, Parkstone, Poole, BH 12 3LL. Telephone: 0845 230 9000, email: learningmatters@bebc.co.uk. You can find more information on each of these titles and our other learning resources at www.learningmatters.co.uk.

Sport and Exercise Psychology

Joanne Thatcher, Melissa Day and
Rachel Rahman

LearningMatters

First published in 2011 by Learning Matters Ltd

British Library Cataloguing in Publication Data
A CIP record for this book is available from the British Library
ISBN: 9781844458394
This book is also available in the following ebook formats:
Adobe ebook ISBN: 9781844458417
EPUB ebook ISBN: 9781844458400
Kindle ebook ISBN: 9780857250452

Cover design by Toucan Design
Text design by Toucan Design
Project Management by Swales & Willis Ltd, Exeter, Devon
Typeset in Garamond Premier Pro by Swales & Willis Ltd, Exeter, Devon
Printed and bound in Great Britain by Short Run Press Ltd, Exeter, Devon
Learning Matters Ltd
20 Cathedral Yard
Exeter
EX1 1HB
Tel: 01392 215560
E-mail: info@learningmatters.co.uk
www.learningmatters.co.uk

FSC
www.fsc.org
MIX
Paper from
responsible sources
FSC® C014540

Contents

Chapter 1
Introduction to sport and exercise psychology

Learning Objectives

This chapter is designed to help you be able to:

1. understand the key aims and concerns of sport and exercise psychology;
2. be aware of elements of this book that are designed to help you learn about and understand the topics we discuss;
3. start to consider the role of sport and exercise psychology in tackling real-life problems and challenges.

Case Study 1.1
Hena

Hena has recently visited her doctor because she has been feeling low in mood and lacking in energy. Her doctor is concerned that she may have mild clinical depression. However, this is not the doctor's only concern. Hena does no exercise and is now at a weight where she is classed as obese. As a result of her weight, Hena has difficulty with some of her daily tasks like walking home with shopping bags. Her blood pressure is 150 mmHg over 100 mmHg (normal blood pressure is 120 mmHg over 80 mmHg), meaning that she is classed as hypertensive.

Case Study 1.2
Sam

Sam is a 14-year-old gymnast who trains five times a week for 2–3 hours each session with his personal coach. Sam's coach thinks that he has the potential to become an elite athlete and this is Sam's ambition. His parents are very supportive of his gymnastics, paying for kit and competition fees, driving him to and from training and competitions and supporting him when he's competing. They and his coach are also keen to ensure that his school work doesn't suffer as he is doing well at school. They also want him to be able to cope with the increasing competition pressure and training demands as he progresses towards the elite level. Other than the support they give him at present they are unsure how best to help him to achieve his ambitions and think that a sport psychologist might be able to help.

Sport and exercise psychology: theory, research and application

These case studies are fictitious but reflect real-life 'problems' that sport and exercise psychologists attempt to help the individual solve, which they do so using both theory and research. Many theories have been developed to explain, understand and change human behaviour and to understand how this behaviour is influenced by a range of different factors, including our thoughts and feelings, social environment, past experiences and personal characteristics. Research tests the proposals of these theories to determine whether or not they can be practically applied, such as in the case studies described above. Sport and exercise psychology research also examines if practical interventions derived from a theory (e.g. a strategy to increase motivation to exercise in Hena's case or to help cope with competition stressors in Sam's case) are effective.

It may not surprise you, given the very dynamic and physical contexts to which sport and exercise psychology is applied, that this is very much an applied field of study. Thus a priority of researchers and academics in this area is to seek to identify how theories that are developed and research findings that are obtained can be applied practically within sport and exercise settings. Throughout this book we consider the key theories used by sport and exercise psychologists to understand, explain, predict and change behaviour and the research that has investigated these theories. In particular, we aim to highlight the practical application of this theoretical and empirical knowledge to help solve problems, such as those presented by our opening case studies.

These case studies illustrate both the similarities and differences between sport psychology and exercise psychology. Try to identify what distinguishes these case studies from each other and their shared commonalities. You may identify that there are more similarities than differences between sport psychology and exercise psychology. Let us first consider their key difference.

Exercise psychology

Exercise psychology focuses on exercise participation and exercise-related behaviours including physical activity, inactivity and sedentary behaviour. This branch of psychology is concerned with:

- understanding and optimising the psychological outcomes and effects of exercise-related behaviours;
- optimising psychological aspects of exercise and physical activity participation;
- understanding the links between exercise and physical activity and mental health and wellbeing;
- improving exercise and physical activity levels in the general population.

Sport psychology

Sport psychology focuses on sport participation and performance at all levels of competition, from recreational to elite level. This branch of psychology is concerned with:

- understanding and optimising the psychological outcomes and effects of sports participation and performance;

- optimising psychological aspects of training and competing in sport;
- understanding the links between psychological characteristics, the use of psychological skills and sports performance;
- improving competitive sports performance.

Although sport psychology and exercise psychology each have a distinct focus, there is clearly a lot of overlap between the two which explains why there are more similarities than differences between them. Some of the key similarities that you may have identified are that both sport psychology and exercise psychology are concerned with:

- understanding people, how they feel, think and behave;
- helping people to solve problems and optimise their experience by changing unhelpful thoughts, feelings and behaviours.

As you will hopefully recognise as you read through the different chapters in our book, while some theories apply specifically to either sport or exercise psychology, many have common application across these two contexts. As you will also see, common methods are used to investigate different psychological phenomena in sport and exercise contexts. These include experimental studies, questionnaire-based cross-sectional research, intervention studies in real life contexts, case studies and qualitative interview studies. Throughout the chapters of the book we explain and provide examples of these different approaches to research to help you see how these different methods contribute to increasing our understanding of the psychological aspects of sport and exercise involvement.

The structure of this book

Our book is divided into two sections: Part 1, Exercise psychology, focuses on the key topics of interest to exercise psychologists and Part 2, Sport psychology, on those of most interest to sport psychologists. In the first section we adopt a process approach to understanding the psychology of exercise behaviour, starting with an examination of the common barriers to physical activity and the effects of physical inactivity on the individual's physical and mental health. Chapter 3 focuses on a key factor in physical activity participation, the role of the self. We consider its role as a factor that might influence physical activity behaviour and be influenced by this behaviour. We then discuss how we can understand physical activity and exercise behaviour using a number of key models and theories. Following this, we examine how these different models and theories might be applied to increase and maintain levels of physical activity and exercise participation. This leads us on to an exploration of the psychological outcomes of exercise participation, both positive and negative, and in clinical and non-clinical populations.

In Part 2 we adopt a similar process perspective to our discussion of sport psychology topics, beginning with an examination of the individual and social factors that might influence the athlete's experience and quality of training for competition. We then consider the competitive environment, examining how and why some athletes cope with the pressures and challenges of sporting competition while others do not. Following this, we consider some of the specific challenges that athletes might face during different transitions that occur as a competitive athlete. These include both transitions that are common to all athletes, such as retirement from competitive sport, and those experienced by some, but not necessarily all, athletes, such as injury. Athletes who cope with competitive challenge, pressure and transitions may go on to achieve excellence in their sport and in Chapter 12 we discuss the characteristics of peak performance and sporting excellence including associated constructs such as mental toughness and flow. In the final chapter in this section of the book, we look at key psychological strategies, focusing specifically on imagery and goal setting, which are techniques that athletes could use to enhance the psychological aspects of their training and competition in an attempt to achieve their peak performance.

Throughout these chapters we return to the case studies with which we opened this chapter and employ the different theories and research findings discussed throughout the book to offer solutions to the problems they present. Our aim in doing so is to emphasise the practical value of sport and exercise psychology knowledge.

It is increasingly apparent that sport and exercise psychology has a key role to play in helping to tackle a number of real life problems and challenges in contemporary society. Although we discuss examples of these throughout our book it is clearly not possible to consider all the potential problems that sport and exercise psychologists could help to address. Throughout the book, however, we offer opportunities for your own critical analysis of and engagement with the topics we discuss through learning activities, reflection points and ideas for further reading. In doing this we hope to offer a starting point for you to be able to consider how problems and challenges in society could be addressed by sport and exercise psychologists. Some of the real life problems we have encountered and attempted to address in our work include:

- What are the barriers to walking in the countryside and how can we help to overcome these?
- How can we help prepare a team for international competition?
- How can we ensure that an athlete is psychologically prepared for the pressures of major competition?
- How can we help a previously injured athlete to overcome their fears of re-injury when returning to sport?
- How can we effectively encourage adults at risk of coronary heart disease to start and adhere to a GP referral exercise programme?

Return to these examples as you read through the different chapters of the book and think about how you might start to address these problems and challenges.

Sport and exercise psychology clearly has a lot to offer society in helping to overcome some of the health problems we currently face, such as rising levels of obesity in the young, and in helping to optimise performance outcomes in one of the world's biggest international businesses: competitive sport. Although elements of sport and exercise psychology stem as far back as the ancient Greek civilisation, Lavallee and his colleagues (2004) note that it is only in the previous century that this has become a formal area of independent academic study. Those of you who are interested in finding out more about the history of the discipline and its development are directed to the further reading listed at the end of this chapter.

All that remains for us to add here is that we hope we have managed to achieve our aims when we set out to write this book. These were to present exercise and sport psychology in an engaging manner which illustrates the practical application of this field and one which encourages our readers to think critically about the theories and research we discuss. If we have achieved these aims then hopefully you will find our book enjoyable and informative.

Further Reading

Lavallee, D, Kremer, J, Moran, AP and Williams, M (2004) Introduction, in *Sport Psychology: Contemporary themes.* Basingstoke: Palgrave Macmillan, pp. 1–17.

We recommend this chapter by Lavallee and his colleagues for its informative and engaging account of how sport and exercise psychology emerged as a discipline, including its development in different countries across the globe.

Part One
Exercise psychology

Chapter 2
Physical inactivity:
effects and determinants

Learning Objectives

This chapter is designed to help you be able to:

1. understand research which suggests that inactivity can contribute to ill-health in the form of chronic disease and its risk factors: anxiety, depression and poor quality of life;
2. critically evaluate the use of cross-sectional research conducted to examine the relationship between physical inactivity and ill-health;
3. identify factors which are likely to predispose individuals to inactivity;
4. consider how this information can be used to implement interventions to increase physical activity levels.

Introduction

For many of us, sport and exercise are sources of fun and enjoyment. However, for a number of people they are far less appealing pastimes. People in developed western countries have become increasingly sedentary in all aspects of daily life, including leisure activities, travel to and from work and during the working day (National Audit Office, 2001). In the UK, only 24 per cent of adults take sufficient exercise to maintain their health (Department of Culture Media and Sport, 2010). This is of concern, as chronic low activity levels are not compatible with good health and commonly result in disease and decreased physical function. The aim of this chapter is to discuss the evidence for the protective effects of physical activity on health and the physiological and psychological effects of inactivity. The second part of this chapter explores the individual, social and cognitive determinants of inactivity. Understanding why people are inactive may enable appropriate interventions to be implemented in order to increase the nation's activity levels and help prevent diseases related to inactivity.

Effects of physical activity on physical and mental health

Learning Activity 2.1

You may recall Hena's case study from the introduction; if not, this is summarised below. Write down which of Hena's symptoms might result from her inactivity and what short- and long-term effects this might have on her physical and mental health. Reflect on your answers as you read through the following sections.

Case Study 2.1
Hena

We first met Hena in Chapter 1. There we learnt that she had recently visited her doctor because she had been feeling low in mood and lacking in energy. Her doctor was concerned that she may have mild clinical depression but he was also concerned about her lack of exercise and her resulting weight and hypertension. As a result of her weight, Hena had difficulty with some of her daily tasks, such as walking home with shopping bags.

Chronic disease, all-cause mortality and physical activity

Evidence suggests that physical activity can protect against numerous chronic diseases, such as coronary heart disease (Lee *et al.*, 2001), diabetes (Maiorana *et al.*, 2001) and breast and colon cancer (Wells, 1999). However, a balanced diet combined with appropriate levels of physical activity is associated with substantial increases in life expectancy (Department of Culture Media and Sport, 2002).

Inactivity, smoking, hypertension and hyperlipidaemia (high levels of cholesterol and fat) now form the four highest risk factors for coronary heart disease, which is the leading cause of death in Europe (European Food Information Council, 2003). Lee and Skerrett (2001) reviewed 44 prospective studies (see Box 2.1) and identified a consistent dose–response relationship (as the amount increases so does the corresponding outcome) between physical activity and/or aerobic fitness and premature mortality (i.e. as the amount of physical activity or fitness increased the risk of premature death decreased). This dose–response relationship provides strong evidence that physical activity protects against the diseases contributing towards premature death.

Box 2.1 Definition: Prospective study

A prospective study is one that is designed to determine whether there is a relationship between different variables. The study follows individuals over time to see what outcomes occur. In this example, the prospective study identified individuals with varying activity levels and followed them over time to see whether they developed any diseases. It is then possible to explore whether there is a relationship between activity levels and the development of certain diseases.

The uptake of activity at a young age also appears to have a protective effect against ill-health in later life. Linstead *et al.* (1991) asked 9484 men to complete a lifestyle questionnaire and revisited the sample over a period of 26 years to examine disease-specific and all-cause mortality (death from any cause). Moderate activity at baseline was associated with a protective effect on cardiovascular and all-cause mortality rates at follow-up with the effects of activity in earlier life persisting into the individuals' 70s and 80s. However, it appears that physical activity need not necessarily be adopted at a young age to protect against disease later in life. Evidence indicates that taking up physical activity in later life can also be protective. Paffenbarger *et al.* (1993) found that men between the ages of 45 and 84 years who began moderate intensity sports added an average of 0.72 years to their lifespan. Although to some it may not seem worth the effort of being active to add less than a year to one's lifespan it clearly demonstrates the effect that activity can have on our health.

Chronic disease risk factors and physical activity

One of the ways that physical activity helps to prevent chronic diseases such as those discussed above is by protecting against many of the risk factors that lead to the development of these diseases. These risk factors include:

- hypertension (high blood pressure);
- hyperlipidaemia (high fats and cholesterol);
- diabetes;
- obesity.

Research by Carnethon *et al.* (2003) explored the role of cardiorespiratory fitness in the development of cardiovascular disease risk factors. Men and women between the ages of 18 and 30 years completed a maximal treadmill test to determine their level of fitness and were subsequently placed into low, moderate and highly fit categories. Participants were followed up at 2, 5, 7, 10 and 15 years after this exercise test. At follow-up the incidence of cardiovascular disease risk factors, such as hypertension, diabetes and hypercholesterolaemia (high cholesterol), were recorded if the condition was not present at baseline. Results indicated that low and moderate fitness levels were associated with a three- to sixfold increased risk of developing hypertension and diabetes at some point in the future. These findings support the contribution of an inactive lifestyle to the development of cardiovascular risk factors and an increased risk of developing cardiovascular disease.

Learning Activity 2.2

Having read about the research by Carnethon *et al.* (2003), consider a potential limitation of this research. Think about some reasons why it is not possible to conclude with certainty that the low to moderate exercise levels of these individuals were the cause of increased cardiovascular risk factors. Discussions later in the chapter will help you to review your answer, however, let's first consider these cardiovascular risk factors in detail.

Blood pressure and physical activity

Hypertension, or high blood pressure, is considered one of the most significant risk factors for cardiovascular disease and stroke. A meta-analysis (see Box 2.2) of 61 prospective studies indicated that the risk of sudden cardiovascular related death decreases linearly with decreasing blood pressure (Lewington *et al.*, 2002). However, exercise has been regularly demonstrated as effective for reducing blood pressure (Pescatello *et al.*, 2004). A meta-analysis by Cornelissen and Fagard (2005) examined 72 trials and found significant reductions in resting systolic and diastolic blood pressure following endurance training. Even acute bouts of exercise have been found to effectively reduce systolic and diastolic blood pressure by an average of 15 mmHg and 4 mmHg, respectively, with effects lasting between 4 and 10 hours and in some cases up to 22 hours following the exercise (Pescatello *et al.*, 2004). These reductions in blood pressure have also been demonstrated with numerous types of exercise including aerobic exercise (Fagard, 2001), moderate physical activity in the form of walking (Kelley *et al.*, 2001) and strength conditioning (Kelley and Kelley, 2000). However, moderate intensity aerobic exercise is the recommended daily activity for effectively reducing blood pressure (Pedersen and Saltin, 2006).

Box 2.2 Definition: Meta-analysis

A meta-analysis is a statistical procedure which combines the results of a number of different studies that address the same research question or hypothesis. The aim of a meta-analysis is to achieve a more powerful effect size than is possible with individual studies. An effect size is a measure of the strength of a relationship between two variables taking into account the sample size of the study. Although each study will determine its own effect size, a meta-analysis will determine an overall effect size which provides an idea of the magnitude of the effect of a phenomenon.

Obesity and physical activity

A large proportion of the UK population are overweight. In 2008, almost 25 per cent of adults in England were classed as obese, with almost 40 per cent having larger than normal waist circumference (National Health Service, 2010). Overweight and obesity result from a positive imbalance between energy intake and energy use (Demaree *et al.*, 2001). The calories that we consume in our diet are either used in the form of energy for us to carry out our daily activities or are stored as adipose tissue (fat) to be used another day. It follows therefore that if we are consistently inactive, the calories we consume are slow to be used and our fat store will increase day by day resulting in weight gain and eventually overweight and obesity.

Slentz *et al.* (2004) conducted a randomised controlled trial (see Box 2.3) to determine the effects of varying intensities and doses of exercise on weight loss without alterations to diet. Participants were randomised to a control group, or one of three exercise interventions lasting eight months. These included low volume moderate intensity exercise, low volume high intensity exercise, or high volume high intensity exercise. All three exercise conditions had a beneficial effect on weight, fat mass and central obesity (fat carried around the waist). The effect did not differ in relation to intensity, however, indicating that even moderate intensity exercise is sufficient to produce these changes.

Box 2.3 Definition: Randomised controlled trial

A randomised controlled trial is a type of research method where people are randomly allocated into a research condition or a control group. The research conditions will involve different forms of an intervention while the control group will receive no intervention. This is considered to be one of the most rigorous types of research design because it eliminates any potential bias of including self-selected groups or similar types of people in one condition or group.

It is clear that exercise of different types and intensities is beneficial for helping people to maintain physical health. Exercise is also beneficial for maintaining mental health, to which we now turn our attention. Specifically, this chapter focuses on health-related quality of life, anxiety and depression.

Health-related quality of life

Health-related quality of life is a multidimensional construct that comprises the following factors: physical functioning (ability to perform all physical activities); role physical (ability to perform daily activities); bodily pain; general health (evaluation of personal health); social functioning (degree of interference in social activities from emotional and physical problems); role emotional (degree of interference in daily activities as a result of emotional problems); mental health (feelings of anxiety or depression); and vitality (Taylor, 1999). Although physical activity can contribute to improved quality of life, research findings on this topic are equivocal. A number of cross-sectional studies have demonstrated improved quality of life in the general population following exercise interventions. Brown *et al.* (2004) found that people who were physically active were significantly less likely to report poor health-related quality of life measured as reporting 14 or more physically or mentally unhealthy days out of the past 30 days.

A longitudinal study by Tessier *et al.* (2007) explored whether there was a relationship between physical activity and quality of life over a three-year period. Benefits were observed in quality of life factors such as vitality, social functioning and mental health, however, these effects were small and did not reach statistical significance. This raises a question with regard to the long-term benefits of exercise on quality of life.

Recently, Bize *et al.* (2007) conducted a meta-analysis of studies exploring the relationship between physical activity and health-related quality of life in the general population. They found a consistent relationship between physical activity and health-related quality of life based on cross-sectional research findings. A problem with cross-sectional research, however, is that we cannot use it to determine cause and effect. Cross-sectional research compares a group of people who exercise and a group of people who do not exercise at one point in time. As a result, the researchers cannot determine whether the active people had higher quality of life because they were active or whether they were active because they had higher quality of life! Cross-sectional research can instead only identify that there is a relationship between the variables being examined. We consider this further as we discuss different research findings which might help you to reflect back on your response to Learning Activity 2.2.

Longitudinal research offers the benefit of allowing us to see how changes occur over time and as a result can be used to identify whether a change in one variable results in a change in another. This helps to determine more conclusive evidence of cause and effect. The longitudinal and randomised control trial studies included in Bize et al.'s (2007) meta-analysis also reported some evidence of a causal relationship between exercise and quality of life. However, the authors highlighted concerns about the methodology of these studies, including unstandardised questionnaires, flawed randomisation (allocation of people into conditions without eliminating bias) or reliance on self-report measures of physical activity and quality of life.

Depression

Anxiety and depression are the most common mental health conditions in the UK, with approximately 15 per cent of people in England reporting some form of these disorders (NHS Information Centre for Health and Social Care, 2007). For this reason it is important to try and determine effective treatments to alleviate the symptoms of these conditions. Although antidepressant medication is known to be effective in the treatment of depression, this type of treatment is often accompanied by adverse side-effects. Exercise has therefore been explored as an alternative treatment and research has compared the effectiveness of exercise and the most widely prescribed antidepressant medication.

De Moor et al. (2006) conducted a population survey to determine whether regular exercise was associated with low levels of depression. Their results demonstrated that regular exercisers were significantly less depressed than those who were inactive, lending support to the mental health benefits of exercise.

Lawlor and Hopker (2001) performed a meta-analysis of 14 randomised controlled trials of exercise for people diagnosed with depression and in doing so compared the effectiveness of exercise in alleviating depression with that of other known treatments. Results indicated that the effects of chronic exercise on depression were similar to those of cognitive therapy and antidepressant medication. However, only one study included in the meta-analysis directly compared the different treatments and therefore these results should be interpreted cautiously. There was no relationship between the type of exercise and the effect on depression. This may indicate that both aerobic and anaerobic exercise have a similar effect on depression. However, the authors also highlighted the need to consider the role of social contact in improving depression.

Exercise interventions in research studies tend to involve a group of people exercising together and therefore in addition to the exercise, provide the participants with social support from other exercisers. This means that it is difficult to exclude the social support as a confounding variable and conclude that the exercise itself provides the observed improvements in depression.

To extend understanding of the relationship between exercise and depression, Dunn et al. (2005) explored the dose–response relationship between exercise and depression. Participants with a mild to moderate major depressive disorder were randomised into one of four aerobic exercise treatment conditions or a placebo exercise control (non-aerobic exercise as a comparison). It is interesting that Dunn et al. decided to use non-aerobic exercise as a control group given the results of Lawlor and Hopker's research, however, this is one way of determining whether any significant difference between the groups is attributable to the aerobic component of the exercise. The exercise conditions were:

1. low dose three times a week;
2. low dose five times a week;
3. public health dose (at the recommended level for health) three times a week;
4. public health dose five times a week.

The placebo control group completed flexibility and stretching sessions on three days of the week. Results indicated that exercise at the public health level was the most effective at reducing depression scores. In contrast, the low dose exercise group varied little from the placebo group, although both these groups did demonstrate decreased depression scores. This suggests that any form of exercise may be beneficial to some degree for lowering depression scores, as was shown in Lawlor and Hopker's (2001) meta-analysis discussed above.

A number of studies have also suggested that maintaining physical activity over several years can provide a reduced risk of up to 22 per cent of experiencing subsequent depression (Dunn *et al.*, 2001). Mutrie (2000) reported on four longitudinal studies that examined the effects of baseline levels of exercise on the incidence of depression in the future. In all of the studies people who were more active at baseline reported lower incidence of depression at follow-up.

Anxiety

Anxiety can be manifest at a number of different levels, however, the two most commonly described are state and trait anxiety (Taylor, 2000). State anxiety reflects the negative perception of a situation expressed as worry, self-doubt and apprehension and is the immediate response to a situation perceived as currently threatening (for example, situations where a person may feel a lack of control). Trait anxiety is a personality characteristic that refers to how likely an individual is to perceive a situation as threatening. Anxiety is a common and normal response to any situation perceived as threatening, however, a distinction must be made between normal levels of anxiety and clinical anxiety disorders (Taylor, 2000). These differ in the intensity of the symptoms and the degree to which normal functioning is impaired (American Psychiatric Association, 2000). Clinical anxiety can not only be debilitating but prolonged inappropriate responses to the anxiety-inducing situation can result in cardiovascular and metabolic changes linked to chronic health problems such as hypertension (Jonas and Lando, 2000). In their population review (discussed in the Depression section), De Moor *et al.* (2006) found that regular exercisers were less likely to suffer from anxiety than inactive individuals, once again demonstrating the protective effects of exercise for mental health. In addition, as we see below, research has demonstrated that exercise can be effective in treating both state and trait anxiety.

Herring *et al.* (2010) recently conducted a systematic review (see Box 2.4) of the effects of exercise on anxiety symptoms in patients with various chronic diseases. They identified that exercise interventions significantly reduced anxiety symptoms in comparison to no treatment. Exercise bouts of more than 30 minutes and interventions lasting no longer than ten weeks were found to be most effective.

Box 2.4 Definition: Systematic review

A systematic review is a type of literature search which aims to address a particular research question. The researcher must try to include relevant literature from all possible databases and include unpublished work such as reports and theses as well as peer reviewed journal articles. Once the collected studies have been reviewed for relevance to the study question and appropriateness of the methodological approaches, the study results are combined to review what types of studies have been conducted in the area and what variables have been explored to identify an overall conclusion on findings related to the study question. The final stage of a systematic review is to identify what has not yet been covered in the research area and make suggestions for future research.

So, how much exercise is necessary in order to achieve these anxiolytic (anxiety-reducing) benefits? Taylor (2000) summarised numerous reviews and studies to examine the effects of acute and chronic exercise on both trait and state anxiety (using cross-sectional and longitudinal designs). Cross-sectional studies of chronic exercise indicated that those who reported being more physically active self-reported lower levels of trait anxiety or stress. Remember, however, that given the nature of cross-sectional research this cannot be assumed to be a causal relationship. It also appears that anxiolytic benefits can be seen from single bouts of exercise. Single bouts of physical activity were found to have small to moderate effects on self-reported anxiety with 19 out of 22 studies reviewed showing an anxiety-reducing effect. Fourteen of the studies examined by Taylor examined reactivity to a psychosocial stressor following a single exercise session and ten of these showed a reduction in reactivity.

Of the 27 longitudinal studies examined by Taylor, 18 showed an effect of an exercise intervention on one or more of various self-report measures of anxiety. A number of the studies focused on whether increasing aerobic fitness was necessary to reduce anxiety. Of the seven studies that specifically examined the effects of fitness change on anxiety levels only three found a positive relationship. This suggests therefore that a change in aerobic fitness is not essential to achieve the anxiety-reducing benefits of exercise. As suggested previously, social support from exercise leaders or fellow exercisers may have a beneficial effect, as might the placebo effect of actively participating in some form of activity. However, of the seven studies that examined the effects of different types of non-aerobic exercise such as weight training and flexibility on anxiety, only one found an anxiety-reducing effect. If you want to find out more about this type of research then take a look at the further reading suggestions at the end of this chapter.

Determinants of physical activity and barriers to exercise

Now we have seen how detrimental inactivity can be for our health, it is hard to understand why so many people remain inactive. Researchers are eager to find out how to encourage people to be more physically active in an attempt to overcome some of the health risks of physical inactivity. Thus they have explored whether there are individual, cognitive and environmental barriers which contribute to the likelihood of being active or inactive. Not surprisingly, the more barriers that we perceive prevent us from exercising the less likely we are to be physically active. It is important therefore for exercise psychologists to identify as many determinants of and barriers to physical activity as possible so that appropriate interventions and strategies can be implemented to overcome these and encourage higher rates of exercise participation.

The main barriers to exercise tend to be time, cost, injuries and health implications (Jewson *et al.*, 2008), lack of motivation and child care needs (Booth *et al.*, 1997), and access to facilities (Giles-Corti and Donovan, 2002). In addition, adolescent girls have identified key barriers such as feeling embarrassed about the way that they look when exercising (Robbins *et al.*, 2003).

Individual determinants and barriers

Case Study 2.2
Hena's case continued

Let's find out some more about Hena . . .

Hena is a 45-year-old mother of three. Although she was born in East London, her family originates from Bangladesh. In school Hena used to participate in PE classes but did no extracurricular activities relating to sport or exercise. She left school with nine GCSEs and has worked in a local shop since, working her way up to branch manager. Given her busy life looking after her husband and three children and working five days a week, Hena finds it difficult to find the time to exercise and has smoked since the age of 15.

When we refer to individual factors, we are referring to the characteristics of individuals who are active or inactive. Research has compared those people who exercise with those who do not to identify whether there are any consistent factors that can predict the type of person who is likely to be sedentary. Other research has offered sedentary individuals an opportunity to become physically active via some kind of intervention. This research has then explored whether there are differences in the type of people who adhere to the programme of exercise and those who do not (e.g. King *et al.*, 2006). However, as discussed previously, the problem with this type of research is that it is cross-sectional and therefore limits the type of conclusions that can be drawn from its results.

The first factor we consider here is age. Research has demonstrated that as we age we are likely to become less active (De Moor *et al.*, 2006). This is perhaps not surprising given that a number of variables change: as we progress from adolescence to adulthood we work more and have more responsibilities reducing our perceived time to exercise. As we further progress from adulthood to older age our physical abilities and health may begin to decline which might place physical barriers on our ability to exercise.

Gender is a slightly more controversial factor influencing our activity levels. Research tends to suggest that gender has more of an influence over the type of activity rather than the level of activity. For example, Leslie *et al.* (2001) identified that men were more likely to engage in activities involving more vigorous and moderate intensity exercise whereas women were more likely to engage in walking than men.

In terms of ethnicity, Bangladeshi and Pakistani groups tend to participate in physical activity the least in comparison to other ethnic groups, while members of the White, Black African and Black Caribbean communities participate in physical activity the most (Sporting Equals, 2007). There also appears to be an interaction between gender and ethnicity, with men in the less active ethnic groups being more active than women (Anderson *et al.*, 2006). This interaction is often attributed to cultural differences causing increased barriers for women. For example, Muslim women may require a female-only exercise environment, which is not always readily available (Ball, 2006).

Level of education has also been identified as a determinant of activity. The higher the level of education a person attains the more likely they are to be physically active (Plotnikoff *et al.*, 2004). This might imply that part of the reason for inactivity is a lack of awareness of the health risks of being inactive. Those people who are more highly educated are more likely to be aware of these risks and as such are taking steps to combat them.

Our economic status plays a role in our likelihood of being physically active. Perhaps surprisingly, blue collar workers (manual workers) tend to be less active than white collar workers (educated professional workers) (Sport England, 2009). There could be a number of reasons for this: it may be that white collar workers have a higher level of education and as discussed above are therefore more aware of the risks of inactivity for their health. Alternatively, it may be that blue collar workers consider their jobs sufficiently active to meet required activity levels, resulting in them doing far less physical activity outside of their jobs. McNeill *et al.* (2006) discuss social economic position (SEP) which relates to a combination of our education level, economic income and occupational status. Their review found that a person's SEP relates to their level of physical activity, with people in the lower SEP tending to report engaging in work-related but not out-of-work activity, lending support to the above proposal.

Exercise history is a determinant of how physically active someone is likely to be later in life. People who have previously been physically active are more likely to be physically active again in the future (McAuley *et al.*, 2007).

Current health status has also been identified as a determinant of physical activity. Although we would hope that unhealthy people would recognise the need to exercise to benefit their health, Sin *et al.* (2004) found the opposite. They identified that people with a high-risk health status for a coronary event were less likely to participate in a cardiac rehabilitation course (including an exercise component) than those with low-risk health status. Although the reasons behind this are unclear, it may be that people with a high-risk health status are more concerned that overexertion will result in a coronary event and as such avoid participating in exercise. In addition to actual health status, perceived health is also a determinant of a person's physical activity level (Plotnikoff *et al.*, 2004). People who are physically active tend to perceive themselves as more healthy. In a similar way, health behaviours are also correlated with activity. For example, smokers are less likely to be physically active whereas those who have never smoked are most likely to be physically active (Plotnikoff *et al.*, 2004). These studies provide clear examples of how cross-sectional research cannot provide us with cause and effect conclusions. For example, are people less active because they are unhealthy or are they unhealthy because they are inactive? To answer such questions, randomised controlled research is required. This example will also help you to reflect on the answer that you gave to Learning Activity 2.2.

Practical application

In this section we have discussed the following individual determinants:

- age;
- gender;
- ethnicity;
- education;
- economic status;
- exercise history;
- health status.

While it is useful to identify a range of individual factors that seem to be related to inactivity, what use can we make of this information? Does this mean that we simply ignore these people and accept that they are likely to be inactive? Although we are unable to change things like people's age or gender we can still use this type of information to identify who should be targeted when we develop interventions to try to increase physical activity participation. For example, using the above information it would be most useful to target an intervention towards a particular age group or ethnic minority who would most benefit from increasing their participation in physical activity. In addition, the knowledge that smokers are less likely to be active might suggest that interventions tackling inactivity should also try to tackle other health behaviours, such as smoking addiction. Chapter 5 further explores the use of physical activity interventions.

Environmental barriers and determinants

Case Study 2.3
Hena's case continued

Hena enjoys living in East London because it is an area with a strong Bangladeshi community. Her two sisters and brother live within walking distance, although Hena usually takes the bus to avoid the poor UK weather. She has a close circle of friends in the community and at work. A few of Hena's work colleagues go to the gym a couple of times a week, however, most of Hena's family and friends lead a similar lifestyle to hers.

So far we have discussed how different individual factors can act as determinants of inactivity. However, not every man is more active than every woman, and not all Bangladeshis are less active than Black Africans, so this must mean that other variables contribute to this relationship between individual factors and physical inactivity. The environment in which we live is also likely to contribute to our level of physical activity. In this section we explore the evidence that suggests a correlation between inactivity and our environment.

The environment created by a western lifestyle is related to lower levels of physical activity. In this environment, unhealthy foods are readily available and modern technology (e.g. TV remote controls) limit the need for even minute levels of physical activity. This increase in sedentary activities and a high fat diet only increases a person's likelihood of being inactive (Koezuka *et al.*, 2006).

The effects of living in a rural or urban area on physical activity have also been explored. The research evidence is contradictory, however, with some findings suggesting that rural areas encourage increased physical activity (Plotnikoff *et al.*, 2004), possibly as a result of the opportunity to walk or exercise in pleasant surroundings, whereas other studies suggest that residents of rural areas report more barriers to exercise (Wilcox *et al.*, 2000) and that higher activity levels are associated with easier access to facilities offered by urban living (Stafford *et al.*, 2007).

Another environmental barrier which appears to contribute substantially to our activity levels is the weather (Tucker and Gilliland, 2007). Bad weather is often reported as a significant barrier determining whether or not people want to engage in physical activity (Salmon *et al.*, 2003). However, it could be argued that it is possible to exercise in leisure facilities such as gyms or swimming pools where the weather would not impact on our exercise enjoyment. Supporting this, although exercise facilities are not a direct determinant of physical activity, it has been found that their availability helps people to reach the recommended daily levels of activity by increasing opportunities for and ease of exercising (Giles-Corti and Donovan, 2002).

Another factor which appears to have a significant relationship with activity levels is the degree of social support that we receive from family and friends (McNeill *et al.*, 2006). In a review of the determinants of physical activity, Trost *et al.* (2002) found that social support was the most consistent predictor of physical activity, while social isolation was significantly associated with inactivity. In addition, Plotnikoff *et al.* (2004) found that the more friends who exercise an individual has, the higher their own level of physical activity.

Practical application

In this section we have discussed the following environmental determinants:

- lifestyle;
- rural and urban living;
- weather;
- social support.

Understanding how the environment contributes to our physical activity participation means that we have the opportunity to modify aspects of the environment and tailor interventions to overcome certain environmental barriers with an aim of increasing physical activity. For example, knowledge that a western lifestyle increases a person's likelihood of being sedentary provides the opportunity for companies to design computer games which encourage more activity while being played. Understanding the difference between rural and urban barriers to physical activity can ensure that governments and councils provide funding for appropriate facilities which are suitable for the community to support and facilitate exercise participation. Social support is also a key aspect of the environment which should be considered in interventions to provide support for participants who are trying to increase their activity levels.

Cognitive barriers and determinants

Case Study 2.4
More about Hena

Having visited the doctor, Hena has been considering ways to improve her health. The doctor has recommended that she tries to increase her levels of physical activity. She used to enjoy exercise at school; however, since then she feels that she is too old and unfit to be able to enjoy exercise. She is embarrassed about her weight and doesn't want to look foolish going to a gym or exercising in her community where she might be seen looking sweaty or out of breath. Despite this she does appreciate that increasing her physical activity might help her but worries that her life is too busy to allow her the time to exercise. Hena therefore intends to try and increase her exercise levels by walking to visit friends and family when the weather and her time permit.

We have discussed a number of factors related to us as individuals and the environment in which we live and which influence our activity levels. In addition, there are a number of cognitive factors which determine our likelihood of being physically active. Cognitive factors refer to the way in which we think or process information.

Enjoyment is a key correlate of physical activity. Salmon *et al.* (2003) identified that those people who reported enjoyment of physical activity were more likely to report high levels of physical activity. This can be explained using a theory called Self-Determination Theory, which is discussed further in Chapter 4 (Deci and Ryan, 1985). This theory proposes that intrinsic motivation to exercise (motivation to participate in exercise for enjoyment) significantly predicts exercise participation (Deci and Ryan, 2000).

Self-efficacy relates to our confidence to be able to do something (e.g. our confidence that we will exercise even when the weather is bad or we are tired). A longitudinal piece of research has demonstrated that the higher our self-efficacy to overcome barriers to exercise, the more likely we are to exercise (McAuley *et al.*, 2007).

The Theory of Planned Behaviour (Ajzen, 1991; discussed further in Chapter 4) proposes that our attitudes, social norms, perceived behavioural control and intentions to exercise all contribute towards our actual exercise behaviour. Our intentions to exercise have been shown to correlate highly with our subsequent exercise behaviour (Rhodes *et al.*, 2006), showing that if we intend to engage in the behaviour we are likely to do so. Our attitudes towards the behaviour also contribute to our likelihood of being physically active (Hagger *et al.*, 2002). Not surprisingly, a negative attitude towards activity is associated with low levels of participation in physical activity. Perceived behavioural control relates to how difficult one perceives it will be to engage in the behaviour. Research by Jewson *et al.* (2008) identified that people with high levels of perceived behavioural control (believed that they had control over the situation enabling them to exercise) were more likely to be physically active than those who had low levels of perceived behavioural control.

Our body image (how we view our physical self) also plays a role in whether or not we choose to be physically active. Research demonstrates that people with a poor body image are less likely to participate in physical activity (Neumark-Sztainer *et al.*, 2006). Although it could be assumed that people with low body satisfaction would be more likely to exercise in order to achieve their ideal body, it is also understandable that these people are less likely to want to be seen in environments with other fit and toned people or in environments such as gyms where they will be surrounded by mirrors (see Chapter 7 for more discussion on this topic).

Practical application

In this section we have discussed the following cognitive determinants:

- enjoyment;
- self-efficacy;
- intentions to exercise;
- attitude and perceived behavioural control;
- body image.

People's cognitions are far harder to change than the physical environment in which they live; however, it is possible to do so. Cognitive behavioural strategies can be implemented which help individuals to alter the way that they appraise situations and strategies can be implemented to help individuals to consider ways to overcome barriers or alter their attitudes. For example, a decision balance sheet can be used where an individual writes a list of pros and cons of exercise so that they can see whether the benefits outweigh the costs of exercising and give further consideration to how they might overcome their exercise barriers (Wankel et al., 1985). These cognitive strategies are discussed in more detail in Chapter 5. If you would like to know more about how interventions can be tailored to suit different people, the article recommended in the Further reading section of this chapter might be of interest to you.

Learning Activity 2.3

Having read about the determinants of inactivity, reflect back on Hena's case, which is outlined on pages 10, 17, 19 and 20. Consider the individual, environmental and cognitive determinants of Hena's inactivity and how these might affect her decision about whether or not to increase her physical activity as recommended by her doctor.

Chapter Review

This chapter first explored the evidence supporting the protective and beneficial effects of physical activity for modifying chronic disease risk factors and protecting against mental health problems such as depression and anxiety (Learning Objective 1). Much of this evidence is cross-sectional in nature and this means that cause and effect cannot necessarily be drawn from these results (Learning Objective 2). However, longitudinal and controlled experimental research also lends support to these findings suggesting that the relationship between physical activity and improved health is reliable. The second part of this chapter explored individual (e.g. age), environmental (e.g. facilities) and cognitive (e.g. attitudes) factors which are believed to be determinants of physical activity/inactivity (Learning Objective 3). These factors can be used to highlight considerations or target audiences for interventions to be most successful (Learning Objective 4).

Learning Activity 2.4
Test your understanding

1. Use the information in this chapter to highlight the short- and long-term consequences of physical inactivity on our physical and mental health.
2. What are the limitations of cross-sectional research for identifying the relationships between individual or environmental factors and physical inactivity?
3. Identify key cognitive determinants of physical inactivity.

Further Reading

- For more information about the benefits of exercise for various health conditions:

Pedersen, BK and Saltin, B (2006) Evidence for prescribing exercise as therapy in chronic disease. *Scandinavian Journal of Medicine and Science in Sports*, 16 (suppl 1): 3–63.
This paper provides a comprehensive review of research which has explored the benefits of exercise interventions for different chronic diseases. The paper also explores the type and duration of training that would be appropriate for individuals suffering from these types of illnesses, as well as the contraindications of exercise for these individuals.

- For more information about the determinants of physical activity:

King, AC, Marcus, B, Ahn, D, Andrea, LD, Rejeski, WJ, Sallis, JF *et al.* (2006) Identifying subgroups that succeed or fail with three levels of physical activity intervention: The activity counseling trial. *Health Psychology*, 25: 336–47.
This paper follows individuals who were classed as being at risk of cardiovascular disease and explores the predictors of their exercise maintenance on an exercise intervention. The study compares the determinants of success on three different types of intervention and explores whether different characteristics are more suited to success with certain types of intervention. This study is therefore a good example of how understanding the determinants of physical activity can be put to practical use.

Chapter 3
Physical inactivity: the role of the self

Learning Objectives

This chapter is designed to help you be able to:

1. understand the definitions of and the difference between self-concept and self-worth;
2. understand the definition of physical self-worth and how this contributes to our global self-worth;
3. understand the reciprocal relationship between physical activity and self-perceptions;
4. understand what is meant by social physique anxiety (SPA) and the role that physical activity can play in improving SPA.

Introduction

Chapter 2 discussed the individual, social and cognitive determinants of physical activity. One individual difference factor is our perception of our self, or self-perception. This chapter examines in detail the link between self-perceptions and physical activity. The chapter discusses what psychologists refer to as 'the self', and how physical activity can be used to improve individuals' global and physical self-perceptions. This chapter considers how low self-worth is related to a fear of negative physical evaluation from others known as 'social physique anxiety'. The chapter concludes with an exploration of how physical activity contributes to improving social physique anxiety.

The self

How we perceive ourselves and how we believe we are perceived by others makes a significant contribution to our decisions to engage in different behaviours (see Chapter 4 for further discussion). Psychologists have therefore spent a considerable amount of time researching how we perceive ourselves, what impact this has on our behaviour and how we can modify our perceptions to improve our own self-image. However, before we can explore the relationship between our self-perceptions and physical activity behaviour we must first understand what psychologists refer to as 'the self'. The self is made up of a number of different components, including self-concept, self-worth and body image. In the sections below we discuss the different factors that contribute to these components.

The self-concept

Case Study 3.1

David and Sabrina were asked to write a brief description of themselves. These are shown below.

- David: *My name is David and I am a Sport and Exercise Science student. I mainly enjoy the psychological aspect of the course and have interests in exercise motivation. In my spare time I enjoy swimming and am the captain of my university's swimming team. I have an older brother who I enjoy mountain walking with in my spare time.*
- Sabrina: *My name is Sabrina and I am originally from the United States, although I am currently studying Sport and Exercise Science in the UK. I would consider myself to be a sensitive and caring individual and I hope to use my degree to pursue a career in counselling. I think that I am relatively attractive and maintain a good figure by attending the gym on a regular basis.*

How we choose to describe ourselves is referred to as the self-concept. According to Shavelson *et al.* (1976) our self-concept is multifaceted and hierarchical. That is, our self-concept is made up of a number of domains which feed into one another to form a pyramid of relationships (Figure 3.1). Self-concept at the peak of the pyramid is a relatively stable construct, but as we move down the hierarchical model through the domains, the sub-domains become more situation specific and are therefore more susceptible to change.

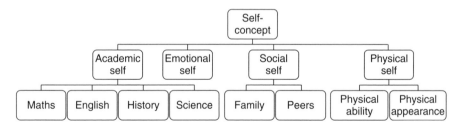

Figure 3.1 The hierarchical self-concept, based on Shavelson, RJ, Hubner, JJ and Stanton, GC. Review of Educational Research, 46(3): 407–441. Copyright 1976. Reprinted by permission of SAGE publications.

According to the model, in forming our self-concept we gather information about our abilities and key roles in four life domains. These are the:

- academic self;
- social self;
- emotional self;
- physical self.

How competent we are in each of these domains and the importance of our role within each domain will impact our overall self-concept. For example, an athlete is likely to be competent in physical activities and their role within this domain is significant within their daily lives. This is likely to contribute towards their description of themselves, or, their self-concept ('I am an athlete'). In a similar way to how the four domains make up the self-concept, the domains are hierarchical and are made up of perceptions of ourselves in more specific settings (Figure 3.1). For example, performance in specific academic subjects will contribute to the academic self, while relationships with friends, family and colleagues will all contribute to the social self (Figure 3.1). The self-descriptions by David and Sabrina in Case Study 3.1 illustrate how people will draw from the relevant sub-domains to form their self-concept.

Having a positive self-concept appears to be important for our psychological and physiological wellbeing and has been linked to affective outcomes. For example, Park (2003) demonstrated that a positive self-concept in adolescent boys and girls had a protective effect against depression and obesity, while a poor self-concept made these adolescents more susceptible to developing depression and becoming obese. Developing a positive self-concept is therefore important for enhancing an individual's physical and psychological health.

Self-worth

Case Study 3.2

Hena

Let's return to Hena who we met in Chapters 1 and 2.

We read in Chapter 2 that Hena achieved good GCSE grades at school and now has a responsible job as a branch manager of a shop. She is a busy mother of three children and lives near to her extended family in East London. She has a close circle of friends both in the local Bangladeshi community and at work, who consider Hena a loyal friend who is always available to listen to their problems and provide a shoulder to cry on. Given that she has little time outside her family and work commitments, Hena does no physical activity and is concerned about her increasing weight. She is now classed as obese and is self-conscious about her appearance.

Learning Activity 3.1

Consider the new information about Hena that is presented in Case Study 3.2 and identify whether she is likely to have high or low self-esteem. Think about what aspects of the case study have led you to your decision and compare your answers with the factors discussed in the section below.

How someone evaluates or sees themselves (self-perception) within each of the domains of the self-concept is a key factor in the development of self-worth or 'self-esteem'. Global self-worth relates to the overall evaluation of how positively or negatively an individual perceives themselves based on their achievements in the domains and sub-domains of the self-concept. Self-worth therefore has the same hierarchical structure as the self-concept (Figure 3.1), being made up of an individual's self-perceptions in the four key life domains which in turn are made up of an individual's self-perceptions in situation-specific sub-domains.

However, not everybody who is good at maths or who is physically strong has high self-worth. This is because being good at maths or being physically strong is not important to everybody. For some people, being academically successful is more important than for others. For those who place high importance on academic achievement, being good at maths is likely to increase their self-worth, while being poor at maths is likely to have the opposite effect. For someone who places little importance on academic achievement, being good or bad at maths is less likely to have the same impact on their global self-worth. Therefore, the higher an individual's self-perceptions within the life domains that are important to them, the more likely they are to develop high global self-worth. Thus if physical ability is considered an important aspect of an individual's self-concept and they perceive themselves to be physically strong and a competent exerciser, this will lead to increased physical self-worth which will in turn contribute to increased global self-worth.

It is widely accepted that self-worth is a strong indicator of emotional stability and has been related to life satisfaction, independence, resilience to stress and high levels of achievement in education and work (Fox, 1997). As a result, self-worth emerges as one of the strongest predictors of subjective wellbeing (Diener, 1984). High self-worth is related to healthy behaviours such as not smoking, greater involvement in sport and exercise and healthier eating patterns (Torres and Fernandez, 1995) while low self-worth is associated with mental illness and lack of mental wellbeing and often accompanies depression and trait anxiety (Fox, 1997).

Box 3.1 Definitions: Self-concept and self-worth

As you can see, self-concept and self-worth are very similar constructs and some researchers believe that the terms are interchangeable because it is virtually impossible to describe ourselves without using a degree of evaluation. However, other researchers do distinguish between the two as we have done in this chapter. It is worth considering this when you read research papers on this topic as the authors may well use the terms interchangeably and so be sure that you are clear about what the paper is discussing. The definitions below highlight the differences between the two constructs discussed in this chapter.

- Self-concept: An overall description of the self based on abilities and key roles in different life domains. For example, 'I am an athlete'.
- Self-worth: An overall evaluation of how positively or negatively an individual perceives themselves. For example, 'I am a good person'.

The physical self

In the sections above we have discussed how self-perceptions and evaluations in the key life domains contribute to our overall self-concept and global self-worth. We also discussed how the importance placed on each of these domains contributes to the impact that our competence has on our global self-worth. One domain appears to have a more consistent impact on our global self-perceptions than other domains: perceptions of the body and aspects of appearance have been found to be the strongest predictors of global-self worth in adults (Harter, 1993; Fox, 1997). Researchers believe that this might be because we use our physical selves as an interface between our inner private selves and other people (Fox, 2000; Thøgersen-Ntoumani *et al.*, 2005). We tend to use our appearance to illustrate our personality by the way we dress or the way we style our hair. Our facial expressions denote the mood we are in and our body language often conveys our opinions about something. Therefore, how people perceive their physical selves is believed to contribute more significantly to their self-concept and global self-worth than the other domains.

Physical self-worth has been found to relate to wellbeing outcomes such as positive affect and emotional adjustment even when global self-worth is statistically controlled for (Van de Vliet *et al.*, 2002). This suggests that how we perceive our physical selves might affect our wellbeing irrespective of how we see ourselves globally and thus demonstrates its importance.

As with the other domains, the physical self is believed to be made up of a number of situation specific sub-domains. The nature and number of these domains varies according to different researchers. For example, according to Fox's hierarchical multidimensional model of the physical self (Fox and Corbin, 1989; Figure 3.2), the sub-domains are sport competence, attractiveness, physical condition and strength.

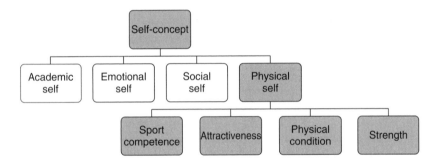

Figure 3.2 Structure of the physical self according to Fox and Corbin. Adapted, with permission, from K. R. Fox and C. B. Corbin (1989) The physical self-perception profile: development and preliminary validation. Journal of Sport and Exercise Psychology, 11(4): 408–430.

Box 3.2 Three scales

- The *Physical Self-Perception Profile* (PSPP; Fox and Corbin, 1989) is a questionnaire designed to measure physical self-perception based on Fox's model of the physical self. The profile consists of five subscales. Four of the subscales are designed to measure perceptions within specific sub-domains of the physical self and measure sport competence, attractiveness, physical condition and strength. The fifth subscale measures overall physical self-worth. The question format is a four-point forced choice scale in which two alternative statements are provided. Individuals are required to select which statement is most like them and then indicate how true the statement is for them (sort of true for me, or really true for me).
- The *Perceived Importance Profile* (PIP) was designed to be used in conjunction with the PSPP and is a measure of perceived importance to allow an assessment of if and how self-perceptions

··· ▶

Box 3.2 continued

in each domain will likely impact on physical self-worth. Earlier in the chapter we discussed the fact that the relative impact of each sub-domain had on a specific domain was based on the perceived importance of that domain by the individual. The PIP determines how important competence in each sub-domain of the physical self is to an individual so that this can be taken into account when determining an individual's physical self-perception and its impact on behaviour and self-worth.

- The *Physical Self-Description Questionnaire* (PSDQ) is based on Marsh and Shavelson's hierarchical model of self-concept (Marsh *et al.*, 1994). It is a 70-item questionnaire measuring 11 subscales: strength, body fat, endurance or fitness, sports competence, physical activity, coordination, health, appearance, flexibility, self-worth and general physical self-concept. Responses lie along a six-point scale ranging from true to false.

Body image

Close your eyes and picture an image of yourself. Now consider what aspects of your body you would change if you had the opportunity. Would you change your nose? Make yourself taller, thinner, more muscular? Most of us could name at least one area of our bodies that we are dissatisfied with.

The image that we hold of ourselves when we look in the mirror, or if we view ourselves in our mind's eye, is our 'body image' and reflects how we feel about our physical self. Body image incorporates perceptions of how attractive we are, how we estimate our body size and our emotions associated with body shape and size (Grogan, 1999). Our body image is often based on comparisons that we make between ourselves and other people, and, with the frequent bombardment of the 'body beautiful' depicted in adverts and magazines, maintaining a positive body image can be difficult. There is even evidence to suggest that we are subliminally fed the concept of what is attractive from a very young age in animated cartoons (Klein and Shiffman, 2006).

Opinion about whether body image is a uni-dimensional or multidimensional construct is mixed. Some believe that body image can be measured simply by evaluating body cathexis (Secord and Jourard, 1953). This is a measure of how satisfied an individual is with different parts of their body. However, the general opinion is that body image is a multidimensional construct made up of factors such as overall appearance, attractiveness, strength, height and weight (Rowe *et al.*, 1999). Understandably there appear to be gender differences in how body image is composed, with men focusing more on strength and women focusing more on weight (Franzoi and Shields, 1984).

Learning Activity 3.2

As a group, collect together a range of magazines. Try to collect a variation including magazines targeting teens, women and men. Compare the differences between the images that are portrayed in these magazines and consider how this might influence the body image of the audience that the magazine is targeting.

Perhaps not surprisingly a poor body image has been shown to be linked to low levels of self-worth. Clay *et al.* (2005) demonstrated that self-worth levels decreased with increasing age among a sample of adolescent girls. Their analysis showed that the decrease in self-worth was related to a decrease in body satisfaction that occurred as girls got older as a result of an increased awareness of sociocultural attitudes towards appearance and comparisons with media models. This demonstrates the important role that our society and media have in influencing young girls' perceptions of themselves and as a result their self-worth.

The self and physical activity

In the previous section we introduced the construct of the 'self', discussed the influence that society could have on our self-perceptions and the effect that our self-worth can have on our wellbeing, physical health and health-related behaviours. In a similar way the relationship between 'the self' and physical activity works in a reciprocal fashion. What we mean by this is that aspects of the 'self' impact on our physical activity behaviour but at the same time our physical activity behaviour can have an effect on our self-concept and self-perceptions. The next section discusses these relationships.

The self influencing physical activity

At first thought we would perhaps expect somebody who is unhappy about their weight to be more likely to exercise in order to lose weight and achieve their ideal body. However, closer inspection suggests that this is not always the case. Annesi (2006) explored the relationship between physical self-concept, self-efficacy and physical activity among children between the ages of 10 and 12 years. The children were taking part in an after-school club which aimed to encourage self-improvement. Sessions included a range of physical activities such as cardiovascular and resistance training on three days of the week but also included sessions on cognitive strategies such as goal setting (see Chapter 6) and discussions surrounding general health and nutrition. The intervention resulted in improvements in physical activity, physical self-concept and self-efficacy, demonstrating that it was successful in encouraging self-improvement. In addition, regression analyses demonstrated that improvements in physical self-concept and self-efficacy predicted increases in physical activity. Therefore, it appears that enhancing an individual's physical self-perception and increasing their confidence in their ability to change their behaviour encourages them to become more physically active.

Using a similar age group, Trautwein *et al.* (2008) explored the relationship between physical self-concept, and the free time physical activity of pre-adolescents using a longitudinal study design. Being in a PE class of high athletic ability resulted in adolescents reporting lower physical self-concept and this was related to lower levels of free time physical activity. Thus it appears that our self-perceptions are based on comparison of ourselves with others and that low self-perceptions make it less likely that an individual will choose to be physically active, supporting the findings obtained by Annesi (2006).

It appears, therefore, that a low-self concept and low physical self-worth make it less likely that individuals will choose to be physically active. A number of factors could contribute to this decision such as the exercise environment. The different factors contributing to exercise behaviour are discussed in Chapter 4.

Physical activity influencing the self

Clearly, low self-perceptions can contribute to low levels of physical activity. However, given the role that physical activity can play in altering an individual's appearance and physical competence, researchers have explored the role that physical activity can play in increasing individuals' self-perceptions, such as self-concept and self-worth.

Physical activity and the self-concept

McDonald and Hodgdon (1991) conducted a meta-analysis to determine the effect of aerobic exercise on adults' self-concept and reported moderate effects, suggesting that participating in aerobic exercise could enhance self-concept. However, a recent review by Spence *et al.* (2005) suggested that the research by McDonald and Hodgdon may have overestimated the effects seen. Criticisms aimed at this meta-analysis included the fact that only aerobic exercise was examined, and only published studies with an increased likelihood of significant results. One of the biggest concerns was the way that self-concept was defined by McDonald and Hodgdon. They combined different aspects of the self such as global self-worth, physical self-perceptions and body cathexis in their definition of 'self-concept'. As we saw earlier in the chapter, these different aspects of the self all have slightly different definitions and as such it might not be appropriate to combine the results of studies measuring all of these and use them to accurately infer effects on global self-concept.

While McDonald and Hodgdon (1991) demonstrated a relationship between aerobic activity and improved self-concept, other researchers have explored whether it is necessary to see a change in physical fitness associated with aerobic activity to achieve improved self-conceopt. In girls between the ages of 14 and 17, both vigorous physical activity and physical fitness (peak oxygen uptake) correlated with physical self-concept (Dunton *et al.*, 2006). However, regression analysis indicated that physical fitness was a stronger predictor of physical self-concept than physical activity, suggesting that physical activity must be at a level to improve cardiovascular fitness in order to impact on the self-concept.

Physical activity and self-worth

A recent systematic review of randomised controlled trials exploring the effects of physical activity on children and adolescents' self-worth was conducted by Ekeland *et al.* (2005). The review supported the suggestion that exercise can improve self-worth but found that the effect was only small. A criticism of the research reviewed by Ekland and colleagues was that none of the studies included in the review followed participants after the intervention. This meant that Ekland *et al.*'s review could only conclude that exercise has a small effect on global self-worth over the short term.

At the other end of the spectrum, McAuley *et al.* (2000) explored changes in self-worth in relation to participation in different types of activity in older adults. Sedentary older adults were recruited to participate in a six-month randomised trial and were assigned to either an aerobic activity programme (walking) or a stretching and toning programme. No control group was used in the trial. Results indicated little difference in the increase in self-worth as a function of exercise type and increases in self-worth were not related to increases in fitness. Overall physical self-worth, esteem related to an attractive body, physical conditioning and strength perceptions all increased over the six-month trial. At six-month follow-up, modest but significant reductions occurred in all measures across the groups. The only difference found between the groups was for physical strength perceptions, where the toning and stretching group demonstrated significantly greater increases during the scheme and a smaller reduction at follow-up than the walking group. Given the nature of the exercise, this is to be expected, therefore overall the type of exercise appeared not to influence changes in self-worth. Without the inclusion of a control group, however, it cannot be concluded fully that the changes seen in self-perceptions were as a result of the intervention. For example, exercising with a group of like-minded people might have alleviated any physical concerns that the participants had and as such increased their self-perceptions, irrespective of the exercise per se.

To address the criticisms aimed at McDonald and Hodgdon's meta-analysis (discussed above), Spence et al. (2005) reviewed the effects of exercise on global self-worth. Their review included both published and unpublished studies (e.g. dissertations and theses) and explored the effects of different forms of exercise such as skills training and cardiovascular-based exercise. A significant but small effect of exercise was found on self-worth but, in contrast to the findings by McAuley et al. (2000), improvement in physical fitness was necessary for the improvement in self-worth to occur. Thus exercise programmes focusing on improving physical fitness resulted in small to moderate effect sizes for self-worth, whereas skills training was found to have no effect on self-worth. However, Spence et al.'s review has been criticised for conceptualising self-worth as a global concept when research has demonstrated that self-worth is a multidimensional construct made up of various sub-domains as discussed earlier in the chapter (Schneider et al., 2008).

Although the studies discussed here have identified positive relationships between exercise and self-worth, the question of causality remains. By this we mean that the studies do not provide conclusive evidence that an increase in physical activity causes an increase in self-worth. Using an adolescent sample, Schmalz et al. (2007) aimed to rectify this problem. The study used a longitudinal design to follow young girls through the adolescent period, taking measures of physical activity and self-worth at the ages of 9, 11 and 13 years. The study used a statistical analysis technique which allows the researcher to explore lagged effects, which means that they can explore how change in one variable influences the change in another variable over time. In this case, they examined how changes in physical activity influenced changes in self-worth over time. Their results demonstrated an effect of physical activity on self-worth, where higher levels of physical activity at 9–11 years predicted increased self-worth at 11–13 years. This relationship was stronger for younger girls (i.e. activity at 9 predicted self-worth at 11 more than activity at 11 predicted self-worth at 13). In contrast to discussions earlier in the chapter, there was no effect of self-worth on physical activity, suggesting that self-worth at an earlier age did not predict physical activity later on.

It appears, therefore, that physical activity can have an effect on an individual's global self-worth. However, given the hierarchical structure of self-worth it is likely that physical activity is more likely to have a direct influence on the physical self than on the global self and therefore affect global self-worth indirectly via modified physical self-perceptions.

Physical activity and the physical self

Schneider et al. (2008) felt that the small effect of physical activity on global self-worth seen in Spence et al.'s review was because these authors did not account for its multidimensional nature. They believed instead that physical activity was most likely to impact on physical self-worth (one of the sub-domains of global self-worth). To explore the impact of physical activity on the physical self-concept of high school children who were not regular exercisers, Schneider *et al.* (2008) conducted a controlled trial using one school as a control group and another school as the intervention group. Children attended a PE class five days a week for 60 minutes. In the intervention PE classes, activities such as yoga and dance were offered and a proportion of the time was spent discussing the health benefits of physical activity. The control group, in comparison, attended usual PE classes with no discussion of these health benefits. Results demonstrated that in the intervention group, those children who increased in cardiovascular fitness reported significant increases in physical self-concept. However, there was no significant difference in global or physical self-concept between children in the intervention and control conditions. This suggests that the determining factor contributing towards the increase in physical self-concept was the increase in cardiovascular fitness and not the intervention per se.

In a similar study, Burgess *et al.* (2006) examined the effect of a six-week aerobic dance intervention on the physical self-worth of adolescents (13–14 years old) who took part in an aerobic dance class twice a week (intervention group) and a swimming class twice a week (control group). An aerobic activity was deliberately chosen as the control group to test the effects of dance on physical self-worth rather than the effects of aerobic versus non-aerobic exercise. The study used a cross-over design and counterbalanced the conditions so that each individual took part in both conditions (within subject design) and as such acted as their own control (see Box 3.3). Measures of physical self-worth were taken prior to the start of the intervention, at the mid point (when participants swapped groups) and again at the end of the intervention. Significant improvements in 'feeling fat', strength and fitness, body attractiveness and overall physical self-worth were identified in the aerobic dance group while significant decreases were seen in all the named variables in the swimming class. It appears therefore that despite both activities involving aerobic exercise, aerobic dance was more successful at improving the body image and self-perceptions of these adolescents. The authors proposed that the non-competitive nature of dance might reduce the anxieties that can be caused by sport and exercise (see sections on social physique anxiety in this chapter and in Chapter 6) and as such provide a more supportive environment for individuals with low body image and self-perceptions to exercise.

Box 3.3

In the study by Burgess *et al.* (2006) students were allocated to either an aerobic dance condition or a normal PE condition (swimming). At the mid point of the study participants swapped so that the dance group took part in the swimming condition and vice versa. This changing of conditions is known as a cross-over design. This means that every participant provided measures in both the intervention and the control conditions and therefore this overcomes many of the limitations of between-subject designs where participants will only take part in one or other of the conditions. However, one problem with within-subject designs (where the same people take part in all conditions) is that the order of the conditions might have an impact on the outcome measures. For example, participants who took part in the dance condition first might have had elevated body image scores following this intervention. This positive effect on body image might have carried over when they then took part in the swimming condition, thus masking the beneficial effect of the intervention. For this reason, counterbalancing is used. ⋯▶

Box 3.3 continued

Counterbalancing involves altering the order in which participants take part in the conditions. In this example, this meant that some participants took part in the dance condition first and then swapped to the swimming condition while the other half of the group started in the swimming class but then swapped to the dance intervention. That way any order effects can be minimised and a more reliable picture of the results can be achieved.

Using a different type of sample, Taylor and Fox (2005) examined the effects of a ten-week exercise referral intervention on adults' physical self-perceptions. Participants, who were between 40 and 70 years old, were randomly allocated to either a control or intervention condition. Both groups attended an initial assessment and received information leaflets on reducing the risks of coronary heart disease. The control group received no further contact or support while the intervention group attended unsupervised exercise sessions twice a week for up to an hour. Participants were encouraged to gradually increase their activity during the ten weeks to aim to participate in 30–40 minutes of aerobic activity during their twice weekly sessions. All study participants completed the Physical Self-Perception Profile (PSPP; Fox and Corbin, 1989) at baseline, 16 weeks and 36 weeks from baseline, thus providing information about the longer term impact of exercise on self-perceptions. At both follow-up points, people in the intervention group were significantly more positive about their physical self-worth, physical condition and physical health than people in the control group. This suggests that participation in the programme resulted in increased physical self-perceptions and that as time progressed participation continued to impact on self-perceptions after the intervention.

Further analysis was conducted to examine any differences in self-perceptions between controls and those who were classed as high (15–20 sessions) or low (0–14 sessions) adherers to the programme. Results indicated that control participants and low adherers both demonstrated significant differences in physical condition from baseline to 16 weeks and in physical health from baseline to 36 weeks. High adherers demonstrated greater improvements in perceived physical appearance than did low adherers between baseline and 36 weeks. This indicates that even small increases in physical activity can impact significantly on some aspects of physical self-perception, while more long-term regular activity is required for improvements in the whole range of physical self-perceptions. The results also demonstrated changes in physical self-perception irrespective of cardiovascular fitness; however, a link was identified between anthropometric changes (changes in weight and body fat) and all subscales of the PSPP. This suggests that the changes in physical self-perceptions may have been linked to the improved body composition as a result of the activity.

Learning Activity 3.3

You might have noticed that a number of the studies discussed so far (e.g. Burgess *et al.*, 2006; Schneider *et al.*, 2008) have focused on the self-perceptions of adolescents. Give some thought to why research might target this group of individuals and how you might expect results to differ between this age group and other ages. Compare your answers with the discussion provided at the end of the book.

The relationship between physical activity, the self and wellbeing

In Chapter 2 we discussed the positive impact that physical activity has on mental health. Earlier in this chapter we also mentioned the benefits that a positive self-concept and self-worth can have on our psychological health. Researchers have therefore considered whether physical self-worth can act as a mediator between exercise involvement and global self-worth and wellbeing.

The self as a mediator of the relationship between physical activity and mental health

Dishman *et al.* (2006) were interested in whether the relationship between physical activity and positive mental health is linked to improvements in physical self-concept. Female adolescents provided measures of depressive symptoms, self-worth and physical self-concept (using the Physical Self-Description Questionnaire; Marsh *et al.*, 1994, see Box 3.2), physical activity and sport participation as well as being assessed for cardiorespiratory fitness and body mass index (BMI). The results demonstrated that girls with higher self-worth reported less depressive symptoms. In addition, physical self-concept mediated the relationship between physical activity and self-worth. This means that those who were more physically active were more likely to have a more positive physical self-concept and as a result higher global self-worth. Given that self-worth was negatively related to depressive symptoms the results suggest that the positive impact of physical activity on mental health might be mediated by improvements in physical self-concept and self-worth. These relationships were observed irrespective of anthropometric measures or BMI, again suggesting that the relationships between physical activity and self-concept are not necessarily linked to bodily changes provided by physical activity as proposed by Taylor and Fox (2005).

Social physique anxiety

Case Study 3.3

Let's return to Hena.

Since her last visit to the GP, Hena has failed to increase her physical activity. Her GP has now advised her to start an exercise referral programme which involves attending a gym twice a week with a trained instructor. Although Hena desperately wants to lose the weight, the thought of attending the sessions terrifies her and brings her out in a cold sweat. She cannot bear the thought of having to wear exercise clothes and attend a gym. She believes that the type of people who attend a gym will be attractive and healthy and will look at her physique and see her as lazy and unattractive. She also cannot bear the thought of exercising in an environment where she will be surrounded by mirrors, forcing her to look at her body while she exercises.

We can see from some of the models of the 'self' that the way others view us is an important factor in how we perceive ourselves and our level of self-worth. For this reason people tend to want to represent themselves in the best possible light so that they are thought of favourably. One way in which people try to maintain a positive image of themselves is by using something called 'self-preservation'. Self-preservation involves people hiding the aspects of themselves that they believe will be viewed unfavourably while promoting the positive aspects of themselves. For example, on meeting a stranger early in the morning, we might aim to override our desire to be our usual grumpy self and put on a cheery smile so that they perceive us to be a likeable individual, rather than the grumpy morning person that we really are! In a similar way, we might not want to place ourselves in situations where we could look foolish or incompetent. For example, an overweight and unfit individual might avoid exercising in the gym because they wish to preserve their self-image rather than have people view them as unfit or unhealthy as they become out of breath.

There are certain situations in which it is extremely difficult to maintain our positive self-image and the more negative aspects of our self are likely to become apparent for all to see. These situations cause the individual to feel anxious and uncomfortable in this environment and to experience social anxiety. Social anxiety can occur as a result of being unable to preserve a positive image of the self and can relate to any of the domains of competence. For example, if we are asked a question in class to which we do not know the answer this is likely to influence our academic self-image. We previously discussed how important the physical self-image is to our global image. It is understandable therefore that in situations which undermine our physical self-image and others' perception of our physical selves we are likely to experience anxiety about our physical self. This is termed social physique anxiety and stems from the fear that others may negatively evaluate our physique. This in turn is likely to have a significant impact on our global self-worth.

Social physique anxiety can have a number of behaviours and cognitions such as whether people choose to exercise, their motives to exercise, where they choose to exercise, what they choose to wear to exercise and how they feel during exercise. Case Study 3.3 describes an individual suffering from social physique anxiety and shows how much of a barrier to exercise social physique anxiety can be. The negative effect of social physique anxiety on exercise behaviour is discussed in more detail in Chapter 6. In this chapter, we focus on whether exercise can be used to improve social physique anxiety.

Exercise and social physique anxiety

So far in this chapter we have discussed how exercise can improve individuals' physical self-perceptions and body image. Exercise also helps people to lose weight and improve the overall condition of the physique (Edmunds et al., 2007). Research has therefore explored whether exercise can in turn reduce individuals' social physique anxiety. Aşçi et al. (2006) suggested that university students with higher levels of physical activity had higher levels of social physique anxiety. On first glance this might suggest that exercise is detrimental to our self-perception and anxieties about our physical selves. This might well be the case since research has demonstrated that certain exercise environments can exacerbate social physique anxiety (see Chapter 6), however, there may be an alternative explanation for this result. It may be that individuals with higher levels of social physique anxiety exercise more in an attempt to change their bodies. It is difficult to say, using cross-sectional research such as this, whether individuals who exercise tend to have more anxieties about their physical selves or whether people who have anxieties about their physical selves tend to exercise more. For this reason, research has begun to employ longitudinal designs, where a repeated measures approach can be used (see Box 3.4). This way, causal relationships between variables, social physique anxiety and exercise in this case, can be explored.

> ## Box 3.4 Definition: Repeated measures
>
> A repeated measures design is a form of research design where the same measures are taken over a period of time during the research. Often research using this method tests the efficacy of an intervention. Participants provide baseline measures of the variables of interest which can then be compared to the same measures taken at the end of the intervention. Any changes seen in the measures from baseline to the end of the intervention can then be attributed to the intervention (if no confounding variables need to be considered and a control group is included that does not receive the intervention).

McAuley *et al.* (1995) invited middle-aged sedentary adults to participate in a five-month exercise programme. The intervention involved participants meeting with an exerciser leader three times a week for one hour of exercise designed to increase their levels of aerobic activity. Measures of social physique anxiety, self-efficacy and outcome expectations (see Chapter 5) and anthropometric variables (e.g. weight, skinfold measures, etc.) were obtained at the start of the programme (baseline) and then again following the five-month programme. The programme was successful at increasing participants' self-efficacy and outcome expectancies. Interestingly, the increases in self-efficacy and positive outcome expectancies predicted decreases in social physique anxiety even when controlling for gender, weight loss and body fat. This demonstrates that the reductions seen in social physique anxiety occurred irrespective of changes in participants' physique and resulted from increased self-efficacy in the exercise environment.

More recently, Lindwall and Lindgren (2005) conducted a controlled trial to determine the effects of exercise on social physique anxiety and self-perceptions in Swedish female adolescents. Schools were randomly allocated to an intervention or control group, and all participants completed measures of the PSPP (Fox and Corbin, 1989) and the Social Physique Anxiety Scale (Hart *et al.*, 1989), were measured for BMI and took part in a submaximal fitness test. The intervention programme involved twice weekly exercise sessions over a six-month period. Participants could choose from a range of activities such as dance, yoga, climbing and karate. The female-only sessions included 45 minutes of the chosen activity as well as a 15-minute discussion on healthy living. Results demonstrated that participants in the intervention group reported more improvements in social physique anxiety and self-perceptions than did those in the control group. In fact the control group demonstrated increases in social physique anxiety during the six-month research period.

Despite these encouraging results, however, when an intent-to-treat analysis (see Box 3.5) was used, the improvements in self-perception were no longer significant. The effect of the intervention on social physique anxiety did remain significant, but social physique anxiety and physical self-perceptions were only weakly related to the physiological measures. This suggests that the beneficial effect of the intervention might not necessarily be attributable to changes in body shape or physical fitness but to a psychosocial effect.

Box 3.5 Definition: Intent-to-treat analysis

Clinical research and research using interventions must account for many influencing factors when analysing the results. For example, people often drop out of interventions before they are completed and so do not provide the measures needed to analyse changes seen during the intervention. This provides the researcher with a dilemma about how to analyse the results. One option is to only use data from people who completed the research. The benefit of this is that there is no missing data. However, a limitation of this is that people who were not doing very well on the intervention or who were not seeing any improvements are likely to be the people who choose to drop out while the people who are doing well will complete the programme. Therefore by only including these people in the analysis, the intervention will look very successful, when in fact this may not be the case. Intent-to-treat analysis aims to overcome this problem by using the data from everybody who intended to take part in the study. Although this is likely to mean that the researcher has to deal with missing data (because some people will only have contributed baseline data), it provides a more accurate representation of all participants. This is therefore a far more rigorous way of analysing the data.

Chapter Review

This chapter began by discussing the factors that make up the self. We discussed how the construct we use to describe ourselves is referred to as our self-concept. This is a multifaceted construct made up of sub-domains which in turn are made up of a number of situation-specific domains. Our roles and competencies within these domains allow us to evaluate ourselves and this contributes to our self-worth (Learning Objective 1). Four main sub-domains are believed to make up the structure of the self-concept and self-worth: social, emotional, academic and physical. The physical self-worth sub-domain is believed to be the most significant predictor of our overall self-worth (Learning Objective 2).

The second part of this chapter discussed the reciprocal relationship between physical activity and the self. Physical activity impacts on aspects of the self and this relationship and an individual's self-concept and self-worth influence their physical activity behaviour (Learning Objective 3). Research has demonstrated that individuals with low-self worth are less likely to participate in physical activity. However, participation in physical activity has been shown to improve an individual's self-worth. Aspects of the self have also been shown to mediate the relationship between physical activity and improved wellbeing.

Finally, this chapter discussed social physique anxiety, which is anxiety stemming from the fear that others might evaluate our bodies negatively. Research has demonstrated that exercise interventions can help to alleviate social physique anxiety; however, some studies suggest that this improvement may be attributable as much to psychosocial variables, such as improved self-efficacy, as it is to the exercise component of the intervention (Learning Objective 4).

Learning Activity 3.4

Test your understanding

1. Compare and contrast the difference between the self-concept and self-worth and describe the relationship between physical self-worth and global self-worth.
2. What is meant by a reciprocal relationship between physical activity and the self and what effect does this have on exercise behaviour?
3. Should an exercise intervention aimed at tackling the obesity epidemic be concerned about improving participants' self-worth. If so, why?
4. What does research suggest about the benefits of different types of exercise on self-worth?

Further Reading

- For more information on the relationship between physical activity and the self:

Goldfield, GS, Mallory, R, Parker, T, Cunningham, T, Legg, C and Lumb, A *et al.* (2007) Effects of modifying physical activity and sedentary behavior on psychosocial adjustment in overweight/obese children. *Journal of Pediatric Psychology*, 32: 783–93.

This study employed a randomised controlled design to test the effects of increasing physical activity and reducing sedentary behaviour in the form of watching TV on obese children's physical and global self-worth. Despite the perceived similarity of increasing physical activity and reducing sedentary behaviour, it is interesting to see the different effects that these behaviours have on aspects of the self.

- For more information on social physique anxiety and its impact on physical activity:

Lindwall, M and Lindgren, E (2006) The effects of a 6-month exercise intervention programme on physical self-perceptions and social physique anxiety in non-physically active adolescent Swedish girls. *Psychology of Sport and Exercise*, 6: 643–58.

Although we briefly discussed this paper in this chapter it is worth reading in full as it provides a good overview of research surrounding physical activity and social physique anxiety and is a study that has used a randomised controlled design.

Chapter 4
Becoming active: models and motives

Learning Objectives

This chapter is designed to help you be able to:

1. be aware of the key models and theories used to predict and explain exercise behaviour;
2. identify the strengths and weaknesses of models and theories of exercise behaviour;
3. understand the importance of self-efficacy in motivational theory.

Introduction

In Chapter 2 we explored the determinants of physical activity and identified a number of individual, cognitive and environmental factors that relate to physical activity level. In addition to identifying these correlates of physical activity, researchers are also interested in what motivates people to be physically active and what processes are involved in changing from being physically inactive to becoming a regular exerciser. Understanding the motives that drive people to engage in physical activity means that we can make interventions more appealing to different individuals. Similarly, understanding the stages of behaviour change means we can target appropriate interventions at the most appropriate time for different individuals.

In this chapter we outline and evaluate a number of models which discuss the stages of behaviour change that we experience when we become physically active. These models are the:

- Transtheoretical Model;
- Theory of Reasoned Action and Theory of Planned Behaviour;
- Self-Determination Theory and Cognitive Evaluation Theory;
- Self-Efficacy Theory;
- Social Cognitive Theory.

Transtheoretical Model

The Transtheoretical Model (TTM; Prochaska and DiClemente, 1983) was designed to explain the processes that people went through while trying to voluntarily stop smoking. The model proposes that during behaviour change, people will move through different stages. Since its use in smoking cessation, this model has been successfully applied to other health behaviours such as physical activity (Daley *et al.*, 2009).

As the model proposes that we move through different stages when changing our behaviour, the model has also been referred to as the Stages of Change model; however, this title only encompasses part of the overall model. As well as the stages of change the model proposes other constructs which are likely to influence behaviour change. These are:

- decisional balance;
- process of change;
- self-efficacy;
- temptation.

In the following sections we examine these constructs in more detail, however, let's start with the key construct in this model: the stages of change.

Stages of change

The stage of change part of the model proposes that there are five stages of behaviour change which people can move through. These are precontemplation, contemplation, preparation, action and maintenance (Figure 4.1). You will notice in the figure that there are no arrows between the stages. This is because people do not have to move through each of the stages in turn but can jump between stages, missing an intervening stage altogether. In addition, there is nothing to stop somebody moving in the opposite direction and becoming less physically active. Prochaska and DiClemente (1986) suggested that people changing their behaviour will move through the stages in a cyclical way, going through periods of growth and relapse. This will occur at a different rate and via different stages for each individual.

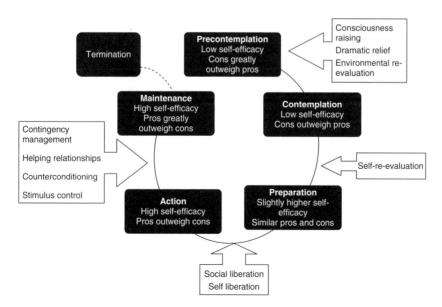

Figure 4.1 Stages of change, including decisional balance and self-efficacy at each stage and the process of change most appropriate for each stage.

- Precontemplation describes somebody who has no interest or desire to become more physically active.
- Contemplation refers to the stage where an individual is considering whether or not to change their behaviour to become more physically active. This stage often involves people considering the benefits and costs of behaviour change.
- Preparation refers to a situation where an individual has decided to become more physically active and is planning to do so within the next month. People in this stage often do something behavioural, such as joining a gym, to prepare themselves for the behaviour change despite not yet having engaged in the behaviour.
- In the action stage the individual has started exercising, but has only been doing so for less than six months. This stage is an unstable one because the individual has only been exercising for a short period of time and as such might still be easily tempted to regress to a preceding stage.
- Finally, the maintenance stage relates to an individual who has been regularly exercising for more than six months and is therefore maintaining the new behaviour. Although these individuals have succeeded in changing their behaviour they are still at risk of relapsing. The novelty of the behaviour might wear off and old patterns might start to remerge.

Once somebody has been in the maintenance stage for over five years they are believed to leave the cyclical stages of change and are said to be in 'termination'. This person no longer feels the temptation to return to their old behaviour and therefore the likelihood of relapse is very slim.

Learning Activity 4.1

Read the case studies below and identify which stage of change each individual is in. Check your answers with those provided at the end of the book.

Case Study 4.1

- Hena *has decided to give the GP referral programme a go. Her husband has helped her to choose some clothes to wear and she starts her first class next week.*
- Tamsin *has been a regular swimmer for the past four years. She finds swimming relaxing and it helps to keep her figure toned.*
- Altab *watched a documentary on the obesity epidemic last night. He realised that he is probably a bit overweight and really should try to do more exercise. He thinks that he might consider doing something once he gets back from his cruise later that year.*

Now that we have considered the stages of change, let's examine the processes that are proposed to predict and differentiate between these stages, starting with decision balance.

Decision balance

When we discussed the contemplation stage above, we identified that people in this stage often evaluated the pros and cons of their behaviour change. This is in essence the decision balance construct of the TTM.

The concept of a decisional balance sheet was first proposed by Janis and Mann (1977). When we are making decisions, we need to balance out the potential benefits and costs to ourselves and significant others. This therefore involves identifying some of the barriers that we have to exercise. If the costs or barriers outweigh the perceived benefits of exercise then it is unlikely that we will decide to adopt the behaviour in question and vice versa.

Although we discussed decision balance as a process within the contemplation stage, it is likely that this decision making strategy is implemented across all five stages of the model. However, the balance of the pros and cons is likely to differ in each stage. Research by Prochaska *et al.* (1994) explored how the decision balance differed for individuals in the different stages. The results are summarised in Figure 4.1. Perhaps not surprisingly, the costs of the behaviour outweighed the benefits for people in the precontemplation and contemplation stages. However, as people progressed through the stages, gradually the differences between the pros and cons reduced until the pros outweighed the cons in the action and maintenance stages.

The second process used to predict and differentiate between the stages is self-efficacy and we consider this construct in the next section.

Self-efficacy

Self-efficacy is the confidence that an individual has that they will be able to carry out a particular behaviour in order to achieve a desired outcome. In this situation, self-efficacy would represent how confident somebody might be that they could become more physically active in order to lose weight.

Similar to the way decisional balance of pros and cons changes across the stages of change, self-efficacy is also believed to change across these stages (Figure 4.1). Not surprisingly, self-efficacy increases as we move through the stages from precontemplation to maintenance. Knowing this allows psychologists to use this information to help people to increase their self-efficacy and in turn move through the stages. Strategies used to increase self-efficacy are discussed in more detail when we consider the processes of change. This is the fourth construct in the model and in the next section of this chapter we look at these more general behaviour change strategies.

Process of change

The processes of change are specific strategies that can be used to help people to move between the stages. One way of doing this is to use strategies to overcome any barriers that prevent us from changing the behaviour (the cons identified in our decisional balance). As mentioned above, others relate to ways in which we can increase our self-efficacy. Prochaska and Velicer (1997) defined ten strategies, which have been divided into cognitive and behavioural strategies, as listed below.

Cognitive processes of change
- *Consciousness raising.* This involves increasing awareness about the causes, problems and consequences of the behaviour.

- *Dramatic relief.* This strategy stimulates an emotional reaction to the behaviour. Media campaigns will often use this strategy by showing personal testimonies of people facing the consequences of a particular behaviour (e.g. smokers with lung cancer) in an attempt to move people emotionally to change their behaviour.
- *Self-re-evaluation.* This involves assessing your self-image while engaging in the behaviour and after the period of behaviour change. For example, forming an image of yourself as an unhealthy and overweight individual prior to any change in behaviour versus a fit and attractive person, after adopting a more active lifestyle.
- *Environmental re-evaluation.* This strategy encourages the individual to consider the effect of the behaviour on significant others. For example, how being inactive might set an unhealthy example for children.
- *Social liberation.* This strategy relates to taking advantages of social opportunities designed to make changing the behaviour more accessible. This might mean individuals taking advantage of promotions at local leisure centres or using cycle paths to cycle to work.

Behavioural processes of change

- *Self-liberation.* This refers to the individual's belief that they can change and employing a strategy encourages the individual to develop a commitment to do so. This might involve making your intentions to change your behaviour public or setting yourself a New Year's resolution.
- *Counterconditioning.* This involves identifying a healthy substitute behaviour that can replace a less healthy behaviour. For example, an individual might decide that every time they want to smoke a cigarette they will go for a ten-minute walk instead.
- *Stimulus control.* This strategy promotes removing cues that encourage unhealthy behaviour and instead using cues to facilitate the new healthy behaviour. This might involve leaving your trainers in your work locker as a cue to go for a walk at lunch time.
- *Contingency management.* Providing rewards for achieving goals for successful behaviour change offers a positive outcome for the efforts involved in behaviour change and in turn is likely to encourage healthy forms of future behaviour. This might come in the form of an unexpected reward such as a compliment from a friend following weeks of hard work at the gym.
- *Helping relationships.* Having people who support your efforts can provide help, advice and reassurance when going through difficult times during the behaviour change process.

Different strategies are believed to be useful for people who are at different stages of behaviour change. Cognitive strategies are believed to be most effective during the early stages of the model, while behavioural strategies are believed to be most effective during the latter stages. This is demonstrated in Figure 4.1 and offers practical implications for interventions that employ these strategies. For example, if we are aiming to encourage sedentary individuals to start some form of activity it would be better to use strategies such as gathering information or social re-evaluation. On the other hand, an intervention aimed at helping already active individuals to remain motivated to exercise should incorporate strategies such as social support or stimulus control.

Learning Activity 4.2

Read the following health promotion interventions and consider which of the processes of change strategies have been incorporated into each intervention. Check your answers with the suggestions at the end of the book.

- *Intervention 1*: A television advert shows an obese lady crying and saying, 'I knew that not exercising would be bad for my heart, but I never imagined it would be bad for his too.' The camera then changes shot to show a little boy who is overweight being bullied in the playground. The slogan, 'Be a role model . . . get active' is then flashed onto the screen.
- *Intervention 2*: A leaflet in a doctor's surgery advertises a local counselling service for individuals who want to lose weight by exercising. The leaflet provides information about the risks of inactivity for one's health, provides a telephone number and details of the meetings that people can attend and includes real life success stories about people who have attended the sessions and successfully lost weight with before and after pictures.

We now consider the final construct that we have all faced at one time or another: temptation.

Temptation

Temptation refers to the urge to relapse to old habits when facing difficult periods in the behaviour change. For example, bad weather and dark evenings in the winter might provide the temptation to resort back to more sedentary behaviour. Giving in to temptation can result in individuals relapsing and moving back to earlier stages within the model. Ensuring that individuals understand when temptation is most likely to occur means that psychologists can ensure that individuals recognise this risk and provide them with strategies (such as those discussed above) to implement to try to overcome temptation.

Evaluation of the Transtheoretical Model

The TTM has been applied across a range of different health behaviours, such as smoking cessation, diet control and physical activity, and has been demonstrated to be useful across a wide range of the population (Nigg *et al.*, 2010). The model is successful at acknowledging individual differences, and since individuals can be placed into one of the five stages, the TTM has been extremely useful for targeting interventions at appropriate participants and applying appropriate strategies to help people to progress towards maintaining a new healthy behaviour (Blissmer and McAuley, 2002).

Despite this, researchers have highlighted limitations to this model. One problem is the application of the model to physical activity. Despite some successful use of the model in this context (e.g. Williams *et al.*, 2008), researchers have highlighted concern that the model is based around behaviour change to stop an undesirable behaviour (e.g. smoking cessation). Trying to initiate the uptake of a healthy behaviour is fundamentally different because the behaviour must be integrated into other aspects of the individual's life and therefore might follow a different mechanism of behaviour change (Nigg *et al.*, 2010).

Although research in the physical activity domain has supported the TTM, much of the research is cross-sectional in nature (Nigg *et al.*, 2010). As such it is difficult to determine the direction of causality between stage of change and self-efficacy and decisional balance. Longitudinal research has therefore been conducted to allow for causality to be explored (e.g. Williams *et al.*, 2008; discussed in Chapter 5).

In addition, research has questioned whether the time frames that Prochaska and DiClemente (1986) propose for the different stages of change have any real basis in observed behaviour change (Sutton, 2000). For example, why is someone classified as being in the maintenance stage after six months of activity rather than five or seven? These numbers appear to be arbitrary, and as such weaken the efficacy of the stages.

A recent meta-analysis by Marshall and Biddle (2001) that explored the efficacy of the TTM supported TTM proposals that physical activity increased with the stages of change. The analyses also highlighted evidence to support the suggested changes in self-efficacy and decision balance according to the stages of change. However, Marshall and Biddle reported conflicting evidence regarding the use of the processes of change in the physical activity domain. Evidence suggested that individuals used all ten processes when undergoing a period of behaviour change, but the proposed patterns of use of cognitive and behavioural strategies at different stages was not supported.

Suggestions have been made that the weakness of the model in the physical activity domain may be the result of the way in which the model has been used. Researchers have tended to explore the component parts of the model in isolation (e.g. using the stage of change but not the processes of change) and as such may not have been using the model in the way it was intended. Nigg *et al.* (2010) suggest that future research should concentrate on validating the entire model within this setting rather than only its component parts in isolation from each other.

Theory of Reasoned Action and Theory of Planned Behaviour

The second theory that we are going to examine is the Theory of Reasoned Action (TRA).

Theory of Reasoned Action

Case Study 4.2
Returning to Hena . . .

We can see from Hena's case study so far that she used to enjoy her PE classes when she was at school. However, she now feels that she is too old and overweight to be able to enjoy physical activity and is concerned about other people's perceptions of her if she started attending the gym. Hena does appreciate the health benefits of exercise and can see the difference it makes to her work colleagues who attend the gym regularly. Despite this, most of Hena's family and friends do not exercise and so it is easy to just follow the crowd and not bother. Even if she wanted to attend the GP referral classes that her doctor has recommended she just can't seem to find the time around her job and three children. Therefore although she did intend to go to her GP referral class this week, as it draws closer she thinks it is unlikely that she will be able to go.

The TRA (Fishbein and Ajzen, 1975; Figure 4.2) is concerned with the social and cognitive factors that predict our voluntary behaviour. Understanding why we do not take part in certain health enhancing behaviours allows us to intervene and use cognitive and behavioural strategies to overcome some of the barriers to exercise.

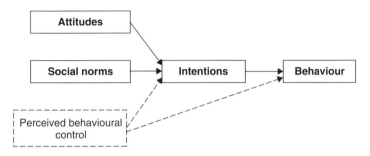

Figure 4.2 Theory of Reasoned Action (in bold) and addition of perceived behavioural control in the Theory of Planned Behaviour (dotted line). Reprinted from Ajzen, I (1991) The theory of planned behaviour. Organizational Behavior and Human Decision Processes, *50: 179–211, with permission from Elsevier.*

The theory proposes that we are rational beings who will use information around us in order to help us decide whether or not to engage in a behaviour. The information that we use is based on two factors: attitudes and social norms. These factors are then believed to influence our behavioural intentions which are an indication of how likely we are to subsequently engage in the behaviour. Read Hena's case study above. In this example, Hena has a mixed attitude towards physical activity classes. This is partly negative as a result of her social physique anxiety (SPA) but also positive as a result of understanding the health benefits of exercise. It appears that her family and friends hold relatively negative attitudes and therefore her social norms are also negative. This is likely to have negative effect on her behavioural intentions. As we see in the case study, this appears to be the case and Hena does not intend to go to her first GP referral class.

Intentions

An individual's intentions to exercise are considered to be a key influence on their likelihood to engage in that behaviour (Armitage and Connor, 2001). An individual with strong intentions to exercise is more likely to commit and put in the effort to do so than an individual with little or no intention, such as Hena. According to the TRA, both the individual's attitudes and social norms (others' attitudes) will determine the degree of somebody's intentions to engage in a behaviour.

Attitudes

Our attitudes towards a behaviour are based on our beliefs about the value of that behaviour. The perceived consequences of engaging in the behaviour will determine how positively we view this behaviour. For example, Hena might believe that exercising after work means that she has less time to spend with her children before they go to bed. In addition, our attitudes are based on what we believe the outcomes of the behaviour will be. For example, Hena might consider the fact that exercising results in upset children who miss their mum and as such this will cloud her attitude towards exercise. Thus attitudes towards a behaviour will be different for each individual.

Social norms

As well as our own attitudes, the theory proposes that the opinions of important others also impact our behavioural intentions. The pressure and social support that we feel from family, friends and society in general will all impact on how likely we are to participate in exercise. For example, a sedentary individual, like Hena, with friends who do not exercise will feel less pressure to exercise given that inactivity is a social norm within their peer group. According to the theory, individuals who perceive a positive social norm towards physical activity are more likely to intend to be physically active, while those who perceive a negative social norm will have less intention to engage in physical activity.

Limitations of the Theory of Reasoned Action

So far we have discussed research that indicates that attitudes and social norms can successfully predict behavioural intentions. However, there are some circumstances where no matter how positive an individual's attitude and peers' attitudes towards a behaviour, factors beyond their control prevent them from carrying out the behaviour. In other words, intentions do not always lead to action. For example, an individual may enjoy the energy that they get from cycling (positive attitude) and have friends who are keen cyclists (positive social norm). They therefore intend to cycle after work (positive intention). However, part way through the working day their boss tells them that there is an extremely important work dinner which they are expected to attend. No matter how positive their own attitudes and intentions or the attitudes of significant others, this situation prevents them from going cycling. It was the acknowledgement of this limitation to the TRA that led to the development of the Theory of Planned Behaviour, which is discussed below.

Theory of Planned Behaviour

The Theory of Planned Behaviour (TPB; Ajzen, 1985) evolved as a result of weaknesses in the TRA. The TPB maintains that behavioural intentions will predict actual behaviour. In addition, the theory supports the proposal that attitudes and subjective norms will predict an individual's behavioural intentions. However, the TPB added an additional concept: perceived behavioural control, as a third predictor of behavioural intentions and actual behaviour (Figure 4.2).

Perceived behavioural control

Perceived behavioural control represents how likely it is that the individual will be able to carry out the desired behaviour (i.e. how much the individual is in control of carrying out the behaviour; Ajzen, 2002). For example, Hena was quick to note that she had little time to commit to exercise as a result of her job and children. Perceived behavioural control is thought to comprise two constructs: self-efficacy (see TTM) and controllability. Controllability relates to how much the individual is in control of carrying out the behaviour (e.g. how easy will it be to find the time to walk 10 miles). The factor that prevents an individual from exercising can be a real barrier, such as childcare in Hena's example; however, this can also be something that the individual perceives to be an obstacle. For example, childcare could be viewed as a barrier that can be overcome as Hena could choose to do some physical activity during her lunch hour. Thus the individual's perception of the severity of the barrier is key to how much it affects their behavioural intentions.

As with attitudes and social norms, the theory proposes that an individual's perceived behavioural control is likely to predict their behavioural intentions. However, unlike attitudes and subjective norms, perceived behavioural control also directly predicts behaviour. This is to account for the fact that although you might intend to exercise, something unexpected and out of your control might arise to prevent this from happening.

Evaluation of the Theory of Planned Behaviour

A number of studies have demonstrated the use of the TPB for predicting a wide range of health behaviours, including physical activity (Hagger *et al.*, 2002) and has been successfully applied in physical activity interventions (e.g. Wyer *et al.*, 2001).

There has also been consistent support for the roles of perceived behavioural control and attitudes as strong predictors of behavioural intentions (Armitage and Connor, 2001). However, some authors suggest that social norms are only weak predictors of intention and as a result have not included this construct in their research (e.g. Sparks *et al.*, 1995). Others argue that the concept of social norms may be too broad as this must account for the opinions of a number of different groups, for example, family and peers, who may have conflicting opinions.

A further limitation of this theory is that although it can be used to predict intentions, actual behaviour is not as well predicted (Godin and Kok, 1996). The TPB proposes that attitudes and social norms can only predict actual behaviour via behavioural intentions. This must mean that there are additional variables which translate intentions into behaviours. Given that the theory makes no attempt to suggest what these additional variables might be, its ability to fully explain behaviour appears to be lacking.

Self-Determination Theory and Cognitive Evaluation Theory

Take some time to think of a sport or exercise that you participate in regularly. Why do you participate in this activity? Do you participate in different aspects of the exercise for different reasons (e.g. training versus matches or competitions)? Keep these different reasons in mind as you read the sections that follow.

Self-Determination Theory

The Self-Determination Theory (SDT; Deci and Ryan, 1985) is a theory of motivation concerned with the regulation of behaviour and the factors that influence this regulation. In a previous section we discussed the fact that people often state a lack of motivation as a key barrier to exercise. However, according to SDT, whether or not we are motivated to participate in a behaviour is less important than what type of motivation we have towards that behaviour. SDT proposes that there are a number of different types of motivation which exist on a continuum. These different types of motivation are explained below.

- *Amotivation* represents a relative absence of any motivation to carry out the behaviour. For example, a sedentary person who has no intention of or interest in exercising is amotivated.
- *Extrinsic motivation* refers to participation in an activity to satisfy an external demand (Ryan and Deci, 2000). Extrinsic motivation can be separated into four forms of behavioural regulation:
  - *External regulation* occurs when the individual's behaviour is controlled by external rewards or the threat of external punishments and this form of regulation undermines intrinsic motivation (Deci *et al.*, 1999). For example, someone who exercises simply for the approval of their family and friends (an external reward) is externally regulated.
  - *Introjected regulation* represents an individual who accepts the value of a behaviour, however, does not truly identify with it. This form of motivation is considered one of the most complex because both positive and negative motives coincide (Koestner and Losier, 2002). For example, an individual may feel that exercise is good for their health (positive feelings) and yet feel that exercise is not supported by their family because it means less time is spent with them (negative feelings). This conflict can result in feelings of guilt or shame (Deci and Ryan, 2000).
  - *Identified regulation* represents a situation where people accept the value of a behaviour. For example, a person may be motivated to go to the gym because they value the benefit that this will have for their health.
  - *Integrated regulation* is the most internalised form of extrinsic motivation. Not only are the values of the behaviour considered important but these are internalised so that the behaviour integrates and correlates with other personal values and beliefs and forms part of one's identity (Ryan and Deci, 2000). Although the behaviour is fully integrated it is still extrinsically motivated because the behaviour is still carried out to achieve a goal that is 'personally important as a valued outcome' (Deci *et al.*, 1991, page 330). For example, an athlete may consider their sporting ability to be part of their identity (i.e. it defines who they are as a person). They might be motivated to exercise in order to maintain their performance and as such their status as an athlete.
- *Intrinsic motivation* is the motivation to do something for its own sake in the absence of external rewards (Ryan and Deci, 2000). Thus, people who are intrinsically motivated will engage in behaviour for the sheer pleasure of taking part.

The different forms of motivation influence the likelihood of carrying out a behaviour. Perhaps not surprisingly, amotivation has been associated with a lower likelihood of people participating in the behaviour (Standage *et al.*, 2003). Although the different forms of extrinsic regulation can be successful in encouraging people to adopt a behaviour, the long-term outcomes of extrinsic regulation vary considerably. An individual who is externally regulated to participate in exercise will do so in order to gain an external reward of some sort. One problem with this type of motivation is that once the offer of this reward is removed, the motivation to participate is lost (Deci and Ryan, 1985). Forms of regulation that are closer to the self-determined end of the scale (i.e. identified and integrated regulation) are positively correlated with future intentions to continue the behaviour (Chatzisarantis *et al.*, 2005) and therefore although these are controlled forms of regulation they are considered to be adaptive. Intrinsic motivation is the most self-determined form of motivation and as expected has the most positive outcomes. For instance, research has demonstrated relationships between intrinsic motivation and increased persistence, long-term participation and wellbeing (Maltby and Day, 2001). The influence of motivational regulations on behaviour and wellbeing is discussed further in a study by Thøgersen-Ntoumani and Ntoumanis (2006) recommended in the further reading at the end of the chapter.

Understanding the different types of motivation that people have to exercise can allow researchers to design specific strategies to help individuals to become more self-determined in their motivation and as such increase their likelihood of continuing to exercise. A sub-theory of SDT is therefore focused on how the environment can encourage or discourage intrinsic motivation, and is discussed below.

Cognitive Evaluation Theory

Cognitive Evaluation Theory (CET; Deci and Ryan, 1985) states that intrinsically motivated behaviour is based on striving to satisfy three innate psychological needs. These are the needs for *competence*, *autonomy* and *relatedness*. If social and/or environmental factors do not satisfy one of the psychological needs then this is thought to diminish motivation (Deci *et al.*, 1991). Autonomy satisfaction results from feeling that the choice to participate in a behaviour is volitional and not controlled by external factors. As you can imagine, autonomy satisfaction is central to SDT as it is virtually impossible to feel self-determined in one's behaviour without feeling that it is your own choice to carry out the behaviour. Competence satisfaction is the perception that you are able to carry out the behaviour and achieve outcomes desired from this behaviour (a concept similar to self-efficacy). Again, this need is extremely important for self-determined motivation because an individual is unlikely to feel self-determined if they are not confident that they can carry out the behaviour in question. Relatedness satisfaction is the need to feel accepted by others and to have supportive relationships (Reis *et al.*, 2000). Humans have a basic need to interact positively with other people and this can be a fundamental aspect of the enjoyment of sport and exercise and thus intrinsic motivation (Markland, 1999).

CET therefore proposes that the environment can either encourage or discourage the satisfaction of the three psychological needs and subsequently intrinsic motivation. Two main types of environment have been the focus of this research: an *autonomy supportive environment* and a *controlling environment*. An autonomy supportive environment focuses on offering choice and opportunities for independent thought. To provide an autonomy supportive environment, leaders should listen and acknowledge feelings, offer positive feedback and provide relevant information when required (Sarrazin *et al.*, 2007). In contrast, in a controlling environment the leader tends to take charge, uses commands and instructions and motivates through threats and criticisms (Sarrazin *et al.*, 2007).

Learning Activity 4.3

Imagine that you are setting up an exercise programme for obese individuals. Consider how you would ensure that your programme meets the participants' needs for autonomy, competence and relatedness satisfaction. Some suggestions are offered at the end of the book.

Evaluation of Self-Determination Theory and Cognitive Evaluation Theory

Evidence has consistently demonstrated the interaction between autonomy supportive environments, increased need satisfaction and feelings of self-determined motivation in physical activity (Edmunds *et al.*, 2006). In addition, research has supported the proposal that intrinsic motivation results in positive outcomes such as increased wellbeing (Maltby and Day, 2001) and persistence (Pelletier *et al.*, 2001), while more controlled forms of regulation result in lower affect (Maltby and Day, 2001). However, some limitations of this approach have been highlighted. The first relates to the influence of introjected regulation on behaviour. SDT proposes that as a more controlled form of regulation, introjected regulation will not encourage exercise behaviour. However, research has demonstrated that introjected regulation can encourage exercise participation, but it is unclear whether this will encourage long-term persistence (Thogersen-Ntoumani and Ntoumanis, 2006).

Cognitive Evaluation Theory proposes that all three needs are equally important for developing more self-determined regulation. However, some researchers believe that individuals are likely to attach different degrees of importance to the three needs (e.g. Vallerand, 2000). For example, Hannah might feel that it is extremely important to be supported during exercise while Sioned might not be at all concerned if she went to an exercise class and did not interact with fellow exercisers. The impact of relatedness satisfaction for these two individuals on intrinsic motivation is therefore likely to be quite different. In addition, the theory fails to account for how external events might impact on an individual's wellbeing even if all three needs are satisfied and the individual is intrinsically motivated towards the behaviour (Buunk and Nauta, 2000). This is similar to the concept of perceived behavioural control discussed in previous sections (see TPB). For example, someone might feel satisfied in autonomy, competence and relatedness to exercise and yet feel depressed because a work commitment prevents them from exercising.

The final criticism of SDT is that it discusses motivation as a trait concept. That is, one has a tendency to be extrinsically or intrinsically motivated towards a behaviour. However, Vallerand (2000) argues that the theory does not take into account how motivation can alter in a specific situation (state motivation). For example, although an individual might normally be intrinsically motivated to swim in their own time, coercion from others to participate in a swimming competition might result in the individual swimming for more external reasons.

Social Cognitive Theory and Self-Efficacy Theory

Case Study 4.3
Let's catch up with Hena . . .

Hena has been invited to be maid of honour at her best friend's wedding. She wants to drop two dress sizes before the wedding, which is in six months. Having attended the GP referral scheme, which wasn't as bad as she imagined, she has been inspired to carry on exercising. She has read in glossy magazines that the new Zumba dance craze is a good way of toning your body while having great fun at the same time. She has done some research and found classes running in her local community. Luckily, the classes run twice a week on evenings when the children are at an after school club. She has always enjoyed dancing and so she is confident that she will be able to master the classes.

Social Cognitive Theory

Unlike the theories discussed so far, the Social Cognitive Theory (SCT; Bandura, 1986) does not propose that a range of factors predict our behaviour. Instead, this theory proposes that personal factors, environmental factors and our behaviour interact and influence each other (Figure 4.3), which is referred to as triadic reciprocal causation.

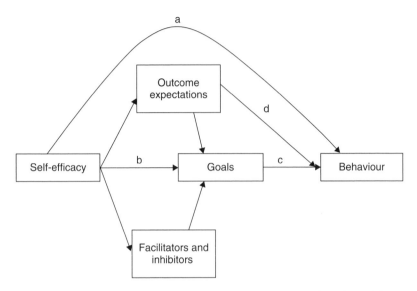

Figure 4.3 Social Cognitive Theory. Adapted from Bandura, A (2004) Health promotion by social cognitive means. Health Education and Behaviour, *31: 143–164. Copyright 2004. Reprinted by permission of SAGE publications.*

According to the theory, personal factors (e.g. self-efficacy and attitudes), are likely to impact our decision about whether or not to engage in a behaviour and are also likely to influence our environment (e.g. the opinions of our family and friends). Likewise both behaviour (e.g. our experiences of exercise) and our environment are likely to influence our own attitudes and self-efficacy (personal factors). As such all of these components will act on each other in a cyclical fashion, feeding into one another and changing the likelihood of engaging in the behaviour in a dynamic way. The theory therefore assumes that we are rational individuals who are able to self-reflect, evaluate our behaviour and consider how to modify that behaviour to reach desired goals. This involves what Bandura terms 'forethought' which requires us to estimate the outcomes of different choices to decide whether these courses of action are desirable. In essence the theory predicts that we evaluate our own actions and compare these with the behaviour required to reach a desired goal. Dependent on the discrepancy between these two we will make a rational decision about what we need to change about our behaviour in order to reach the desired goal.

Bandura (2004) proposes that the key determinants involved in health behaviour are:

- *Self-efficacy.* In Hena's case (see above) she was confident that she could master Zumba dance and therefore had high self-efficacy in relation to this behaviour.

- *Outcome expectations.* This refers to whether or not the individual feels that the behaviour will lead to the desired outcome. Hena had read positive information about the success of Zumba dance for losing weight and therefore would have high expectations that attending would lead to her desired goal of losing weight.
- *Cognitive goals.* These are the goals that the individual wishes to meet and can be immediate goals (proximal) or more long-term goals (distal). Hena's long-term goal was to drop two dress sizes in time for the wedding while her short-term goal was to regularly attend the Zumba dance classes.
- *Facilitators and impediments.* These are the personal and situational facilitators and barriers that might enable or prevent the individual from participating in the behaviour. These contribute to the individual's evaluation about whether or not to engage in the behaviour. In Hena's case, she had no other commitments on the evening of the classes and therefore had no obvious barriers that would stop her from attending.

Our self-efficacy is believed to directly predict our behaviour as well as predict it indirectly via its influence on the outcome expectation, our goals and the facilitators and inhibitors (Figure 4.3). For example, feeling confident that she could master the Zumba dance would increase Hena's self-efficacy that she could achieve her long- and short-term goals, would increase her expectation that the dance classes would successfully help her to lose weight and would make it less likely that she would perceive barriers to participating in the classes. In turn, all of these factors will increase her likelihood of attending the classes. Anderson *et al.* (2010) implemented SCT constructs into a physical activity and nutrition intervention. Adults participating in the intervention provided measures of self-efficacy, outcome expectations, social support and self-regulation at the start of the intervention and at seven months, and provided measures of physical activity and nutritional intake at 7 and 16 months following the intervention. The study examined whether the changes seen in SCT variables from baseline to seven months mediated (see Box 4.1) the effect of the intervention on changes in physical activity and nutrition seen from 7 to 16 months. Results demonstrated that social support increased individuals' self-efficacy, lending support to the SCT proposal that environmental and personal factors interact with each other. Self-efficacy mediated the effect of the intervention on physical activity behaviour (Figure 4.3, pathway a) and increased the likelihood of goal setting (Figure 4.3, pathway b). Therefore, the intervention helped to increase individuals' self-efficacy which in turn increased goal setting and thus physical activity (Figure 4.3, pathways b and c). Outcome expectancies predicted physical activity (Figure 4.3, pathway d), but was not identified as a mediator between the intervention and physical activity.

For more information on the application of SCT using a clinical sample of diabetes patients see the further reading at the end of the chapter.

Box 4.1 Definition: Predicting between variables

When examining predictions between variables, some variables will predict the outcome variable directly, such as self-efficacy directly predicting behaviour. Other variables will predict the outcome variable indirectly via another variable, for example self-efficacy also predicted behaviour via cognitive goals. In other words, increased self-efficacy results in exercise if goals are set. The middle variable (e.g. cognitive goals in this example) is said to be a mediator.

This section identified how self-efficacy is considered a central personal factor within the SCT. As such, Bandura further expanded on the concept of self-efficacy within the Self-Efficacy Theory which is discussed in the section below.

Self-Efficacy Theory

Self-Efficacy Theory (Bandura, 1977) employs the framework of the SCT but focuses specifically on the influence that self-efficacy has on our behaviour. The theory proposes that three cognitive processes, namely, self-efficacy expectations, outcome expectancy and outcome value, all contribute to determine behaviour.

Self-efficacy expectations refer to the beliefs and expectations of an individual that they are able to carry out the necessary behaviours in order to achieve a desired outcome. The more confident an individual is that they can achieve the behaviour successfully the more likely they are to engage in the behaviour. Outcome expectancy relates to whether or not the individual feels that the behaviour will lead to the desired outcome. People are far less likely to engage in a behaviour that they do not believe will help achieve their goal. Outcome value relates to the value placed on the desired outcome. That is, how much an individual wants to achieve the desired outcome. If an individual is doing something to please someone else rather than because they truly want to, they are far less likely to persist at this activity. Therefore, the more competent or self-efficacious an individual is, the more challenging the goals they are likely to set and the more persistent and motivated they are likely to be to achieve them (Sniehotter *et al.*, 2005).

Knowing that self-efficacy is an important predictor of behaviour, however, is of no real benefit to us unless we can identify how to increase an individual's self-efficacy in order to increase the likelihood of participation. We consider strategies to enhance self-efficacy in the section below.

Developing self-efficacy

Bandura (1997) proposed that self-efficacy could be developed from a number of different sources:

- *Performance accomplishments*: Successfully performing a behaviour is likely to increase our self-efficacy for that behaviour. Therefore setting realistic goals which we are likely to achieve is one way of increasing self-efficacy. However, achieving success in a situation with little challenge is less likely to increase our self-efficacy than achieving success when we have had to overcome challenges and barriers to do so.
- *Vicarious experiences*: This refers to observations that we have made about other people's attempts at carrying out the behaviour. If we have observed numerous people failing to achieve the behaviour then this is likely to reduce our own self-efficacy that we can do it and vice versa.
- *Verbal persuasion*: This refers to positive feedback or encouragement. Being told that you are good enough to achieve something by a reliable source (a coach or medical professional) is likely to increase one's self-efficacy.
- *Physiological arousal*: Within an exercise context, an individual's physiological arousal is also believed to contribute towards their self-efficacy, however, this is very much based on an individual's appraisal of the situation. For example, feeling your heart pumping might indicate that you are working to the desired level to increase fitness and as such boost your self-efficacy to exercise. Alternatively, the same

physiological cue could signify a lack of fitness to a sedentary individual and as such decrease their self-efficacy to exercise in the future.

- *Emotional arousal*: This is based on how our mood primes the types of memories that we have about an event or experience like exercise. A negative mood is more likely to prime us to remember negative memories where we have previously failed at similar behaviours and thus reduce our feelings of self-efficacy. On the other hand a positive mood is more likely to prime us to remember events with a positive outcome and therefore increase our self-efficacy.

Evaluation of Social Cognitive and Self-Efficacy Theories

A review of studies using outcome expectancies to predict physical activity behaviour has supported the relationship between self-efficacy and outcome expectancies in accordance with SCT. However, interventions aiming to change outcome expectancies by educating individuals about the benefits of physical activity have been unsuccessful (Williams *et al.*, 2005). This raises questions about the inclusion of this construct when applying this model to physical activity behaviour. As a complete model, researchers argue that SCT is so broad and loosely organised that it has little practical use, as taking into account all environmental and personal factors makes testing the theory in full virtually impossible. This means that researchers have tended to focus on aspects of the theory (e.g. self-efficacy) in isolation from the rest of the model, making the results of these investigations less valid.

Self-Efficacy Theory has been applied within exercise rehabilitation and has been shown to moderately predict outcomes such as performance in walking programmes (Subramanian *et al.*, 2008). Ashford *et al.* (2010) conducted a systematic review to explore the best facilitators of change in self-efficacy. In support of the theory, these authors identified that vicarious experiences and encouraging awareness of performance accomplishments via positive feedback were associated with higher levels of self-efficacy. Verbal persuasion on the other hand was associated with lower self-efficacy, suggesting that this form of strategy is less effective.

Chapter Review

This chapter has introduced some of the key models and theories used to predict physical activity behaviour. These were the Transtheoretical Model, Theories of Reasoned Action, and Planned Behaviour, Self-Determination Theory and Cognitive Evaluation Theory, Social Cognitive Theory and Self-Efficacy Theory (Learning Objective 1). Although all of these theories have been widely used within the context of physical activity, each has its own limitations which should be considered when using the theory to predict behaviour change (Learning Objective 2). Each theory has a slightly different focus in relation to behaviour change, but some overlaps between theories were highlighted in this chapter, most importantly, the common inclusion of self-efficacy into these theories of behaviour (Learning Objective 3). The definition and conceptualisation of self-efficacy may vary between models but each consistently includes the concept of confidence in our ability to carry out a behaviour. Models and theories of behaviour provide an important insight into the possible variables which explain an individual's reasons for participating in health related behaviours such as physical activity. Understanding the variables that are likely to contribute to behaviour change provides information to underpin interventions and devise appropriate strategies to help encourage individuals to change their behaviour to adopt a more healthy lifestyle. The recommended reading at the end of this chapter suggests a review article which provides an overview of many of the theories discussed in this chapter which you might find useful.

Learning Activity 4.4
Test your understanding

1. Use the information in the chapter to identify some of the common variables used across the different models of behaviour change.
2. Provide a definition of self-efficacy and identify the role of self-efficacy in the different models and theories discussed in this chapter.
3. A number of theories discuss the effects of individual and environmental variables on exercise intentions or behaviour. How do the effects of these two types of variables differ between the different models?
4. What are the benefits of understanding the variables that predict exercise behaviour?

Further Reading

-   For an overview of the application of some of the models and theories discussed in this chapter:

Taylor, D, Bury, M, Campling, N, Carter, S, Garfied, S, Newbould, J *et al.* (2006). A Review of the Use of the Health Belief Model (HBM), the Theory of Reasoned Action (TRA), the Theory of Planned Behaviour (TPB) and the Trans-Theoretical Model (TTM) to Study and Predict Health Related Behaviour Change. London: Department of Health and National Institute of Clinical Excellence.
This document provides an overview of the key theories of behaviour change as well as documenting how they have been employed in research in the health care setting.

-   For more information about SDT:

Thøgersen-Ntoumani, C and Ntoumanis, N (2006) The role of self-determined motivation in the understanding of exercise-related behaviours, cognitions and physical self-evaluations. *Journal of Sport Sciences*, 24: 393–404.
This study employed a longitudinal design to explore the use of psychological need satisfaction and motivational regulations as predictors of exercise behaviour and wellbeing.

-   For more information about Social Cognitive Theory:

Plotnikoff, RC, Lippke, S, Courneya, KS, Birkett, N and Sigal, RJ (2008) Physical activity and social cognitive theory: A test in a population sample of adults with type 1 or type 2 diabetes. *Applied Psychology*, 57: 628–643.
This study implemented a longitudinal research design to test the use of SCT for explaining exercise behaviour in a sample of diabetes patients.

Chapter 5
Changing and maintaining physical activity

Learning Objectives

This chapter is designed to help you be able to:

1. understand the strategies used to encourage behaviour change and increase self-efficacy and motivation;
2. understand how these strategies are underpinned by the behaviour change theories discussed in Chapter 4;
3. describe the different types of physical activity interventions;
4. understand the need for individually tailored interventions that integrate behaviour change strategies.

Introduction

In this chapter we discuss some of the strategies that are used to help overcome cognitive barriers to physical activity, increase motivation and self-efficacy, all with the aim of increasing physical activity participation. In the second half of this chapter we explore the different types of interventions that are used to increase physical activity levels. These interventions range from targeting small groups in local communities to larger scale interventions that target the whole nation via media campaigns.

Cognitive behavioural strategies

You may recall in Chapter 4 that we discussed a number of the key theories that describe the behavioural and cognitive processes involved in behaviour change. However, these theories are not much use to us if we do not know what we can do to increase our self-efficacy or to change our attitudes, for example. A number of cognitive behavioural strategies have been suggested to increase motivation and self-efficacy and/or change our attitudes towards the behaviour in question. A number of these key strategies are discussed here:

- decision balance and processes of change;
- goal setting;
- self-monitoring;
- stimulus control and reinforcement;
- increasing self-efficacy.

Decision balance and the processes of change revisited

In Chapter 4 we introduced the Transtheoretical Model (Prochaska and DiClemente, 1983) which includes cognitive and behavioural strategies to increase self-efficacy and the likelihood of successful behaviour change. Although we introduced these in the previous chapter, we consider these in more detail here.

Decision balance

A significant factor which limits attempts at behaviour change is the individual's perceptions of the barriers to changing their behaviour. Individuals who see barriers as insurmountable are more likely to struggle to see the point of changing their behaviour. A decisional balance sheet (Janis and Mann, 1977), however, encourages individuals to actively consider the potential benefits and costs of changing their behaviour for themselves and significant others. The individual compiles a list of all the benefits of changing their behaviour and all the barriers preventing them from doing so (see examples below and Chapter 4 for an overview).

Case Study 5.1
Example of Hena's decision balance sheet

Pros of walking to work each day:	Cons of walking to work each day:
I will be healthier	*Bad weather*
I will lose weight	*I will have to get up earlier*
I will feel a sense of accomplishment even before	*I might look untidy when I get to work*
I start my day!	*I might be tired when I get to work and therefore be less productive*

The decision balance sheet can work in two ways. In its simplest form, if an individual can see that their list of benefits outweighs their list of costs then this can change their perceptions of the behaviour change so that they view the decision to change their behaviour more favourably. However, it may be that the lists of benefits is shorter than the list of costs, as in the example above, but committing these to paper allows the individual to evaluate whether some of these are more important than others. For example, the benefit of being healthier would normally outweigh the cost of bad weather and as such will help the individual to rationalise the magnitude of their barriers and costs and therefore change their perceptions to view their barriers more realistically.

However, people are more complex than this and not every individual will compile a list comprising more benefits than costs or be able to realistically weigh up these costs and benefits. In these situations the decision balance can work in a slightly different way. Having taken time to think through the barriers preventing behaviour change, the decision balance sheet can be used as a resource to help consider strategies that will help the individual to overcome the barriers that have been identified and reinforce reasons for changing their behaviour. For example, on days when an individual is at risk of relapsing to their old habits, reading through the list of benefits can remind them of their goals and provide them with the necessary motivation to complete the intended physical activity.

Learning Activity 5.1

Revisit the decision balance sheet in Case Study 5.1. Discuss in a group the different ways that you could use the decision balance to help Hena to start walking to work.

Processes of change

We introduced the processes of change as cognitive and behavioural strategies that could be used to move individuals between the different stages of the Transtheoretical Model. To summarise, these were:

- Cognitive processes of change:

  - consciousness raising,
  - dramatic relief,
  - self-re-evaluation,
  - environmental re-evaluation,
  - social liberation.

- Behavioural processes of change:

  - self-liberation,
  - counterconditioning,
  - stimulus control,
  - contingency management,
  - helping relationships.

Williams *et al.* (2008) compared the psychosocial predictors (e.g. decision balance and processes of change) of exercise adoption and exercise maintenance. Sedentary participants were recruited and those who had either successfully adopted physical activity six months later (active six months) or remained inactive at six months but planned to adopt physical activity (inactive six months) were also asked to provide data 12 months later. Participants' decision balance and processes of change provided at the six-month time point were then used to predict physical activity status at 12 months (active/ inactive). Results demonstrated that both decision balance and processes of change at six months significantly predicted physical activity status at 12 months. There was no difference between the effects seen for those who were already active at six months and maintaining their physical activity (active six months) and those who planned to adopt physical activity (inactive six months). This is contrary to previous research (Prochaska *et al.*, 1994; discussed in Chapter 4), which has suggested that the cognitive processes of change are more applicable for those in the contemplation, preparation and action stages of change while the behavioural processes are more applicable for those in the maintenance stage of change.

Goal setting

Case Study 5.2

Revisiting Hena . . .

When we last visited Hena, she was intending to start Zumba dance classes. She has been going to the classes for the last three weeks and enjoys the sessions. However, she is a little disappointed that her goal of dropping two dress sizes is taking longer than she anticipated. She is therefore considering whether it is really worth the effort and is thinking of giving up and returning to her sedentary lifestyle.

We all have our reasons for wanting to exercise, whether to keep fit, relieve stress, get into the football team or simply to be the best athlete that we can be. Having a goal that we are trying to achieve can be extremely motivating and as such goal setting is a popular strategy to encourage behaviour change. For example, having the goal of running a marathon or losing three stones can spur us on to start exercising more regularly. These are known as distal or long-term goals and represent what we are trying to achieve in the long term. However, one problem with distal goals is that they take a long time to achieve. As a result, people can become despondent and as their motivation dwindles so does their exercise behaviour. We saw this in Hena's case where her long-term goal of dropping two dress sizes was taking longer than she thought. As a result she was reconsidering her decision to attend dance classes.

For this reason, goal setting works best if the distal goals are broken down into a number of proximal or short-term goals which are easier to achieve in a short space of time. For example, Hena could be encouraged to set some proximal goals, such as losing a centimetre from her waist and hips in a fortnight. This is far more achievable in the short term and successfully achieving a proximal goal increases self-efficacy for achieving distal goals and helps the individual to increase their perceived behavioural control (see Theory of Planned Behaviour, Chapter 4). Once the proximal goal is achieved a series of other proximal goals leading to the distal goal can be set. This way motivation is maintained and the likelihood of achieving the distal goal is increased.

Case Study 5.3

As his New Year's resolution, Solomon has set himself the challenge of cycling from Land's End to John O'Groats by the end of the year. He has not cycled for some time so set himself some short-term goals to achieve this:

- *to start cycling in preparation;*
- *to occasionally cycle with his friend Bob who will help to motivate him;*
- *to cycle 25 miles and then build up the distance over the next few months.*

Learning Activity 5.2

In the following section we consider key principles of goal setting. After reading this section, reflect back on Solomon's goals to see if his short-term goals will help him achieve his long-term goal.

For goals to be successful, they must demonstrate a number of criteria:

- *Meaningful*: There is little use setting short-term goals which are unrelated to the long-term goals or that do not have real meaning for the individual. For example, there is little use setting an individual a long-term goal of being able to achieve 60 minutes on a running machine if they hate running but want to lose some weight.
- *Realistic*: Goals must be realistically achievable. Setting a goal that is unachievable will only result in disappointment, reduced motivation and the individual will inevitably give up.
- *Challenging*: Although a goal should be realistic it must also be somewhat challenging to drive the individual towards their long-term goal and increase self-efficacy as goals are achieved.
- *Specific*: For a goal to be successfully achieved it must be sufficiently specific for the individual to be clear about what they are trying to achieve. Take Solomon's short-term goals, for example, the time frames and distances are somewhat vague. This makes it difficult to accurately determine whether or not a goal has been achieved and what to do to achieve the goal.
- *Measurable*: Similarly, the goal must be measurable to clearly identify whether or not it has been achieved. A goal which simply states, 'Solomon will start cycling', for example, is difficult to measure. Is trying his bike out one morning sufficient to meet this goal or does he need to cycle regularly to achieve this?
- *Within a time frame*: Setting a time frame for achieving goals also provides clarity for the individual. For example, Solomon has all year to reach his long-term goal and therefore could argue that he could still achieve his first short-term goal even if he hadn't started cycling by October! The time frame should be short enough to provide regular feedback to the individual and therefore help to maintain their motivation, but should also be long enough for short-term goals to be successfully achieved.
- *Independent of others' input*: Goals which rely on other people are out of our own control. This means that even if we are motivated to achieve the goal, we could be unsuccessful as a result of being let down by other people. This is likely to be detrimental for our self-efficacy and motivation.
- *Flexible*: When setting goals we must be mindful that factors out of our control are sometimes unavoidable. For example, setting a goal that we will go to the gym for 60 minutes every Tuesday night meets a number of the requirements outlined above. It is measurable, is within a time frame, is specific and so on. However, an important social event might be scheduled one Tuesday making it difficult to achieve the goal. Being flexible that the goal can be met on a different night means that it is still achievable and is therefore more likely to be attained.

Despite the popularity of goal setting as a behavioural strategy in physical activity interventions, limited research in the exercise domain has tested the efficacy of goal setting, unlike the wealth of research in sporting and occupational contexts. Dishman *et al.* (2009) used a successful workplace physical activity intervention to examine whether there was a relationship between goal setting and physical activity level. The 12-week intervention implemented personal goal setting as a behavioural strategy and results demonstrated that individuals who set higher goals maintained high levels of self-efficacy, commitment and intention to reach their goals and achieved higher physical activity levels measured as number of steps taken.

Shilts *et al.* (2004) conducted a review of interventions using goal setting as a strategy to change dietary and physical activity behaviour. Six out of the eight studies that used goal setting to increase physical activity supported the effectiveness of goal setting with adults. The review also examined findings pertaining to results in relation to a number of factors: feedback mode (whether the intervention used rewards or feedback), type of goal setting (whether the goals were self-set, assigned by leaders or were collaborative), and properties (difficulty, goal specificity). Assigned goal setting was more effective than self-set goals in some cases, however, the results were inconclusive and the authors proposed that this was likely to be affected by factors such as the type of dietary or physical activity behaviour being changed and the readiness of participants to change. A number of studies reviewed also compared the effectiveness of setting proximal and distal goals. Results of one study indicated that distal goals led to more weight loss but resulted in higher attrition (drop-out). In contrast, three other studies found no differences between setting distal and proximal goals. The authors warned however that these results should be interpreted carefully given that one of the studies that compared proximal and distal goals included self-assigned proximal goals and as such the results may have been confounded by this additional parameter of goal setting.

Self-monitoring

One of the reasons that people are often unsuccessful at changing their behaviour is that the original motivation to change dwindles and relapsing back to old habits is far too tempting. Self-monitoring can help to maintain the original motivation and help discover ways to overcome the temptation to relapse. It requires individuals to keep a diary of their thoughts, feelings and behaviour relating to the behaviour change. For example, the individual records what exercise they did, how many steps they walked, how they felt before exercising, and/or how they felt after exercising. In addition, they make records about days that they did not exercise, what they were doing on those days and how they felt as a result of not exercising. Below is an example of what Hena's diary might look like.

Case study 5.4
Hena's diary

Date: June 3rd

Exercise goal: Walk to my brother's house   *Goal achieved? Yes*

How did you feel before exercise?

I really didn't want to walk today. I didn't sleep very well last night and was quite tired but I persevered.

How did you feel after?

Once I got to Aman's house I felt completely invigorated. The fresh air had cleared my head, I was really proud of myself for walking even though I didn't want to. I felt ready to tackle the day!

Date: June 6th

Exercise goal: Walk to work   *Goal achieved? No*

How did you feel before exercise?

I really didn't want to exercise again today. It was raining a bit and I didn't want to get wet on the way to work. I also had an important meeting to prepare for and so needed to get into work early.

How did you feel after?

I feel really guilty for not having exercised today and have been miserable all day because of it.

I am disappointed with myself for not sticking to the regime and now I am behind on my weight loss target. I was also really stressed about this meeting and a walk would probably have done me good.

Learning Activity 5.3

Think about how Hena could use her diary to help motivate her to exercise in the future and prevent the risk of relapsing back to her sedentary lifestyle. Compare your ideas with the section below.

You will see from Hena's example that people are likely to have days where they meet their targets and feel great and days when they don't and so feel less pleased with themselves. The aim is that on days when an individual might not feel like exercising, they can refer back to an excerpt like 3 June in the example, and remind themselves of how good they felt after they had made the effort to exercise. Or, they could read the excerpt from 6 June and remind themselves of the negative feelings that they had on the day that they did not exercise.

Another way that monitoring can be used is to help identify behavioural cues that might result in not achieving an exercise goal. Looking back through the diary for common trends that are apparent on the days that they failed to exercise could provide someone with the information that they need to overcome the temptation not to exercise. For example, Hena might look back and identify work pressures and poor weather as cues that prevent her from exercising. This provides her with the opportunity to identify some strategies to overcome these barriers. For example, she might decide to leave some spare clothes at work so that if the weather is poor she is able to change out of wet clothes.

Using a sample of patients with type 2 diabetes, Gleeson-Kreig (2006) examined the effect of a self-monitoring intervention for increasing physical activity levels. All participants met with a researcher to provide demographic information, measures of physical activity and self-efficacy and were randomly assigned into an intervention or control group. All participants were provided with information about what constituted moderate physical activity (defined as using large muscle groups and at least equivalent to brisk walking). In addition, those in the intervention group were asked to keep a record of any moderate physical activity lasting longer than 10 minutes each day, providing information such as the type of exercise and duration, and to return these records every two weeks. Neither group received any structured physical activity prescription. After six weeks participants met with a researcher and provided follow-up measures of physical activity and self-efficacy. There was no significant difference in physical activity levels between the intervention and the control group, but the intervention group reported higher self-efficacy to exercise. These results may suggest that self-monitoring is beneficial for increasing an individual's self-efficacy for behaviour change, however more structured support might be necessary to translate the self-efficacy into actual behaviour. In addition, participants simply reported exercise behaviour and provided no information regarding the individual's cognitive appraisal of the situations. It may be, therefore, that the intervention failed to use the self-monitoring strategy to its full effect.

Stimulus control and reinforcement

Stimulus control and reinforcement are based on the behavioural psychology of learning (Skinner, 1953). According to learning theory we react to certain cues in the environment. For example, seeing an advert for our favourite chocolate bar on the television might provide us with the cue that we fancy a treat! On this basis, some mass media campaigns use this strategy to try to encourage people to exercise. For example, one environmental cue might be to see a flyer advertising an aerobics class. Cues can also come from external sources such as a phone call from a friend asking you to accompany them on a walk. They may also be more internal and based on the physiological feeling of being full and lazy after a Sunday roast prompting you to exercise!

Understanding our responses to environmental cues allows us to implement deliberate strategies to provide prompts to participate in desirable behaviours and avoid undesirable ones. For example, we might leave a pair of trainers in our work locker so that when we see them we are presented with a cue to go to the gym after work. This is known as stimulus control. This strategy can also be used to help people overcome the temptation to return to old habits. For example, if we know that when we get in from work and make ourselves a cup of tea we feel relaxed and no longer motivated to go out for a run, we can decide to avoid the cue of a cup of tea and instead implement a competing cue such as changing into our running clothes straight away.

Reinforcement is a strategy based on a form of learning first identified by Skinner (1953) known as operant conditioning. When we discussed goal setting earlier, we noted that long-term goals are less motivating than short-term goals which are achieved more quickly. One reason for this is that we gain a sense of achievement from reaching a target goal which acts as a reinforcer or a reward for the behaviour that led to goal achievements. Operant conditioning identifies four types of reinforcement:

- positive reinforcement;
- negative reinforcement;
- positive punishment;
- negative punishment.

According to Skinner, when we are rewarded for behaviour (positive reinforcement) or if something negative is removed when we perform a behaviour (negative reinforcement) we are more likely to perform that behaviour again. In a similar way, if we are punished for a behaviour (positive punishment), or if something positive is removed when we perform the behaviour (negative punishment) we are less likely to perform that behaviour again. Figure 5.1 provides an example for each of these cases.

Using this strategy, we can establish rewards for when goals are met and/or punishments can be determined for when we fail to achieve our goals. Above we discuss self-imposed rewards or punishments to encourage or discourage the desired behaviour. However, rewards and punishments can also come from external sources which may be unexpected. For example, after their first exercise session, someone who is sedentary might experience a degree of muscle pain the next day. This could act as positive punishment (adding something that reduces the likelihood of exercising again). Knowing how operant conditioning works means that strategies can be implemented to try to overcome positive and negative punishment, for example ensuring that people understand that this pain is expected from exercise and is short lived.

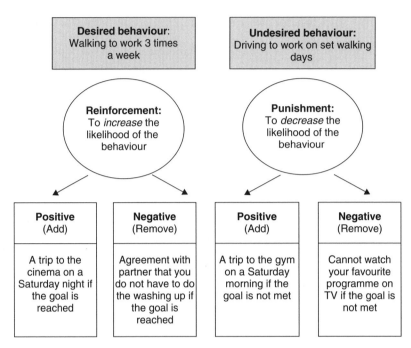

Figure 5.1 Operant conditioning.

Many physical activity promotion interventions will offer incentives for people to take part and rewards such as t-shirts when people reach their goals (e.g. Hardman *et al.*, 2009). However, reinforcement must be used cautiously to encourage behaviour change. Although offering rewards for behaviour can encourage participation in the short term, these rewards can undermine intrinsic motivation (the motivation to do something for its own rewards; Deci and Ryan, 2000). Rewards can remove the sense of autonomy, and once the incentive is removed the behaviour will no longer be desirable and as such rewards are unlikely to increase participation in the long term (Deci and Ryan, 2000). Despite this, interventions have successfully used reinforcement to encourage exercise adoption, following which individuals were taught to use autonomous behaviour change strategies to maintain the behaviour (e.g. Lawton *et al.*, 2009).

Behaviour change interventions

So far in this chapter we have discussed different strategies that are designed to help people through a period of behaviour change. However, changing behaviour is not an easy process for people to undergo alone. For this reason a range of interventions are now available to help people with this process. This section starts by exploring the considerations that are necessary when designing an intervention. These include the target audience, the setting and the target level of the intervention.

Target audience

When planning an intervention with the purpose of increasing individuals' physical activity it is first important to consider who the intervention is aimed at. For example, Chapter 2 discussed a range of personal characteristics which correlate with inactivity. These include age, gender and ethnicity, for example.

The target audience is likely to impact on a range of different aspects of the intervention, from the activities included to how the intervention will be advertised, how the participants will be recruited and the intensity of the exercise. It is well established that men are more likely than women to engage in more negative health-related behaviours and less likely to engage in positive behaviours such as exercise interventions (Gijsbers van Wijk *et al.*, 1995) and therefore novel ideas are needed to try to encourage men to participate. For example, in general men tend to prefer sporting activities in comparison to women (Martinez-Gonzales *et al.*, 2001) and as such interventions with a more competitive and sport-related nature might appeal more to men.

Another consideration when planning an intervention is the target participants' current level of activity. The stages of change in the Transtheoretical Model are often used for this purpose to target individuals in a specific stage. For example, an intervention aimed at individuals in the contemplation stage is likely to be very different from an intervention that targets individuals in the action stage (see Chapter 4 for a reminder of the stages of change).

Blissmer and McAuley (2002) compared a stage-matched intervention with a stage-mismatched intervention, standard care and control conditions. Those in the stage-matched intervention received written information designed to help move them to the next stage of the Transtheoretical Model. Similarly, those in the mismatched intervention condition received written information but the information was tailored for people in a different stage to themselves. Those in the standard care condition received a manual by the American Heart Association which included information about lifestyle improvement. Those in the control condition received a health care pamphlet which provided health-related information but no guidance on behaviour change. Results demonstrated that the stage-matched and standard care interventions led to greater increases in activity compared with the mismatched and control conditions.

There are other cognitive factors which require consideration. For example, individuals' attitudes, self-efficacy for change and outcome expectations are also likely to impact the success of an intervention. Although it is perhaps unlikely that an intervention will only deliberately target individuals with a certain degree of self-efficacy or a certain attitude, having an understanding of an individual's cognitive beliefs about exercise is useful for determining which strategies are likely to be most beneficial for them. For example, knowing that a participant has low levels of self-efficacy means that an intervention can employ relevant strategies such as positive feedback or goal setting to help increase self-efficacy. For more information about selecting appropriate behaviour change strategies based on the characteristics of the participant and tailoring interventions to the appropriate audience refer to the further reading recommended at the end of this chapter.

Intervention settings

Having established who our intervention is targeting, the next decision we need to make is where the intervention should take place. A number of factors should be considered here, including how easy it will be for people to attend the facility or whether specific audiences have particular needs which must be addressed. Here we outline a number of potential intervention settings.

Home-based interventions

Home-based interventions are, not surprisingly, based in people's homes. A programme of exercise that can be easily implemented in or from the home is designed. Activities tend to make use of the home environment, including chair exercises, walking up and down the stairs, or sometimes walks in the local vicinity. This type of intervention is ideal for elderly participants or participants with mobility difficulties who might be unable to attend sessions elsewhere. Home-based exercise can also overcome the time constraints faced by people with family commitments.

The benefits of this approach are the easy access to exercise and the exercise can often be accommodated into an individual's daily routine. In Chapters 3 and 6 we also discuss how social physique anxiety can prevent individuals from exercising. Home-based exercise means that the individual can exercise in privacy and therefore also overcome this barrier.

One limitation of home-based exercise is the isolation. Having other people exercising around you or sharing in the experience can motivate and provide social support for individuals during a period of behaviour change. Home-based exercise does not offer this support, although some exercise schemes have overcome this problem by providing telephone support or visits from exercise leaders/researchers (Conwell et al., 2010).

Conwell et al. (2010) explored the efficacy of a ten-week home-based physical activity programme to improve insulin sensitivity in obese young people (aged 8–18 years). A home-based intervention was selected as this provided a cheap and convenient intervention for the entire family, meaning that the intervention was feasible for families to maintain. A researcher conducted semi-structured interviews with each participant to develop a personalised programme of activities that the individual enjoyed. They also helped to identify periods that were suitable for substituting sedentary behaviours with more active pursuits. Support was provided in the form of twice weekly visits from the researcher and behaviour change strategies were also implemented: rewards and setting goals of step counts to achieve, measured using a pedometer. Results demonstrated that the intervention was successful in increasing participants' daily step count and these benefits were maintained at ten-week follow-up.

Community-based interventions

A number of interventions target individuals in their local community. These are often based in community centres, places of worship, leisure centres or local parks. In Chapter 2 we highlighted that accessibility to facilities was a significant barrier to exercise. Locally based interventions benefit from being easily accessible for most individuals but have the added benefit of encouraging communities to support each other. For example, in Chapter 2 we discussed how certain ethnic groups are known to be less physically active than others. A local community intervention specifically targeting these individuals can be made more culturally relevant and mean that they have the support of other individuals from their community who face similar barriers and share similar experiences.

Another consideration of community-based intervention is that the exercise leaders can often be from the local community too. The benefit of this is that the leaders are more aware of the needs and values of the community and therefore are often more successful at encouraging attendance and adherence to the exercise programme.

Van der Bij et al. (2002) compared the effectiveness of different types of interventions for increasing physical activity in older adults, including home-based interventions, group interventions and educational interventions to increase awareness of physical activity but which did not involve exercise. Both home-based and group-based interventions resulted in high participation rates in the short term (over 80 per cent), but adherence dwindled as the intervention progressed. Educational-based interventions led to much lower and more varied adherence rates ranging between 35 and 96 per cent. However, educational and group-based interventions appeared to be the most effective for increasing physical activity levels in the short term. Few of the studies reviewed by Van der Bij *et al.* explored the effectiveness of interventions in the long term, but of those that did, no significant difference between the intervention types was seen, suggesting that any differences in physical activity levels seen may be short lived.

Work-based interventions

Chapter 2 highlighted time constraints as a key barrier to exercise, therefore given that many of us spend approximately half of our waking hours at work (Department for Work and Pensions, 2005) interventions in this setting offer an excellent opportunity to increase physical activity without impinging too much on individuals' time. In addition, active employees take significantly less time off work as a result of sickness in comparison to inactive co-workers (van Amelsvoort *et al.*, 2006). A number of employers are therefore willing to invest in interventions to increase physical activity in the workforce, which in turn should benefit them through fewer days lost due to ill-health (Sustrans, 2008).

Lawton *et al.* (2009) reported on a successful work-based intervention aimed at increasing the activity levels of employees to the recommended daily level of 30 minutes of moderate intensity exercise. The intervention was based on the Theory of Planned Behaviour (Ajzen, 1985) and therefore aimed to improve attitudes, perceived social norms, increase perceived behavioural control and intentions to be physically active. Worksites were matched into pairs according to size and function and then randomised into either a control or intervention condition. The intervention condition incorporated a range of cognitive and behavioural behaviour change strategies, such as a launch week to increase awareness and gain public support, rewards such as fridge magnets and self-monitoring. The programme was delivered by facilitators who had been trained in the use of these strategies. At baseline, three and nine months following the programme, participants were given a health check and asked to self-report their physical activity, complete questionnaires measuring quality of life, wellbeing and job satisfaction. Although there was no significant difference in physical activity levels between the control and intervention conditions, systolic blood pressure and resting heart rate were lower in the intervention group, indicating improved cardiovascular health.

Health centre interventions

Although the health benefits of exercise have been well documented, exercise is not necessarily safe for all individuals without medical guidance. From a subjective perspective, exercising with a known medical condition can be frightening and disconcerting for an individual who is unaware of the level of exercise suitable for them. For this reason, GP referral or exercise on prescription and exercise rehabilitation programmes are designed specifically for clinical populations. Patients who are either at risk of cardiovascular disease or who have a condition which would benefit from increased levels of physical activity (e.g. depression, obesity, osteoporosis) are referred by a medical professional to a supervised exercise programme. Trained exercise leaders assess the individual's capabilities and medical health and develop a structured exercise programme designed to help with their medical condition.

Given the clinical status of these participants, these interventions are often conducted in health care environments such as hospitals and GP surgeries. Health centre-based interventions may offer benefits as the patient feels a sense of reassurance that they are within close proximity to a medical professional should they require assistance. This may also add credibility to the intervention as it is recognised by medical professionals and therefore increase the likelihood of patients attending and adhering to their programme of exercise.

One limitation of this type of intervention is the risk that patients fail to transfer the exercise skills and behaviours they have developed in the health setting to the outside world and as such never feel confident to exercise independently, for example in their local leisure centre. This therefore limits the degree to which these interventions encourage long-term behaviour change. The National Institute for Clinical Excellence recommendations suggest that referring patients on to an exercise specialist in the community can help to overcome this problem and facilitate longer term participation (NICE, 2006). In response, a number of GP referral and rehabilitation interventions are now run by trained staff in community leisure centres (e.g. Taylor and Fox, 2005; discussed in more detail in Chapter 3).

School-based interventions

Schools provide an opportunistic setting to implement interventions with a captive audience who must participate in PE classes to meet national curriculum guidelines. Numerous interventions targeting young people have therefore integrated the intervention into existing PE classes (e.g. Harrison *et al.*, 2006). These interventions usually aim to offer something different from the traditional PE class to encourage increased physical activity outside of the classroom or to encourage less able students to engage more fully in PE classes (e.g. Burgess *et al.*, 2006; discussed in Chapter 3). Interventions in this setting often make use of an educational approach as this is the norm in the school environment. The aim of this approach is to change students' perceptions of physical activity and health-related behaviours so that they are more likely to adopt a healthy lifestyle in the future.

A recent systematic review of the effectiveness of physical activity interventions that target school children was recently conducted by Sluijs *et al.* (2007). Interventions that were based in schools were found to be most effective compared to those in other settings but more so if families and communities were also involved in the intervention. One of the studies included in the review aimed to increase levels of physical activity and decrease levels of TV viewing in children with a mean age of 10 years (Harrison *et al.*, 2006). Children were randomly assigned into either a control group who received the usual PE national curriculum or an intervention condition who received a PE intervention which integrated a number of the strategies discussed in this chapter. These included goal setting and self-monitoring in an attempt to increase self-efficacy, promote self-reflection and decision making. The parents of children in the intervention group were also asked to support them in their attempt to change their behaviour. At follow-up, children in the intervention group had significantly higher levels of self-reported physical activity and self-efficacy for physical activity, however there was no significant difference in the amount of time spent watching television. Thus the intervention was successful in increasing healthy behaviour but unsuccessful in encouraging children to decrease an unhealthy behaviour.

Learning Activity 5.4

Read the following three examples and consider how you would design relevant interventions. You might want to consider how you will recruit your participants, where you will hold the intervention, the types of activities you will offer, how often the sessions will run and what strategies you will employ and why. Compare your ideas with the previous sections and the section that follows.

- *Intervention 1*: The aim of this intervention is to increase the activity levels of adolescent boys and girls ranging from 12 to 16 years.
- *Intervention 2*: This intervention is aimed at anybody who has risk factors for heart disease, including overweight, hypertension and high cholesterol.
- *Intervention 3* is aimed at increasing physical activity in the elderly and reducing the incidence of falls. The audience is likely to include people who were once very active and people who have done very little prior exercise.

Intervention levels

So far we have discussed the importance of identifying the target audience of an intervention and where best to locate the intervention. In addition, interventions can be aimed at different levels in relation to the number of participants and the degree of supervision that is offered.

Helping an individual

Some interventions work on a one-to-one basis where an exercise professional will meet with an individual to discuss their individual requirements (e.g. Conwell *et al.*, 2010). Specific strategies can be implemented to encourage increased physical activity and individual programmes of exercise can be delivered. One benefit of this type of intervention is that it is extremely individualised and as such should provide the individual with every opportunity of success. However, this type of intervention provides limited support (other than that of the exercise leader).

Helping a group

Other interventions include exercise classes for small groups of individuals at a similar stage of behaviour change. This provides a support group and a social component to the exercise. This can be important for fostering a sense of belonging and confidence in the exercise environment (see SDT; Chapter 4). A number of interventions also offer social support by organising buddy systems, mentor programmes or group activities to encourage group cohesion (e.g. Silva *et al.*, 2008).

As well as targeting different numbers of individuals, interventions also differ in the level of support offered by an exercise leader. In some situations, exercise leaders only meet with the participants to initially assess their exercise abilities and to determine their goals. Once this is done, the participants are provided with a tailored exercise programme and are then expected to exercise independently. Others provide more support by including telephone consultations during the programme to offer advice and guidance while others involve supervision throughout with classes taking place in the presence of the exercise leader (e.g. McAuley *et al.*, 1995; detailed in Chapter 3). Fully supervised classes are far more expensive to run and as such are not as easy to sustain.

National campaigns

On a much larger scale, interventions can also aim to target the whole population. Government policy or the mass media are usually the best ways to do this as these allow a message to be broadcast on a large scale. The government has acknowledged the problems associated with physical inactivity and the consequences that this is having on the country's health and economy. As a result a number of government policies have set out action plans to increase the physical activity within the population (e.g. Welsh Assembly Government, 2010). These strategies involve developing and maintaining environments where people feel safe and find it easier to exercise (by developing play areas and cycle paths), providing opportunities for low income families to exercise together and building more physical activity into the National Curriculum.

Mass media campaigns tend to take the form of health promotion adverts on television or poster campaigns which aim to highlight a particular issue. For example, Huhman *et al.* (2008) launched the 'VERB' campaign which aimed to get children between the ages of 9 and 13 years physically active every day. The one-year campaign involved using paid advertisements, poster campaigns in schools and internet activities to promote physical activity as fun, 'cool' and a good way of spending time with friends. At the end of the year campaign results demonstrated that 74 per cent of children surveyed were aware of the campaign, demonstrating that the marketing was effective. Physical activity levels increased most in younger children (9–10 years), girls, children from less educated families, children from densely populated urban areas and children who were less active at baseline. The increase in activity level was related to exposure to the campaign such that greater exposure was associated with more free time physical activity.

However, other mass media campaigns have been less successful. Hillsdon *et al.* (2001) discuss the 'Active for Life' campaign in England which aimed to increase adults' physical activity levels via television advertising. Levels of awareness of the campaign were much lower (38 per cent) compared with the VERB campaign and there was no evidence that physical activity levels had increased as a result of the campaign. Clearly mass media campaigns can be useful but need to be targeted appropriately.

Chapter Review

This chapter discussed a range of cognitive and behavioural strategies designed to help individuals to change their behaviour. These included decision balance, processes of change, goal setting, self-monitoring, and stimulus control and reinforcement (Learning Objective 1). These strategies often have theoretical underpinnings (e.g. processes of change from the Transtheoretical Model) or aim to increase an individual's self-efficacy for change (Learning Objective 2). No one strategy is usually sufficient to change behaviour and as such interventions will often combine strategies to maximise their effect. The second half of the chapter explored the different types of interventions that can be implemented and the considerations that are necessary when designing interventions. We discussed the target audience, setting and level of the intervention (Learning Objective 3). The chapter also highlighted how careful consideration of the components of an intervention and the integration of appropriate behaviour change strategies can all contribute to the likely success of an intervention (Learning Objective 4).

Learning Activity 5.5
Test your understanding

1. How do the strategies of behaviour change discussed in this chapter relate to the models and theories of behaviour change discussed in Chapter 4?
2. How can theory be used to help select the target audience of an intervention and how does this information benefit an intervention?
3. How can community level interventions be used to inform national policy on behaviour change?

Further Reading

- For more information on using behaviour change strategies:

Michie, S, Johnston, M, Francis, J, Hardeman, W and Eccles, M (2008) From theory to intervention: Mapping theoretically derived behavioural determinants to behaviour change techniques. *Applied Psychology: An International Review*, 57: 660–680.
This paper explores how to integrate behaviour change strategies and determinants of behaviour to optimise behaviour change.

- For more information on tailoring health behaviour change interventions:

Noar, SM, Benac, CN and Harris, MS (2007) Does tailoring matter? Meta-analytic review of tailored print health behavior change interventions. *Psychological Bulletin*, 133: 673–693.
This paper provides a comprehensive review of the methods used in health behaviour printed interventions. It also uses a meta-analysis to examine whether there are differences in the outcomes of printed interventions based on demographic variables or target behaviours and the effect of tailoring and employing theory-based interventions on their success.

Chapter 6
Being active: negative effects

Learning Objectives

This chapter is designed to help you be able to:

1. understand how exercise may relate to poor body image, social physique anxiety and negative affect;
2. identify criticisms of research into affective responses to exercise;
3. develop an understanding of the circumplex model of affect (Russell, 1980).

Introduction

Let's return to Hena: in Chapter 3 we learnt that she is categorised as obese and is self-conscious about her appearance, resulting in low physical self-perceptions. She hasn't been physically active since school PE lessons and now just walking up the stairs makes her feel sweaty and out of breath. Because of her high blood pressure, her GP has advised her to exercise. The thought of this makes her feel anxious, concerned about looking a fool and about others laughing at her, and worried that she may not be able to deal with the physical effort involved in exercise.

Hena's is a very real experience for some people and, as Backhouse *et al.* (2007) point out, understanding these experiences may help to explain a curious conundrum: as exercise psychologists we know that exercise offers a number of psychological benefits (indeed we discussed some of these in Chapter 2), however, as we also saw in Chapter 2, a large percentage of the population is not physically active or fails to adhere to exercise programmes. Clearly, for some people, exercise is not a positive experience and there are a number of negative psychological responses to exercise that may help to explain the currently low levels of and adherence to physical activity in the general population. In this chapter, we consider some of these responses and the factors that may influence them. Specifically, we examine factors that may result in poor body image, social physique anxiety and negative affect in exercisers.

Body image and exercise

When was the last time you saw an image of a good looking, young, slim, toned and tanned individual in adverts on TV or in magazines? Probably only hours, maybe even minutes ago. More so than ever, we are constantly bombarded with images and messages of the 'ideal' body and how to achieve it. It is little wonder then that many of us are preoccupied with how we look, whether or not we measure up to this 'ideal' and how attractive we appear to others. The images we see often depict unachievable and unrealistic images of the 'ideal' physique. As a result many people are dissatisfied with their physique and have a poor body image. As we saw in Chapter 3, exercise may help some people to develop a positive body image; for others, however, participating in exercise seems only to add to the problem of a poor body image and body dissatisfaction. In the next chapter we explore the extreme consequences of body dissatisfaction and the role of exercise in the conditions that can develop from this dissatisfaction. First, let us consider why for some people exercise has a negative effect on body image and serves to increase body dissatisfaction.

Think back to Hena for a moment. In Chapter 3 we read that although Hena desperately wants to lose weight the thought of attending the GP referral sessions terrifies her. She cannot bear the thought of having to wear exercise clothes and attend a gym and thinks that she will be surrounded by attractive, healthy people who will look at her physique and see her as lazy and unattractive. She also cannot bear the thought of exercising in an environment where she will be surrounded by mirrors, forcing her to look at her body while she exercises. As we see in the following sections these are some of the factors that can lead to body dissatisfaction from exercise.

When is exercise related to body dissatisfaction?

Research in this area suggests that there are five main reasons why exercise may be associated with body dissatisfaction and a poor body image:

- the individual's motives to exercise;
- where the individual exercises;
- the type of exercise the individual participates in;
- the characteristics of the exercise leader and the exercise class;
- whether exercise is central to the individual's lifestyle or occupation.

Box 6.1 Definition: Body image dissatisfaction

Body image dissatisfaction is *dissatisfaction with one's body size, shape or some other aspect of body appearance* (Gardner, 2001, page 193).

Exercise motives and motivation

Research has shown that when people are motivated to exercise for appearance or weight-related reasons, like our case study example Hena, they may suffer from high levels of body dissatisfaction or poor body image. Although researchers have not always measured exactly the same body image perceptions, this relationship has been demonstrated in both genders and across a wide age range. For instance, based on questionnaire responses in a sample of men and women aged between 16 and 60 years, exercising to control weight or improve body tone was associated with lower levels of body satisfaction (Tiggeman and Williamson, 2000). As we would expect, these motives were stronger in women than in men. Strelan and his colleagues have replicated this finding (Strelan *et al.*, 2003; Strelan and Hargreaves, 2005) and have developed this further by examining the mediating role of self-objectification.

> ## Box 6.2 Definition: Self-objectification
>
> Self-objectification is *our internalisation of society's view of the body as a sexual object, so we see ourselves as something to be looked at and evaluated in relation to how we look* (Fredrickson and Roberts, 1997).

Using a similar questionnaire-based methodology, Strelan *et al.* showed that in a sample of young women (16–25 years) those who scored higher on self-objectification were more dissatisfied with their bodies if they reported weight and appearance-related reasons for exercising. In other words, although exercise could have helped to reduce their levels of self-objectification and improve body image, this was not the case. A later study by Strelan and Hargreaves (2005) included both males and females aged between 18 and 35 years and found the same relationship between self-objectification, weight and appearance-related reasons for exercise and body esteem in men and women, although the relationship was less strong in men.

What these results suggest is that women, and to a lesser degree men, who self-objectify (who focus on their external appearance and its evaluation by others) and who exercise primarily for body-related reasons are likely to have a poor body image. Importantly, as the authors suggest, exercising for these reasons seems to heighten the negative influence that self-objectification has on body esteem (our evaluations of our body).

Location and type of exercise

Where people exercise has been shown to relate to their body dissatisfaction. Prichard and Tiggemann (2008) used questionnaires to assess a number of exercise variables in women aged 18–71 years, including exercise motives, type of exercise they participated in and the location in which they most often exercised. The more time these women spent exercising within a fitness centre compared with other environments (e.g. cycling or playing hockey) the lower their body esteem. The authors speculate on why women who exercise more often in a fitness centre are more dissatisfied with their bodies: maybe it is because of the number of mirrors in these environments, or the emphasis placed on weight loss in the fitness environment. There may of course be other reasons, like the presence of more fit, toned individuals than we might normally encounter, including other exercisers and instructors.

The type of exercise that these women did was also related to their body esteem as women who participated more in cardiovascular-based activities (e.g. treadmill running) reported lower levels of body esteem. Not surprisingly, these women were more likely to have weight and appearance-related motives to exercise. Thus, as the authors note, cardiovascular exercise participation is associated with greater body image concern because of these motives to exercise.

Exercise leader characteristics

We have already suggested a potential role for exercise instructors in influencing women's body dissatisfaction and in fact, research evidence provides some support for this suggestion. In a study by Martin Ginis *et al.* (2008), women exercised to either one of two 30-minute exercise videos which included the same exercise workout led by an exercise instructor who had a lean, toned physique. In one video the exercise instructor wore tight-fitting exercise attire that emphasised her lean and toned physique. In the second, she wore baggy clothing that hid her physique. Participants reported greater body dissatisfaction after exercising to the exercise video when the instructor wore clothing that emphasised her physique compared with when the same instructor wore loose-fitting clothing that de-emphasised her physique.

Exercise-related lifestyle or occupation

Just as the exercise leader may influence others' body image following exercise, being an exercise leader itself may be related to body dissatisfaction. Thøgersen-Ntoumani and Ntoumanis (2007) administered questionnaires to a sample of mostly female aerobics instructors. They found that those who were more motivated to exercise due to internal pressure to develop the 'ideal' body type and so develop their own self-worth (introjected regulation as defined by Self-Determination Theory, Deci and Ryan, 1985; see Chapter 4) were more likely to have higher levels of body dissatisfaction. A similar finding was identified by Yager and O'Dea (2009) when male and female trainee health and physical education teachers were compared with those training to teach other subjects; body dissatisfaction was higher in those training to teach health and physical education. To find out more about how research in this area is conducted and alternative findings to those we have discussed here, consult the further reading listed at the end of this chapter.

You may have noticed that the majority of studies in this area have focused on women, which reflects the greater emphasis that our society places on body image in women, but men are unfortunately catching up in this regard! As researchers begin to include males in studies in this area evidence that some male exercisers exhibit high levels of body dissatisfaction is growing, sometimes with severe consequences, as we will see in the next chapter.

What else have you noticed about these studies? Take a moment to think about the research design of these studies; in particular, consider which of these studies are observational/descriptive and which are experimental (i.e. have manipulated a variable to examine its effects on body image). In fact, with the exception of Martin Ginis *et al.*'s (2008) study which examined the effects of exercise leader characteristics on body image (by changing, or manipulating, these characteristics), all of these studies are observational/descriptive. This means that these descriptive studies offer only correlational evidence about the relationship between body image, exercise motives and motivation, occupation, and exercise type and location. Thus we know that poor body image is related to these factors and we might quite reasonably speculate that exercise location, for instance, causes body dissatisfaction. However, we cannot say with certainty that the exercise participation, type, location etc. is the cause of this body dissatisfaction. For example, we know that women who exercise more in a fitness centre have lower body esteem than those who exercise more in other environments (Prichard and Tiggeman, 2008). However, we do not know if exercising in a fitness centre causes this body dissatisfaction; instead it could be that high levels of body dissatisfaction result in women exercising more in a fitness centre. Although there are a number of reasons, as we have discussed, to suggest that the exercise environment causes high levels of body dissatisfaction, until we conduct experimental studies to examine this relationship we can only say with certainty that the two variables are related to each other.

Social physique anxiety and exercise

Social physique anxiety (SPA) is very closely related to poor body image and body dissatisfaction but can you remember its definition from Chapter 3? There we defined SPA as anxiety stemming from the fear that others may negatively evaluate our physique and while much more research has shown that SPA can be decreased through exercise, some studies have shown that in some exercise settings and for some exercisers, SPA might actually increase.

When is exercise related to social physique anxiety?

Before we address this question, consider the following scenarios:

Scenario 1   Females exercising in an environment where all the exercisers are female, or, where all the exercisers are male, or, with an equal mix of males and females.   Males exercising in an environment where all the exercisers are female, or, where all the exercisers are male, or, with an equal mix of males and females.

Scenario 2   An aerobics class where the exercise instructor adopts an enriched leadership style by supporting, interacting with and motivating participants.   An aerobics class where the instructor adopts a bland leadership style, by providing technical instructions, focusing on participants' mistakes, and not encouraging or interacting with them.

Scenario 3   An aerobics class where class members interact with, encourage and positively reinforce each other and the instructor, creating a relaxed and comfortable environment.   An aerobics class where class members do not interact with, encourage or positively reinforce each other and the instructor, creating an environment that lacks warmth and communication.

Scenario 4   Exercisers who are confident of presenting a positive image of themselves during exercise (e.g. fit and toned) and are confident that exercise will help them to convey this image. They also use imagery to see themselves as fit, full of energy and competent.   Exercisers who lack confidence in presenting a positive image of themselves during exercise (e.g. fit and toned) and lack confidence that exercise will help them to convey this image. They do not often use imagery to see themselves as fit, full of energy and competent.

Learning Activity 6.1

Identify the scenario from each pair where you think participants are most likely to experience SPA, and why. Check your responses with the information below on studies which have investigated these questions.

Scenario 1: Other exerciser characteristics

Male exercisers asked to anticipate their SPA in each of these settings reported the same SPA in response to each setting. Female exercisers, in contrast, anticipated that their SPA would increase from the all female, to the mixed sex to the all male setting (Kruisselbank *et al.*, 2004).

Scenario 2: Exercise leader

Male and female undergraduates who exercised in a class where the instructor adopted an enriched leadership style experienced less physique-related social anxiety than those whose instructor adopted a bland style of leadership (Martin and Fox, 2001).

Scenario 3: Interactions with others

Unexpectedly, physique-related social anxiety was higher when people exercised in a class where members interacted with and supported each other. Maybe this was because individuals received more personal attention and so liked each other more. Both factors may have increased people's desire to impress others, increasing physique-related social anxiety (Martin and Fox, 2001).

Scenario 4: Exercise self-perceptions

Female exercisers who reported higher levels of confidence in presenting a positive image of themselves as an exerciser both during and via exercise and who used imagery to see this image had lower SPA than less confident women who used imagery less (Gammage *et al.*, 2004a). This was also the case for female exercisers in an experimental study whose confidence in portraying positive images to others during an anticipated aerobics class was manipulated to be high or low (Gammage *et al.*, 2004b).

In addition, as we saw with body image, SPA is lower in those who exercise for intrinsic reasons such as enjoyment, but higher in those who place internal pressure on themselves to exercise, resulting in guilt if they don't (Thøgersen-Ntoumani and Ntoumanis, 2006). This manuscript is included in the further reading recommended for this section as it offers a useful example of how different theories can be used together to underpin a research study.

Also similar to body image research, most of the research into SPA has focused on females and not all studies allow us to draw conclusions about the causal relationship between exercise and increased SPA. Some exceptions do exist, however, where quasi-experimental and experimental designs have been used (e.g. Martin and Fox, 2001). These findings on body image and SPA offer initial insight into why some people experience negative psychological outcomes from exercise. Based on this evidence, we can propose ways to intervene to try to minimise these effects (see below). It is important to note that the effectiveness of these suggestions needs to be examined in research before we can adopt them in practice.

Practical application

Research into the links between exercise, body image and SPA offer a number of practical applications for people like Hena, who clearly suffers from SPA which is a key barriers to exercise for her. We could focus on the exercise environment by encouraging Hena to exercise in locations other than a fitness centre where her physique may be emphasised to others or we could encourage her to find women-only sessions or areas in fitness facilities. We also could encourage Hena to develop non-appearance related motives to exercise such as enjoyment or health benefits or help her to increase her exercise self-efficacy using strategies such as using positive imagery to see herself as a competent exerciser. We may instead centre our attention on the exercise leader, ensuring that they do not emphasise the 'ideal' physique to exercisers and provide support for class members during exercise classes.

As already mentioned, we will return to body image perceptions and exercise in the next chapter. We now turn our attention to the effect of exercise on negative affect, or put more simply, negative feelings.

Negative affect and exercise

In Chapter 2 we presented a large body of research that supports the notion that exercise results in positive affect, or, makes us 'feel good'. However, as we noted at the start of this chapter, Backhouse and her colleagues (2007) comment that a large percentage of the population, including males and females across all age groups, are still not physically active. So, we are faced with a paradox: if exercise is 'good for us' and makes us 'feel good', why are so many people inactive (Backhouse et al., 2007)? Possibly the answer lies in the fact that while exercise does mostly increase positive affect there is also evidence that exercise can, in some instances, result in increased negative affect. Nevertheless, the message that exercise is beneficial is one that prevails among exercise scientists, educators and practitioners, with some good reason of course as we know that exercise offers a number of psychological, social and physical benefits. However, if we ignore the factors that are associated with negative affective responses to exercise, we do not know which factors to modify to try to limit their influence.

There are a number of reasons outlined by Backhouse et al. (2007) to explain why this somewhat simplistic conclusion that exercise makes us feel better pervades in the field of exercise psychology:

- there is a tendency to ignore findings that conflict with this conclusion;
- particularly early research did not measure all possible affective responses that might be experienced by a range of people, above all, potential negative responses. Affect measures used in exercise studies have generally been developed using healthy college students whose affective responses to exercise may not reflect others' responses, for instance, elderly women;
- not all studies, again, particularly earlier ones, have measured affect during exercise, only obtaining responses before and after exercise;
- researchers tend to group all the participants in a study together (the nomothetic approach) which masks differences in responses between individuals. Group-based analysis may show no change in positive affect due to exercise, however, in reality, half the participants reported an increase in positive affect and half a decrease, cancelling each other out when viewed overall.

You can read more detailed discussion of these comments in Backhouse *et al.*'s original paper which is identified as the further reading for this section. Backhouse *et al.* (2007) highlight that, in their view, a general response to exercise simply does not exist. Instead, how different individuals respond to exercise depends on the interaction between the person, including their appraisals of the situation and the exercise and the environment. Below we consider some research that has demonstrated this to be the case, and, as Backhouse *et al.* have emphasised, illustrates that whether or not exercise is good for you depends on a range of factors.

The key factors identified by research that may result in negative affective responses to exercise can be grouped as follows:

Exercise factors:	exercise intensity
	exercise mode
Person factors:	fitness/training status
	self-efficacy
	personality
Environment factors:	leadership style
	mirrored environments

The following sections consider research evidence in relation to each of these factors.

Exercise factors

Exercise intensity

In studies conducted by Rose and Parfitt (2007) and Kilpatrick *et al.* (2007) positive affect was significantly lower when people exercised at high compared with lower exercise intensities. The males and females in Kilpatrick *et al.*'s study reported less positive affect during a hard, short bout of ergometer cycling compared with a longer, moderate intensity bout. Throughout the short, hard bout of exercise positive affect also decreased but this decrease was not maintained 10–15 minutes after the exercise bout.

As recommended by Backhouse *et al.* (2007), Rose and Parfitt (2007) examined interindividual variability in their subjects' (sedentary women) affective responses to different exercise intensities, including a self-selected intensity. The group-based analysis only revealed a decrease in positive affect between the 10th and 15th minutes and pre- to post-exercise in above lactate threshold running (high-intensity exercise). However, take a look at Table 6.1. This shows the percentages of women who reported increases, decreases, fluctuations (both increases and decreases throughout the exercise) or no change in positive affect at different exercise intensities.

It is clear from these data that affect did not remain as stable as the group-based result would suggest. In particular, at the lower exercise intensities, a good deal of interindividual variability (variability between individuals) of responses was observed. This led Rose and Parfitt to conclude that, although exercising at the same relative intensity, each individual had a 'unique affective experience' (page 305).

	Below LT (low intensity)	At LT (moderate intensity)	Above LT (high intensity)	Self-selected intensity
Increased positive affect	42.1%	21.1%	78.9%	47.4%
Decreased positive affect	31.6%	42.1%	10.5%	26.3%
Fluctuations in positive affect	10.5%	15.8%	5.3%	5.3%
No change in positive affect	15.8%	21.1%	5.3%	21.1%

Note: LT = lactate threshold.

Table 6.1 Percentages of participants reporting increases, decreases, fluctuations and no change in positive affect during treadmill running at different exercise intensities (Rose and Parfitt, 2007)

Exercise mode

A second exercise factor influencing affective responses to exercise is exercise mode. Most of us tend to prefer certain types or modes of exercise over others, for a whole host of reasons. Moreover, as you have no doubt experienced, when you take part in a type of exercise that you prefer, you enjoy it more, feel better about yourself and generally 'feel better' as a result, compared with when you take part in less preferred forms of exercise. Research has confirmed these observations, demonstrating that our affective response to exercise differs when we perform our preferred versus our non-preferred mode of exercise. For instance, Parfitt and Gledhill (2004) found greater psychological distress when low active adults performed their non-preferred compared with their preferred mode of exercise.

This effect is not restricted to low active individuals as Daley and Maynard (2003) demonstrated that active males reported greater negative affect during and after exercise which participants had not chosen to do, compared with when they performed exercise they had chosen from a number of options. Interestingly, they also reported a greater increase in negative affect following non-preferred exercise compared with a control condition of watching TV. So while we may derive other health benefits from performing exercise that we do not like, to improve your feeling state, you may be better advised to watch TV!

Person factors

Fitness/training status

As discussed in the section above, the intensity at which people exercise can influence their affective response. In addition, as Backhouse *et al.* (2007) highlight, exercise intensity and fitness/training status interact to influence this response. Studies have shown that less fit and untrained individuals report a more negative affective response to exercise than those who are fit or trained. Boutcher *et al.* (1997) compared positive and negative affective responses in trained and untrained males during and after treadmill running that progressed in intensity from light to moderate to hard. During the moderate and hard intensity exercise the trained males reported an increase in positive affect in relation to pre-exercise level whereas the untrained males' positive affect decreased in comparison to pre-exercise. Negative affect also demonstrated different patterns of change between the two groups with no changes reported by the trained males whereas in comparison with pre-exercise the untrained males reported less negative affect at all exercise intensities.

Similar results were obtained in a sample of unfit and highly fit females who performed moderate and high intensity exercise on a cycle ergometer (Blanchard *et al.*, 2001). No change in psychological distress was reported by both groups of women following moderate intensity exercise or by the highly fit group following high intensity exercise. However, the unfit women experienced a significant increase in psychological distress from pre- to post-exercise when they performed high intensity exercise. In addition to this physical attribute, as the following sections discuss, psychological person factors can influence our affective responses to exercise.

Self-efficacy

As we would expect, individuals with low self-efficacy to exercise have been shown to experience negative affective responses to exercise. For instance, McAuley *et al.* (1999) manipulated college women's self-efficacy for exercise by providing them with false feedback about their own performance in relation to comparative norms on a submaximal cycle ergometer test. Those women who had manipulated low levels of self-efficacy reported significantly greater psychological distress and fatigue following receipt of this information, and after performing a stepping task in a subsequent session. Although the women were reminded of their apparently poor performance on the ergometer test prior to the second session their efficacy on this second exercise was not manipulated. These results therefore indicate the potential transfer of low self-efficacy and its effects across different exercise activities.

A similar effect was seen in adolescents during submaximal treadmill exercise as lower pre-exercise self-efficacy (not manipulated in this case) was associated with feeling worse during exercise (Robbins *et al.*, 2004). As the exercise progressed, feeling state became more negative, and interestingly an effect of maturation status was revealed. Those adolescents experiencing the early stages of puberty felt worse than those in the middle and later stages of puberty.

Personality

In addition to the modifiable person factors of self-efficacy and training or fitness status, Schneider and Graham (2009) have demonstrated that the more stable personality characteristic of approach or avoidance action tendency is related to affective response to exercise. They compared the affective responses to moderate and high intensity exercise in adolescents in relation to their tendency to approach goals, experience positive emotions and focus on achieving possible rewards and to avoid threatening stimuli, experience negative emotions and focus on avoiding possible punishment. Adolescents with a high avoidance tendency and those with a low approach tendency reported more negative feelings during both moderate and high intensity exercise. These authors concluded therefore that adolescents who focus on potential punishment (e.g. in this case feeling tired because of the exercise) find exercise less pleasurable and so are at increased risk of becoming sedentary.

Environment factors

Leadership style

We have already seen that the exercise leader can influence body image and SPA and the same is true for negative affect. Female college students completed an aerobics class with a leader who emphasised either health or appearance aspects of exercise (Raedeke *et al.*, 2008). In the health-oriented class the instructor made comments focusing on the health benefits of the exercise (e.g. improving posture) and wore baggy clothing to de-emphasise her slim, toned physique. In contrast, in the appearance-oriented class she wore tight clothing to accentuate her physique and focused her comments on the appearance-related benefits of exercise (e.g. losing weight). Following the appearance-oriented class the women reported greater physical exhaustion than following the health-oriented class. These women all had high SPA so results may not extend to exercisers who are not high in SPA. There is also the possibility that in the appearance-oriented class the women worked harder as the focus on exercise as a means of improving appearance, coupled with their high SPA, motivated them to do so. Although each class included the same exercise routine no measures of subjective effort or objective energy expenditure were obtained to rule out this possibility.

Mirrored environments

Research has also shown that in addition to the characteristics of the exercise leader the physical characteristics of the exercise environment can influence affective responses to exercise. Focusing on sedentary women, Martin Ginis *et al.* (2007) also found an effect of exercise environment on physical exhaustion. These women cycled in one of four conditions: alone in front of a mirror, alone with no mirror, with other exercisers in front of a mirror, and with other exercisers and no mirror. Only when the women cycled with other exercisers in a mirrored environment did they report increases in physical exhaustion. When we consider that this condition reflects the real life exercise environment of most gyms it is perhaps not surprising that some women remain sedentary.

Again, however, subjective or objective measures of work output were not taken, therefore we cannot rule out variations in actual or perceived work rate as explanations for this effect. In addition, women who exercised in front of mirrors in the presence of other exercisers also made more social comparisons of their fitness and appearance with others who were present. It is possible that these social comparisons motivated them to work harder in this condition. Clearly, research that includes subjective and objective measures of work output would help to further understand this effect.

The studies above offer some useful results to help us to try and optimise affective responses to exercise in individuals like Hena. First, as she is unfit we need to ensure that she begins with exercise that for her is at a moderate intensity. As we saw above with body image and SPA, we might encourage her to use imagery to see herself as a confident, competent exerciser, to try and increase her self-efficacy. We could also help her to find environments to exercise in other than the gym where she will be faced with mirrors and other exercisers who she feels may be negatively evaluating her physique.

Research Focus: Does exercise make people feel better?

Backhouse *et al.* (2007) examined both group and individual affective responses to exercise, using the circumplex model of affect (Russell, 1980). This model proposes that we can encompass affective responses into a 'global affective space' with two dimensions: affective valence (pleasure–displeasure) and perceived activation (low arousal–high arousal; Figure 6.1).

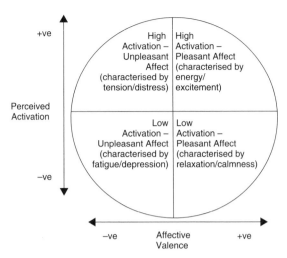

Figure 6.1 The circumplex model of affect (Russell, 1980).

The individual's affective state can be located anywhere in this space, resulting in different kinds of affect based on different combinations of experienced pleasure–displeasure and arousal levels (see Figure 6.3). As this model does not identify specific affective responses, theoretically, measurement of these two dimensions will cover the whole spectrum of potential affective responses with the added advantage of requiring individuals who are exercising to answer only two questions.

Twelve recreationally active males completed the Loughborough Intermittent Shuttle Test (Nicholas *et al.*, 2000) and reported their affect at the following time points: pre-exercise, every 15 minutes during exercise, on reaching fatigue, and 15 minutes post-exercise.

Group-based responses demonstrated that affect and perceived activation did not change from pre- to post-exercise but perceived activation increased from pre-exercise to all time points during exercise, and affect decreased from 60 minutes onward (Figure 6.2).

Figure 6.3 depicts the individual responses of two participants, whose responses differ in both magnitude and direction from the group response. For participant a, perceived activation was consistently low with little variation during exercise and only small changes in affect. Participant b's profile is different again, from both participant a's and the group's.

Responses pre- to post-exercise could suggest that the exercise did not influence affect but during exercise the participants progressed through all four quadrants of the circumplex model, suggesting a range of feelings was experienced. Individuals' response patterns reveal even more variability. While most participants' responses matched the group average, some demonstrated distinctly different responses, as the examples in Figure 6.3 illustrate.

Backhouse *et al.* (2007) concluded that their results show that exercise does not always make us feel better as our response to exercise is influenced by a range of person, environment and exercise factors. Their results also reinforce the need to address the criticisms of research in this area, as discussed above.

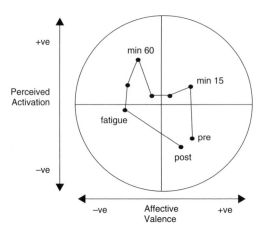

Figure 6.2 Group-based results from Backhouse et al. *(2007). Reprinted with permission from Human Kinetics from Backhouse, SH, Ekkekakis, P, Biddle, SJH, Foskett, A and Williams, C (2007) Exercise makes people feel better but people are inactive: Paradox or artifact?* Journal of Sport and Exercise Psychology, *29: 498–517.*

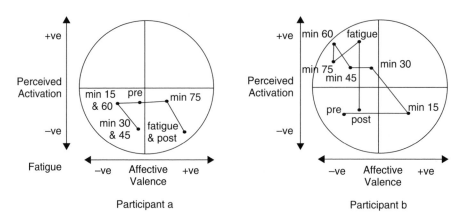

Figure 6.3 Examples of individual responses to exercise. Reprinted with permission from Human Kinetics from Backhouse, SH, Ekkekakis, P, Biddle, SJH, Foskett, A and Williams, C (2007) Exercise makes people feel better but people are inactive: Paradox or artifact? Journal of Sport and Exercise Psychology, *29: 498–517.*

Learning Activity 6.2

What limitations of Backhouse *et al*.'s (2007) study can you identify? Check your ideas with those provided at the end of the book.

Learning Activity 6.3

Conduct a study to examine the effect of different modes of exercise on affective responses (e.g. cycling, running, walking, weight training, etc.). Try to collect measures pre-, during and post-exercise and measure both affective valence and perceived activation using the following scales:

Displeasure   −5   −4   −3   −2   −1   0   +1   +2   +3   +4   +5   Pleasure
Feeling Scale (Hardy and Rejeski, 1989)

Low arousal   1   2   3   4   5   6   High arousal
Felt Arousal Scale (Svebak and Murgatroyd, 1985)
Use the circumplex model to plot your responses for different exercise modes and consider comparisons you could make (e.g. males vs. females, preferred vs. non-preferred exercise, aerobic vs. strength exercise). Don't forget to examine individual as well as group-based responses.

Unlike the majority of studies into body image and SPA which we examined, studies that have examined negative affect and exercise have employed quasi-experimental or experimental research designs. Thus, we can say with greater certainty that the exercise, person or environment factor examined in these studies had a causal effect on study participants' responses. However, it is important to note that these different studies used different participants (e.g. adolescents, women high in SPA) therefore further studies are needed to see if their findings can be generalised to other populations. A second important observation we can make is that not all individuals respond to exercise in the same way, thus there is a great deal of interindividual variability in affective responses to exercise and future studies need to account for these individual differences.

Chapter Review

We first identified a number of reasons why exercise may be associated with body dissatisfaction (Learning Objective 1): exercise motives and motivation, the exercise leader, location and type of exercise. High social physique anxiety is also associated with exercise motives and leader characteristics, in addition to the types of interactions with others in the exercise class and, in women, to the gender composition of the exercise environment and exercise-based self-perceptions (Learning Objective 1). We discussed reasons why exercise may lead to negative affect (Learning Objective 1), including exercise intensity and mode, exercise self-efficacy, personality and fitness level, and, characteristics of the exercise leader and environment. We also considered criticisms of this latter body of research (Learning Objective 2) including limited measures of affective responses and a lack of measures during exercise. Our brief consideration of the circumplex model of affect (Learning Objective 3) identified that this model proposes two dimensions: affective valence and perceived activation, to encompass a whole range of possible affective responses.

Learning Activity 6.4
Test your understanding

1. Identify the reasons discussed in this chapter why some people who exercise may suffer from body dissatisfaction.
2. Define social physique anxiety (SPA) and identify two reasons why exercise may be associated with high SPA.
3. Discuss one person, one exercise and one environment factor which may be associated with a negative affective response to exercise.
4. Draw and briefly explain the circumplex model of affect (Russell, 1980).

Further Reading

- For more on exercise-related lifestyle/occupation:

Prichard, I and Tiggemann, M (2005) Objectification in fitness centers: Self-objectification, body dissatisfaction and disordered eating in aerobic instructors and aerobic participants. *Sex Roles*, 53: 19–28.

This article examines self-objectification, exercise motives and behaviours in female aerobic instructors and participants. It provides an illustrative example of correlational research in this area and presents some contradictory findings with aerobic instructors to those discussed above.

- For more on social physique anxiety:

Thøgersen-Ntoumani, C and Ntoumanis, N (2006) The role of self-determined motivation in the understanding of exercise-related behaviours, cognitions and physical self-evaluations. *Journal of Sports Sciences*, 24: 393–404.

This article examines physique related concerns in a large group of exercisers and uses Self-Determination Theory and the stages of change model that we have encountered in Chapter 4 to do so, providing a useful illustration of how theory can help us to understand different phenomena.

- For more on negative affect and exercise:

Backhouse, SH, Ekkekakis, P, Biddle, SJH, Foskett, A and Williams, C (2007) Exercise makes people feel better but people are inactive: paradox or artifact? *Journal of Sport and Exercise Psychology*, 29: 498–517.

Although we have already examined the empirical study described by Backhouse and colleagues it is worth reading in more detail their comments on the literature in this area which comprise the first half of this article.

Chapter 7
Being active: harmful effects

Learning Objectives

This chapter is designed to help you be able to:

1. identify some of the cognitive and behavioural effects of the drive for muscularity, particularly in males;
2. define muscle dysmorphia and identify the effects and possible causes of this condition;
3. discuss the relationship between exercise and eating disorders, including the role of psychological factors in this relationship;
4. outline a potential psychobiological explanation for exercise dependence;
5. distinguish between primary and secondary exercise dependence.

Introduction

In Chapter 6 we considered a number of potential negative effects of exercise, including negative affect, body dissatisfaction and social physique anxiety (SPA). In this chapter we continue our discussion of negative or harmful aspects of exercise participation. However, unlike in Chapter 6 where we focused on non-clinical, or healthy, populations, in this chapter we focus on clinical populations. In other words, we turn our attention to the more extreme harmful effects that are associated with exercise. These centre, not surprisingly, on body dissatisfaction. Specifically we examine the links between exercise and eating disorders, exercise and muscle dysmorphia and the phenomenon of exercise dependence. Although these conditions are seen in competitive athletes, as in Chapter 6, we mostly restrict our discussion to non-competitive exercisers and exercise settings.

Exercise and muscularity

We noted a number of studies in Chapter 6 that examined links between exercise, SPA and body dissatisfaction, the majority of which focused on females. This focus is led by the fact that until recently, society's emphasis has been on the female body, with media representation of an 'ideal' body that for many women is increasingly unattainable. However, physical appearance and the need to achieve the 'ideal' body are increasingly emphasised for men, leading to increasing prevalence of body dissatisfaction among males. Whereas most women still express a desire to lose weight and be thinner, and so do some men, an increasing element of body dissatisfaction in men reflects a desire to be more muscular.

Cash (2002) noted that the percentage of men who reported dissatisfaction with their degree of muscle tone has risen from 25 per cent in 1972 to 32 per cent in 1985 to 45 per cent in 1996. We can speculate that with society's increasing emphasis on physical appearance, this figure has since risen yet further. Confirming these data, McCabe and Ricciardelli (2004) conducted a review of studies into body image dissatisfaction in males which suggested that, particularly in adolescence and adulthood, many males are dissatisfied with their bodies and express a desire to be more lean and muscular. There are limitations to this body of research (e.g. the interchangeable use of different terms, like heavier and bigger) but it does serve to inform us that body dissatisfaction is certainly not the sole preserve of females. This body dissatisfaction may lead to an increase in the drive for muscularity (e.g. Martin *et al.*, 2006) which has associations with both negative cognitions and behaviours. For instance, in a sample of regularly exercising male college students those who felt that being muscular had a number of positive attributes reported higher levels of SPA. Their mean SPA was moderate and their body image was positive, nevertheless, these men reported high levels of motivation to be muscular, suggesting that the high level of SPA experienced by some is an indication of their dissatisfaction with their degree of muscularity (Martin *et al.*, 2006).

McCabe and James (2009) examined if the motive to exercise to lose weight and increase muscle is related to extreme behaviours to achieve this (e.g. excessive exercise and the use of food supplements). In a sample of male and female fitness centre users, compared with women, men reported using more strategies to increase muscle, including taking food supplements and steroids. This gender difference aside, both men and women who exercised mainly to increase muscularity (or to improve sporting ability) were more likely to report using these strategies to increase muscle. Similarly males and females with a higher body mass index (BMI; therefore likely to have a more muscular physique) reported greater use of strategies to increase muscle, including taking food supplements. This latter relationship was stronger in males, and interestingly, greater use of food supplements subsequently led to excessive exercise in males but not females. As McCabe and James (2009, page 276) caution therefore, 'engaging in relatively innocuous exercise and eating behaviours may lead to more problematic behaviours'. Thus, a drive for muscularity is not inherently detrimental to the individual as it may lead him or her to engage in healthy levels of health-related behaviours such as exercise. However, as we have seen, this drive may be associated with unhealthy self-perceptions or behaviours. Taken to the extreme, this desire to be more muscular may result in a pathological disorder known as muscle dysmorphia.

Muscle dysmorphia

Muscle dysmorphia has been defined as a pathological (i.e. medical) condition where the individual is preoccupied with not being muscular or large enough (e.g. Pope *et al.*, 1997). Their life is focused on activities to try and increase muscle mass such as weight lifting and dieting (Pope *et al.*, 1997). Paradoxically, many men who suffer from muscle dysmorphia are in fact very muscular, more so than most men (Olivardia, 2007), illustrating the degree of cognitive distortion that they experience. Box 7.1 summarises the diagnostic criteria for muscle dysmorphia, as listed in the *Diagnostic and Statistical Manual of Mental Disorders* (American Psychiatric Association, 2000).

Box 7.1 Definition: Muscle dysmorphia

An individual with muscle dysmorphia:

- has an obsessive belief that he or she should be more lean and muscular, often accompanied by a regimented diet and excessive weightlifting;
- has at least two of the following characteristics:

  (a) excludes themselves from social, career or other activities to pursue a fixed training regime;
  (b) feels uncomfortable and avoids situations where their body is on display;
  (c) is affected in work and social situations by their poor body image;
  (d) continues to diet and work out excessively or use steroids even though they are aware of the health dangers of this behaviour;

- is preoccupied with the belief that they are too small and insufficiently muscular.

(Adapted from Leone *et al.*, 2005)

Effects of muscle dysmorphia

People with muscle dysmorphia experience both cognitive and behavioural effects. The key cognitive and behavioural effects are discussed by Olivardia (2007) and summarised in Table 7.1.

Cognitive consequences	
Preoccupation with appearance	Constant thoughts and anxiety about appearance, approximately 5.5 hours a day, compared with 40 minutes a day in non-MD male weight lifters (Olivardia *et al.*, 2000).
	A sense of failure as an individual if they do not achieve 'perfection,' derived from overvaluing appearance (Olivardia *et al.*).
	Difficulty concentrating and distractability as thoughts are preoccupied with appearance (Pope *et al.*, 2000).
Cognitive distortion	An all or nothing, or polarised, view of themselves and their behaviour (e.g. a missed workout or diet infringement means the individual feels like they're back to square one).
	Projecting own beliefs onto others so that if they see themselves as small and skinny, then so must others.
	Inaccurate body assessments that exacerbate negative aspects and ignore any positive ones.
Personalisation	Interpreting others' behaviour as confirmation of their own distorted body image. For instance, the MD sufferer may believe that someone they see laughing and joking with friends is actually laughing at them.

	Often, the individual has no control over these thoughts, increasing feelings of helplessness and anxiety.
Diet preoccupation	MD sufferers are preoccupied with consuming the correct balance of nutrients to optimise their physique.
	As a result they often decline dinner invitations as they are unable to ensure that what they eat will aid them in their quest to gain muscle.
Behavioural consequences	
Excessive exercise	MD sufferers exercise to the point of missing important life events even though, contrary to what observers think, they may not always enjoy working out and feel trapped by the behaviour.
Appearance checking	MD sufferers often check their appearance in mirrors or any available reflective surface.
	This checking is fuelled by anxiety and is never sated as they are never satisfied with the image that is reflected back at them.
	Often, the MD individual will avoid mirrors completely.
Steroid use	Steroid use is high in men with MD, reaching approximately 50%, substantially greater than the 7% of comparison men who reported using steroids (Olivardia *et al.*, 2000).
Poor functioning in different life domains	Excessive concern about their physique may cause MD sufferers to avoid social situations, such as a beach party, where their physique is on show, and they may conceal what they perceive as a poor physique with baggy clothing.
	School and work performance may suffer as the individual spends time working out or thinking about their appearance when they should be focused on their job or schoolwork.
	Interpersonal relationships may suffer, first, because social invitations may be declined in favour of exercising and second, when attending social events, the individual is preoccupied with anxiety about their physique. Significant others may become exasperated by the constant reassurance the individual seeks about their body, and sexual relationships may suffer due to anxiety about appearance or an unwillingness to expend energy that could be used in a workout.

Table 7.1 Key cognitive and behavioural effects of muscle dysmorphia (MD)

One of the case studies presented by Pope *et al.* (1997, page 554) in their seminal work offers a colourful depiction of this condition. See below for a summary of this case study.

Case Study 7.1
Muscle dysmorphia

Mr A weighed 92 kg and was 168 cm tall with 17 per cent body fat. Although his body fat percentage was only slightly below average, his fat free mass index was 28 kg/m², indicating hypermuscularity. In fact, such a muscle mass is far in excess of that which could normally be achieved without taking anabolic steroids or similar drugs. Until recently Mr A had indeed taken anabolic steroids regularly for a number of years. Regardless of his actual body dimensions Mr A felt he was much fatter and was unhappy with his physique.

He constantly thought about increasing his muscularity and weighed himself and checked his appearance numerous times each day although he tried in vain to stop himself from doing so. He exercised excessively, weight lifting every day and the thought of being unable to made him feel anxious and depressed.

He wore baggy clothing to hide what he perceived to be a small physique and his fear of others' perceptions of his physique affected his social life and relationships. For instance, he missed a college reunion to avoid being seen as 'small' (page 554) by his old college friends and did not eat out in restaurants to ensure that his dietary intake helped him to minimise fat and enhance his muscularity.

Causes of muscle dysmorphia

Evidently, muscle dysmorphia and its associated behaviours and cognitions may have serious consequences for the individual's physical, psychological and social health and wellbeing. There is currently less available evidence to explain why individuals develop the condition. However, Grieve (2007) has proposed a model that identifies factors which may lead to the development of muscle dysmorphia and suggests how these factors may be related (Figure 7.1).

According to Grieve (2007) ideal body internalisation, body dissatisfaction and body distortion are the most important factors in the model as it is mainly through these that the remainder exert their effects. Although there is evidence to support links between some of these factors and muscle dysmorphia, as Grieve notes, many of the relationships in the model have not yet been tested in research. Moreover, those relationships that have been supported in research have been examined in populations with subclinical levels of muscle dysmorphia, therefore research is needed that includes those who are at risk of, or are suffering from, clinical levels of muscle dysmorphia.

Our discussion has focused on muscle dysmorphia in males as its prevalence is greater in males than in females, however, cases have been reported in females. In fact, Pope *et al.*'s (1997) original paper identified muscle dysmorphia symptoms in 32 of 38 competitive female bodybuilders and presented a disturbing case study of one female with muscle dysmorphia who experienced serious health problems because of her steroid use and restricted diet but continued with these behaviours nonetheless. Considering the increasing pressure placed on women to not only be thin but also muscular, and the increased muscularity of female athletes, it seems that researchers would do well to include females in their studies on muscle dysmorphia.

Dealing with muscle dysmorphia

We can use the diagnostic criteria for muscle dysmorphia to identify individuals who may be suffering from this condition. Leone *et al.* (2005, page 355) identify specific questions that can be asked that focus on social avoidance, time spent on appearance and diet and drug use (e.g. 'How frequently does your

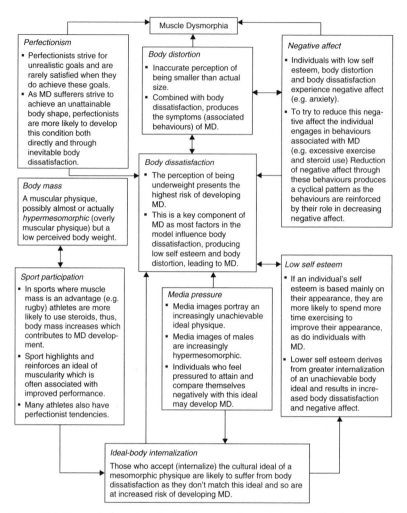

Figure 7.1 Factors influencing the development of muscle dysmorphia. Reprinted with permission from Taylor & Francis from Grieve, FG (2007) A conceptual model of factors contributing to the development of muscle dysmorphia. Eating Disorders, *15: 63–80.*

appearance make you feel distraught, depressed, or anxious?'). We might focus interventions to prevent or treat muscle dysmorphia on the factors proposed to be most influential in its development: body dissatisfaction, body distortion and ideal body internalisation. Reshaping the individual's distorted body image is clearly a key step in helping sufferers to deal with muscle dysmorphia. As muscle dysmorphia is a clinical condition, its treatment would be undertaken by someone who is qualified to do so, such as a clinical psychologist. However, we can try to prevent it developing in individuals who may be at risk. We may help them to enhance their self-esteem through non-appearance based sources (e.g. acting as a role model for younger exercisers or athletes) or help them to realise that media-presented images of the ideal body are not the norm, are mostly unattainable and often artificially produced.

Of course before we can fully address this issue a huge change is needed at a societal level in the way we view our bodies and appearance (Leone *et al.*, 2005) to rid our society of harmful and unrealistic portrayals of the 'ideal body'. Leone *et al.*'s paper is listed in full in the further reading at the end of this chapter and you may want to consult it to obtain more detail about these suggestions.

Learning Activity 7.1

1. In groups of three, locate the following articles, two of which we have considered in this chapter:

   - Martin, JJ, Kliber, A, Kulinna, PH and Fahlman, M (2006) Social physique anxiety and muscularity and appearance cognitions in college men. *Sex Roles*, 55: 151–158.
   - McCabe, MP and James, T (2009) Strategies to change body shape among men and women who attend fitness centers. *Asia-Pacific Journal of Public Health*, 21: 268–278.
   - Pickett, TC, Lewis, RJ and Cash, TF (2005) Men, muscles, and body image: Comparisons of competitive bodybuilders, weight trainers, and athletically active controls. *British Journal of Sports Medicine*, 39: 217–222.

2. In your groups of three, select one paper each and read through the Introduction, Method and Results sections. Note at least three strengths and three limitations of the study. Discuss your critical analysis of the three studies, highlighting strengths and limitations that differ and are common between the three studies.

3. Now read through the Discussion sections of the papers and compare your critical comments with those made by the authors.

Eating disorders and exercise

When Pope and his colleagues introduced the idea of muscle dysmorphia in 1997 they used the term 'reverse anorexia' to describe this condition as it shares clear similarities with anorexia nervosa. What are the key similarities and differences between these two conditions? You probably identified that both conditions involve obsessive behaviours, a preoccupation with appearance and a restricted diet. However, there is a key difference between muscle dysmorphia and anorexia nervosa. The former involves a preoccupation with becoming larger (more muscular) and the use of exercise and large intakes of food to optimise muscular development. The latter involves a preoccupation with becoming smaller (thinner), restricted calorie intake and often involves the use of exercise to lose as much weight as possible. This suggests a potential link between exercise and eating disorders which we consider in the following sections.

Eating disorders in exercisers

Holme-Denoma *et al.* (2009) suggest that exercisers may be more at risk of suffering from an eating disorder than non-exercisers, and independent exercisers may be at equal risk of suffering from an eating disorder as competitive sports participants. In a sample of 274 female undergraduate students, independent exercisers (those who do not exercise in a class or with others) reported a higher drive for thinness (one subcomponent of eating disorder symptoms) than both non-exercisers and club level athletes. Interestingly though, body dissatisfaction was lower in exercisers than in club level athletes, possibly suggesting that these athletes' dissatisfaction stemmed from a desire to be more muscular and not thinner, emphasising our earlier call for research to examine this condition in females as well as males. This study also found that bulimic symptoms were higher in exercisers, club and university level athletes than in non-exercisers.

We have already mentioned a few different terms so far, for instance, eating disorder symptoms, drive for thinness, bulimic symptoms, anorexia nervosa, and before we go any further let us ensure that you are clear on what we mean by these terms. Berger and her colleagues (2007) provide explanations, based on the American Psychiatric Association's DSM-IV criteria (1994), which are summarised in Box 7.2.

Box 7.2 Definitions: Summary of eating disorders

Anorexia nervosa (AN)	The individual is visibly underweight, usually 15% below comparable norms. Nevertheless, she or he has an extremely distorted body image, seeing her/himself as overweight and has an extreme fear of becoming fat. In females, the menstrual cycle stops and extreme cases may result in organ failure and death.
Bulimia nervosa (BN)	The individual is obsessed with their body but instead of the self-starvation of AN sufferers, BN sufferers lack control over their eating, resulting in bingeing and purging. Bingeing involves eating large quantities of food in secret and in a short space of time. Purging of this food to prevent weight gain may include the use of vomiting, laxatives, strict dieting or vigorous exercise.
Binge eating disorder (BED)	Similar to BN, this disorder involves lack of control over eating and rapid consumption of large quantities of food over a short duration. The binge eater often suffers from guilt, embarrassment and disgust and therefore eats alone. The binge eater eats until uncomfortably full and when she or he is not hungry but does not purge him/herself of food to compensate as do people with BN.
Disordered eating (DE)	Many people are not diagnosed with a clinical eating disorder such as AN or BN but nevertheless engage in disordered eating. This label reflects the fact that eating disorders exist on a continuum with an absence of any disorder at one end and a full clinical disorder at the other (see below). In between, individuals may have unhealthy attitudes towards their weight and food and may engage in some unhealthy eating behaviours but they do not meet the criteria for clinical diagnosis of an eating disorder.

Disordered eating can be described as a continuum as shown in Figure 7.2.

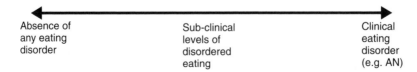

| Absence of any eating disorder | Sub-clinical levels of disordered eating | Clinical eating disorder (e.g. AN) |

Figure 7.2 Continuum of eating disorders.

Physical activity in the development of eating disorders

Instead of examining eating disorders in exercisers, other researchers have examined this relationship from an alternative perspective by exploring exercise levels in patients suffering from a clinically diagnosed eating disorder. A comparison between adolescent patients with anorexia nervosa and a healthy control group identified that the anorexia patients were more physically active and reported more obligatory commitment to exercise (Davis *et al.*, 2005). That is, they felt they had to exercise and stick rigidly to a strict exercise regime.

In this study, Davis *et al.* (2005) retrospectively compared physical activity levels in adolescent patients with anorexia nervosa prior and subsequent to the onset of their condition to those reported by healthy adolescents. Exercise increased with age in all respondents but more so for the anorexia patients, with a dramatic increase in patients' physical activity approximately one year prior to their diagnosis as anorexic. In conclusion, these authors suggested that high levels of physical activity play a role in the development of anorexia nervosa.

Eating disorders and excessive exercise

We have established that there is a relationship between exercise and eating disorders and researchers have also noted that exercisers with an eating disorder often exercise excessively. For instance, Lejoyeaux *et al.* (2008) identified that 42 per cent of 300 fitness room users were exercise dependent and reported a higher level of bulimia nervosa symptoms than non-exercise dependent respondents.

You may have noted that in this chapter alone we have used a number of different terms to describe very similar but different phenomena: excessive exercise, over-exercise and exercise dependence. Cook and Hausenblas (2008) highlighted that research in this area has used inconsistent definitions and measures of excessive exercise, resulting in mixed findings that may not represent the true picture of the link between excessive exercise and eating disorders. Even a casual perusal of the literature will reveal even more terms used in this area: obligatory exercise, compulsive exercise, exercise addiction, obsessive exercise and so on. Although not identical these are similar concepts and we do not have the scope to define and discuss all these terms in this chapter; instead, we focus on excessive exercise and exercise dependence. Excessive exercise describes exercise levels above those recommended for health and as such exercise interferes with the individual's lifestyle, for instance, missing important social events. The individual will also continue to exercise when it is inadvisable to do so, for instance, when ill or injured (American Psychiatric Association, 2000). Exercise dependence is defined in a later section when we consider this phenomenon in more detail. You may want to find definitions of the additional terms listed above in existing research.

Psychological factors involved in the relationship between excessive exercise and eating disorders

Research has revealed an important role played by psychological factors in the relationship between excessive exercise and eating disorders. Key factors identified to date include:

- compulsion to exercise;
- exercise motives;
- guilt experienced following a missed exercise session.

Compulsion and motives to exercise

Adkin and Keel (2005) examined the links between excessive exercise, compulsion to exercise and eating disorders in relation to exercise motives. In people who exercised for appearance-related reasons such as to lose weight, time spent exercising was negatively related to reported symptoms of bulimia nervosa whereas a compulsion to exercise was positively related to bulimia symptoms. In other words, people who had a compulsion to exercise were more likely to report disordered eating whereas those who spent a great deal of time exercising were less likely to report disordered eating. No such relationships were revealed in people who exercised for non-appearance related reasons such as challenge and fun, and who reported disordered eating symptoms. These results suggest that: (1) exercise behaviour (excessive exercise) is not necessarily related to disordered eating but exercise cognition (compulsion to exercise) is; (2) this relationship may only be apparent in people who have appearance-related motives for exercise, and (3) compulsion to exercise is not necessarily related to disordered eating in exercisers, as we explore further when we examine the phenomenon of exercise dependence.

Exercise and guilt

Think about how you feel when you miss an exercise session you had planned; do you feel annoyed, restless or conversely, sluggish? Do you worry about your lost fitness or do you simply think little of it? Do you ever feel guilty when you miss an exercise session? For some people this guilt is related to adverse health consequences in the form of disordered eating.

From a Self-Determination Theory perspective (see Chapter 4; Deci and Ryan, 1985), people who experience guilt when they miss an exercise session are likely to report high levels of introjected regulation, reflecting a motivation to exercise because of pressure the individual exerts on themselves to do so. In their study of aerobics instructors Thøgersen-Ntoumani and Ntoumanis (2007) found that instructors with more introjected regulation to exercise had increased risk of developing an eating disorder. This bolsters support for the notion that self-imposed guilt from missing exercise and internal pressure to exercise are implicated in the link between exercise and eating disorders.

Clearly, the relationship between exercise and disordered eating is not straightforward and is not explained simply by the amount of exercise we do. Psychological factors such as exercise compulsion and exercise motives play a role in this relationship; hence, we cannot ignore these factors if we want to fully understand this relationship. Research conducted by Davis and her colleagues provides further insight into this complex relationship by considering common personality characteristics which underpin eating disorders and excessive exercise, as discussed in the next section.

Obsessive compulsive disorder, eating disorders and excessive exercise

There is a common obsessive compulsive underpinning of excessive exercise and eating disorders, and psychological factors mediate the relationship between these two behaviours, in particular, compulsion to exercise and intense guilt following missed exercise sessions (Cook and Hausenblas, 2008). Box 7.3 provides an explanation of what we mean by a mediator. Anorexia nervosa patients who exercise excessively have a more obsessive compulsive personality (Davis and Kaptein, 2006) and higher levels of perfectionism (a personality factor associated with the development of an obsessive compulsive personality disorder; Davis et al., 1998) than those patients with anorexia nervosa who do not exercise excessively. These obsessive compulsive personality characteristics were reflected in an obsessive (according to the authors, almost pathological) attitude towards exercise in the patients with anorexia nervosa included in Davis *et al.*'s study.

Box 7.3 Definition: Mediator

A mediator is something that explains how or why one thing influences another and therefore can be considered as a mechanism by which this influence occurs (Frazier *et al.*, 2004). Exercise compulsion is a potential mediator between, or explanation for, the relationship between exercise behaviour and disordered eating.

As well as sharing personality characteristics, eating disorders and excessive exercise result in similar physiological and behavioural outcomes. Davis and Claridge (1998) observed excessive exercise levels in eating disorder patients which they explained via shared biological mechanisms. Both excessive exercise and starvation stimulate the release of endorphins (i.e. 'feel good' hormones); subsequently high endorphin levels result in increased physical activity and self-induced starvation as the individual tries to produce more of these 'feel good' hormones. When we consider this shared biological factor it's easy to see how these two behaviours so often coexist.

Dealing with disordered eating and exercise behaviours

Yager and O'Dea (2008) conducted a review of 27 health promotion and health education programmes implemented in universities and designed to improve body dissatisfaction, eating and exercise behaviours. They identified a number of limitations of these interventions, such as a focus predominantly on female, self-selected participants; nevertheless they identified two intervention approaches which seem to be most effective: cognitive dissonance education-based approaches and media literacy approaches.

- *Cognitive dissonance education-based approaches*: When there is a mismatch between an individual's health-related beliefs and behaviours (e.g. I should exercise but I don't; termed 'cognitive dissonance') this can lead to psychological discomfort and motivate the individual to change either their beliefs or behaviour to reduce this inconsistency and any resulting psychological discomfort (Stice *et al.*, 2000). Interventions that have adopted this approach have involved, for instance, asking female university students to develop an educational programme that reduces the internalisation of a thin ideal in female high school students. Such approaches have proved to be successful in reducing the internalisation of thin ideals, body dissatisfaction, dieting and disordered eating in female undergraduates.
- *Media literacy approaches*: These approaches focus on educating the individual to critically evaluate media representations, such as the thin ideal body for women and the muscular ideal body for men, thus resulting in rejection of these media representations. These interventions have demonstrated success in improving body image and reducing the internalisation of thin ideals but less success in changing related behaviours such as disordered eating. Yager and O'Dea highlight that these relatively brief interventions compete with a lifetime of pervasive exposure to media representations of the 'ideal' body which may explain their mixed success. However, it seems that combined, cognitive dissonance

and media literacy based interventions have the potential for modifying disordered eating and the attitudes and beliefs that underpin this behaviour in university populations.

Yager and O'Dea's paper is listed in full in the further reading at the end of this chapter and you may want to consult it to obtain more detail about these and other interventions that have been used to address these problem behaviours.

Exercise dependence

Given the seemingly consistent finding that excessive exercise and eating disorders very often go hand in hand, there is some debate over whether excessive exercise, or, more precisely, exercise dependence, exists as a condition separate from an eating disorder. In other words: can someone be dependent on exercise without suffering from an eating disorder, or, if someone is exercise dependent, do they necessarily also suffer from an eating disorder? This debate describes two forms of exercise dependence as identified by Veale (1995):

- primary exercise dependence;
- secondary exercise dependence.

Exercise dependence is a condition where the individual engages in excessive and unhealthy levels of exercise and experiences withdrawal symptoms (e.g. irritability) when they are prevented from exercising. This rarely happens though, as these individuals will exercise when ill or injured or even when doing so interferes with other areas of their life. Just like people with muscle dysmorphia, individuals who are exercise dependent will forego social invitations, will arrange their working life, and maybe even their career, around exercise.

We have already seen that exercise dependence very often coexists alongside an eating disorder, and this is termed 'secondary exercise dependence'. Excessive exercising is considered a symptom of the individual's eating disorder. The individual is not dependent on the exercise itself, but is thought to be dependent on the effects of his or her exercise on body weight and shape; in other words, its secondary effects, hence the label secondary exercise dependence. In contrast, someone who does not have an eating disorder but is exercise dependent is 'primary exercise dependent' as they are dependent on the exercise itself and not its secondary effects such as weight loss or toning.

The development of exercise dependence

Why some people, and not others, develop primary exercise dependence, is not yet fully understood. Hamer and Karageorghis (2007) presented an analysis of competing psychobiological explanations for exercise dependence. They conclude their analysis by suggesting that the most plausible potential mechanism to explain exercise dependence involves the overproduction of a chemical in the brain called interleukin-6 (IL-6); this theory is known as the Cytokine Hypothesis. We do not have the scope to consider the competing explanations and why they are considered less plausible by Hamer and Karageorghis, but you can consult this paper to review these alternatives.

The Cytokine Hypothesis

Cytokines are chemicals that transmit messages between the immune system (the body's system for fighting infection) and the brain, ultimately resulting in changes in the activity of neurons in the brain and impacting on behaviour (Hayley *et al.*, 2003). Interleukin-6 is the first cytokine released when the individual exercises and has a protective, anti-inflammatory effect (Tilg *et al.*, 1997; Petersen and Pedersen, 2005). Production of this cytokine also increases fatigue, anxiety and depression and has detrimental effects on concentration and sleep (Späth-Schwarbe *et al.*, 1998; Reichenberg *et al.*, 2001). As Hamer and Karageorghis (2007) note, these negative effects have been observed when habitual exercisers are deprived of exercise. Moreover, some research has shown that athletes suffering from overtraining syndrome (characterised by persistent decreases in performance despite being rested) demonstrate overproduction of and/or intolerance to IL-6 during exercise (Robson, 2003).

Given these effects, Hamer and Karageorghis (2007) propose that IL-6 may be a psychobiological mechanism that underpins the development of exercise dependence. They propose that in people who are exercise dependent, exercise results in the overproduction of IL-6 with its negative effects on psychology and behaviour. The individual has to exercise to relieve these symptoms, consequently producing more negative effects, resulting in more exercise and so the cycle continues. They also note that the consistent link between exercise dependence and eating disorders may offer further support for this hypothesis. IL-6 production is increased by low muscle glycogen levels (Keller *et al.*, 2001), likely to be evident in eating disordered individuals, thus stimulating overproduction of IL-6. Also in support of their hypothesis they offer the finding that exercise-induced increases in IL-6 also result in the secretion of cortisol, which is implicated in a number of addictions (e.g. alcohol dependence; Kiefer and Wiedemann, 2004).

As is the case with all these suggested mechanisms, more evidence is needed before we can accept or reject this hypothesis as an explanation for exercise dependence. However, as Hamer and Karageorghis (2007) suggest, methods exist to measure levels of IL-6, making this a potentially exciting period for this area of research.

Primary exercise dependence: fact or fiction?

Just as there is no clear evidence to suggest exactly which mechanism leads to or underpins exercise dependence the debate as to whether primary exercise dependence does indeed exist is still ongoing; let us turn to that debate now.

Bamber and colleagues (2000a) screened almost 200 female exercisers for exercise dependence and eating disorders. The women also completed a battery of tests measuring a range of psychological and behavioural variables (e.g. psychological distress and physical activity). Based on their eating disorder and exercise dependence status the women were assigned to one of four groups:

- Group 1: Eating disordered but not exercise dependent ($n = 14$);
- Group 2: Exercise dependent but no eating disorder ($n = 43$) (primary exercise dependent);
- Group 3: Eating disordered and exercise dependent ($n = 27$) (secondary exercise dependent);
- Group 4: Neither an eating disorder nor exercise dependent ($n = 110$).

Group 3 (eating disordered and exercise dependent) showed the highest levels of psychological morbidity (e.g. high levels of psychological distress). Group 2 (exercise dependent but not eating disordered) showed a similar psychological profile to group 4 (neither eating disordered nor exercise dependent). Considering these results, what conclusions would you draw from this research?

You may have identified, as did Bamber *et al.* (2000b) that exercise dependence is not a distinct pathological condition and is less prevalent than previously suggested. Bamber *et al.* (2000a) conducted a follow-up qualitative study to their quantitative examination of exercise dependence which reinforced these quantitative findings. They interviewed four women from each of their four groups about their eating and exercise behaviours and cognitions. For group 2 (designated in their quantitative study as primary exercise dependent) they found results that contradicted earlier findings. Two of the women who were thought to be primary exercise dependent, based on questionnaire data obtained in their earlier study, were not dependent on exercise. For instance, although exercise was important to them they did not report intense withdrawal symptoms when prevented from exercising, and they did not organise their lives around exercise. The remaining two women in this group did show evidence of exercise dependence, but contrary to earlier quantitative results, did also have an eating disorder. Thus these women were secondary not primary exercise dependent, questioning the diagnoses of primary exercise dependence in Bamber *et al.*'s (2000b) initial study. These findings were supported by a later study (Bamber *et al.*, 2003). A case study of one woman, classified as secondary exercise dependent (Bamber *et al.*, 2000a) as summarised below, provides a stark illustration of the potential severity of this condition.

Case Study 7.2
Secondary exercise dependence

Annie (a pseudonym, or false name) was one of the women classified as secondary exercise dependent as she clearly suffered from an eating disorder and exercised excessively to help her to maintain her low body weight. Although Annie was not diagnosed with an eating disorder on the basis of her responses to an eating disorder questionnaire administered in Bamber et al.*'s (2000b) initial study, her responses during interview and the researchers' observations of her physical appearance confirmed that this was indeed the case. Her BMI was 16.8, below the criterion level of 17 for a diagnosis of anorexia nervosa, and the researchers noted that she was 'visibly underweight' (page 426). This illustrates the possible problems with conducting research in this area as questionnaires may not always be the best method for identifying an eating disorder. The respondent may actively deny there is a problem or may do so unconsciously as they do not see their behaviour as problematic.*

When interviewed, Annie reported a history of anorexia with her weight falling to 35 kg when she was 23 years old and she was currently on the waiting list for a private eating disorder clinic. She expressed an intense fear of gaining weight and losing control over her eating and was no longer aware that her eating behaviours and cognitions were abnormal as for her, they had become the norm. For instance, her diet consisted of lettuce and bran cereal and although she occasionally binged on whisky and chocolate she generally felt that she did not deserve food and would calculate the exact amount of calories she needed to burn to allow her to eat a bar of chocolate.

Her exercise behaviour was extreme and regimented. At 5 a.m. every day she cycled for 32 minutes, followed by 30 minutes of calisthenics and 30 minutes of weight training. She walked up to 4 hours a day and spent the afternoons horse riding, grooming and mucking out horses in her role

as a professional horse rider. Her need to exercise above all else was summed up in her comment,
'Its [sic] exercise or nothing' (page 426), as was her extreme distress at her condition with the
realisation that, 'I know it will kill me, I know the anorexia will kill me in the end' (page 426).

Understanding exercise dependence: the way forward

Having considered evidence presented in favour of the existence of primary exercise dependence as a pathological condition separate from an eating disorder and evidence presented against this proposition we appear to be no closer to answering the seemingly simple question of whether or not primary exercise dependence does exist. A systematic review conducted by Hausenblas and Symons Down (2002) suggests that some of the problems in addressing this question may stem from methodological concerns with studies in this area. Their review included 88 papers published between 1970 and 1999 so does not include the specific studies we have considered but nevertheless highlights potential explanations for the mixed findings to date, and how these might be resolved. Hausenblas and Symons Down's comments on these methodological limitations of previous research are discussed in more detail below.

Limitation 1: Operational definitions

Different definitions of exercise dependence have been used in different studies (e.g. psychological, behavioural, physiological). This clearly makes comparison of findings difficult but is also likely to lead to different findings across studies because researchers have defined exercise dependence differently and not because of true differences in findings.

Limitation 2: Measurement

The use of different and inadequate measures of exercise dependence is a key reason for the inconsistent findings in this area, again limiting the degree to which findings can be compared across studies. Many studies have included insufficient participants who are truly exercise dependent.

Limitation 3: Research designs

Three approaches to research have been used in this field, to compare:

- exercisers with eating disorder patients;
- excessive with less excessive exercisers;
- exercisers with non-exercisers.

The lack of experimental designs, comparable control groups and controls for participant biases in these approaches are contributing factors to the inconsistency of findings within this area.

Clearly this is a complex issue that requires further research that pays close attention to these limitations. The need for more research in this area is highlighted further when we consider recent research which presents initial findings linking exercise dependence to another potentially harmful behaviour: alcohol consumption.

Wider implications of exercise dependence?

Martin *et al.* (2008) conducted a preliminary study that examined potential links between exercise dependence and alcohol consumption. They questioned students who exercised at least occasionally about their alcohol consumption, alcohol-related problems and symptoms of exercise dependence. The results revealed small but significant relationships between some aspects of exercise dependence, alcohol-related problems and amount of alcohol consumed. These findings led the authors to suggest that:

- people who exercise to decrease anxiety and feel happier about their life may use alcohol in the same way, or, may exercise to feel better about and compensate for the negative effects of excess alcohol consumption;
- people who exercise to control their weight may do so to combat the effects of gaining weight through alcohol consumption;
- people who exercise to experience the structure and predictability that a regular exercise regime offers may do so to compensate for a lack of structure and unpredictability when drinking.

Given that individuals may develop dependence on exercise or alcohol these preliminary findings make sense. However, the authors do not report the levels of exercise dependence symptoms and alcohol use and problems, thus we cannot be sure if any of the participants were in fact dependent on exercise or had significant problems related to alcohol. Take a moment to reflect on some of the additional limitations of this research; consider the implications of the following: the use of self-report measures and the study's cross-sectional design.

In your reflections you may have identified that the use of self-report data may mean that some participants could have under (or over) estimated their alcohol consumption or inaccurately reported their alcohol-related problems to present socially desirable responses. We are also unable to determine if exercise dependence and alcohol consumption and problems are causally related and how this relationship might develop over time as this was a cross-sectional, descriptive study. Nevertheless, this initial study has highlighted that exercise dependence may be related to other behaviours which are detrimental to one's health and has identified an area that clearly warrants attention in future research.

Dealing with compulsive exercise

Dalle Grave *et al.* (2008) conducted an evaluation of a cognitive behavioural intervention with females who were diagnosed with a clinical eating disorder, approximately 45 per cent of whom were also classified as compulsive exercisers. The treatment programme examined by Dalle Grave *et al.* (2008) consisted of 13 weeks of an inpatient three-stage programme:

- *Stage 1* focused on educating patients, helping them to engage with the programme and encouraging them to change their behaviour as much as possible in the early stages of the programme, including compulsively exercising to control shape and weight.

- *Stage 2* focused mainly on modifying the patient's eating disorder pathology, for instance, their overemphasis on eating and controlling weight.
- *Stage 3* focused on helping patients to continue to make progress and organising follow-ups after the treatment programme had finished.

BMI significantly increased in those patients who completed the programme, and, most noticeably, in compulsive exercisers. This increase in BMI was related to reduced levels of disordered eating, such as self-induced vomiting, and decreased frequency and amount of exercise. This cognitive behavioural intervention therefore does demonstrate some success in helping these eating disordered patients who exercise compulsively to reduce their levels of exercise.

Learning Activity 7.2

Produce a list of five bullet points highlighting key points that we have considered about exercise dependence that stand out for you. Share your ideas with a partner and check the accuracy of your lists with the sections above.

Chapter Review

We first discussed the increasing levels of body dissatisfaction in males and the links between a drive for muscularity, social physique anxiety and the use of food supplements, steroids and excessive exercise (Learning Objective 1). We then defined muscle dysmorphia as a preoccupation with being insufficiently lean and muscular and considered the cognitive and behavioural effects of muscle dysmorphia, such as preoccupation with appearance and steroid use (Learning Objective 2). We examined Grieve's (2007) model of proposed physical, psychological, social and cultural causes of muscle dysmorphia, identifying that ideal body internalisation, body dissatisfaction and body distortion are likely to be the most influential factors in the development of this condition (Learning Objective 2). We then saw that eating disorders and exercise are closely linked, particularly in excessive exercisers, and indeed, exercise participation may lead to an eating disorder (Learning Objective 3). We examined this relationship in more detail, considering the key role of psychological factors such as compulsion to exercise (Learning Objective 3). We considered the cytokine hypothesis as a potential psychobiological explanation for the development of exercise dependence (Learning Objective 4). This involves the overproduction of IL-6 during exercise, producing negative effects that the individual attempts to reduce through further exercise (Learning Objective 4). Finally we distinguished between primary exercise dependence as a dependence on exercise itself and secondary exercise dependence which coexists alongside an eating disorder and therefore represents dependence on the secondary effects of exercise such as weight loss (Learning Objective 5).

Learning Activity 7.3

Test your understanding

1. Discuss the strategies exercisers might use to increase muscularity.
2. Describe muscle dysmorphia and identify at least one cognitive and one behavioural effect of this condition.
3. Identify as many factors as you can from Grieve's (2007) model of muscle dysmorphia development. What does he suggest are the three most influential factors, and why?
4. Why have some researchers suggested that physical activity and exercise may lead to the development of an eating disorder?
5. What psychological factors may be important in explaining the link between exercise and eating disorders?
6. What is the difference between primary and secondary exercise dependence?

Further Reading

- For more on muscle dysmorphia:

Leone, JE, Sedory, EJ and Gray, KA (2005) Recognition and treatment of muscle dysmorphia and related body image disorders. *Journal of Athletic Training*, 40: 352–359.

This paper discusses interventions and guidelines that athletic trainers can use for identifying the symptoms of and dealing with muscle dysmorphia in athletes but nevertheless offers some useful advice that could also be applied to exercisers.

- For more on eating disorders and exercise:

Yager, Z and O'Dea, JA (2008) Prevention programs for body image and eating disorders on University campuses: A review of large, controlled interventions. *Health Promotion International*, 23: 173–189.

Reviews different intervention approaches for helping students to reduce body image concerns and eating disorders and concludes by describing an intervention developed by the authors.

- For more on exercise dependence:

Bamber, D, Cockerill, IM, Rodgers, S and Carroll, D (2000) 'It's exercise or nothing': A qualitative analysis of exercise dependence. *British Journal of Sports Medicine*, 34: 423–430.

The illustrative case studies in this article provide a stark account of the lifestyles and attitudes of people who are exercise dependent.

Part Two
Sport
psychology

Chapter 8
Training for competition: individual factors

Learning Objectives

This chapter is designed to help you be able to:

1. describe Vealey's model of sports confidence and understand sources of self-confidence;
2. use Bandura's theory of self-efficacy to suggest how an athlete's self-efficacy could be improved;
3. understand the potential negative and positive effects of motivational climate;
4. outline the different types of attentional strategy and when they are most appropriately used;
5. understand the impact that anxiety can have on attention.

Introduction

This opening chapter on sport psychology begins with an exploration of the individual factors that may impact on sports performance. Whereas previous chapters have focused on the exercising individual, our focus now shifts to the sports performer or athlete. Thus we now start to investigate some of the factors that may impact on how well someone performs in the sporting environment.

Often, the key goal in sport is to improve performance. Sport science research informs us that there are a number of different approaches that we can take to improve performance. Sports biomechanists may look to change technique by correcting faults or improving efficiency. Sports physiologists aim to improve fitness levels or increase strength by developing physical training programmes. Alternatively, sport psychologists focus on enhancing the psychological skills and characteristics of the athlete. Therefore knowing the optimal psychological skills and characteristics for achieving high levels of performance is an essential first step.

Research in sport psychology has identified that a number of psychological constructs relate to performance. This opening chapter focuses on those constructs that may be particularly relevant in the training environment. We first focus on 'individual factors' and discuss why individual athletes differ in their self-confidence and levels of motivation and how these differences may influence their preparation and training for competition. One of the most consistent research findings in the sport psychology literature is that self-confidence correlates with successful sporting performance via an influence on an athlete's thoughts, feelings and behaviours, all of which will determine sporting performance (Vealey, 2001). It is possible to increase an athlete's self-confidence by using psychological techniques, therefore we explore psychological techniques for increasing self-confidence based on Vealey's (2001) model of sport confidence and Bandura's (1977) self-efficacy theory.

Vealey's (2001) integrative model of sport confidence suggests that factors such as motivational climate and the individual's goals and expectations influence the development of self-confidence. Therefore, we consider how different training environments (e.g. one in which personal achievement is valued) influence self-confidence.

Another individual factor that may impact on the athlete's performance is their level of concentration and their attentional strategy. Of major interest in sport psychology research is the type of attentional strategy that an athlete adopts while performing, particularly in events which may include some physical pain such as endurance events. You might want to consider your own attentional strategy if you were about to complete a 5-mile run. You may decide to concentrate on internal sensations such as your racing heart or the sensation in your legs, or you may try to ignore these internal cues and focus externally on something such as the contours of the course you are running. In this chapter we explore whether one of these strategies will lead to superior performance. We also examine the impact that anxiety may have on attention. The overall aim of this chapter is to examine the impact of these individual factors and how we can use theory and research related to these to optimise performance in the training environment.

Throughout this chapter we also use the example of our gymnast, Sam. Although Sam has natural ability in gymnastics he sometimes lacks belief in his own abilities. When he is faced with tough competition he tends to underperform and does not commit to skills that he is able to do in training. Let's explore how psychological theory may help Sam to have more self-belief.

What is self-confidence?

Self-confidence is a commonly used term in everyday language. Often we may describe that we are feeling self-confident about winning a particular match, or that our favourite sports team or athlete is looking confident before a big match. But what do we mean when we use this term? Think about an athlete or team that you may perceive as being particularly self-confident. This athlete or team may have a strong belief that they will win before they even start to compete. You may have even heard them in the media talking about how well training has been going and how confident they are that they will play well.

Sport psychologists define self-confidence in a very similar way, proposing that it represents the belief that we can successfully perform a desired behaviour. Consequently a self-confident sprinter who is aiming to win the race will believe that she can sprint faster than her opponents. Similarly a self-confident gymnast who is aiming to perform a new tumble will believe in his own ability to execute the skill.

Box 8.1 Definition: Sport confidence

Vealey (1986) conceptualised sport confidence as 'the belief or degree of certainty individuals possess about their ability to be successful in sport' (page 222).

Learning Activity 8.1

Think about the last time that you felt self-confident when you were playing sport. To help you do this try to picture a particular experience you have had. This may have been a time when you were playing in a certain team, or when you were attempting a particular skill in training. Now consider how you felt when you were self-confident and answer the following questions:

- What kind of thoughts were going through your mind when you were feeling confident?
- How did being self-confident make you feel (physically and emotionally)?
- How did you behave?

You may have noticed from these questions that there are three factors which can be influenced by self-confidence. These include an individual's thoughts, feelings and behaviours. First, the self-confident athlete may have thoughts that are positive, for example, their self-talk (an athlete's internal dialogue) may reflect their confidence in their own abilities; they may also interpret difficulties as challenges to overcome rather than as threats (Lazarus, 1999). Confident athletes will be more skilled in using the cognitive resources that will help them to achieve sporting success (Vealey, 2001), for example, they will make more adaptive attributions (reasons for success and failure) and use of their attentional skills. Second, the self-confident athlete may feel more positive or have more adaptive emotions; these may include feeling calmer under pressure or feeling more assertive (Mellalieu *et al.*, 2006). An athlete who lacks self-confidence may experience upset, anxiety and dissatisfaction. Finally, the self-confident athlete may engage in behaviours that enable them to pursue their goals, for example, adopting a particular game strategy, working more persistently towards a goal, or increasing the amount of effort they expend to achieve their goal (Hays *et al.*, 2010).

The relationship between high levels of self-confidence and performance has been well supported (e.g. Feltz and Lirgg, 2001; Hays *et al.*, 2009). However, it is also important to note that the relationship between self-confidence and performance is represented by an inverted 'U'. Consequently although performance increases as self-confidence increases, overconfidence can also negatively impact on performance. Figure 8.1 demonstrates the inverted U relationship.

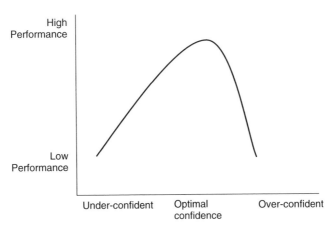

Figure 8.1 The inverted U relationship between self-confidence and performance.

The inverted U relationship shown in Figure 8.1 suggests that there is a threshold of self-confidence beyond which performance will start to deteriorate. This concept is also central to theories of anxiety and performance such as catastrophe theory (Hardy and Fazey, 1987; Hardy, 1996; see also Chapter 10). Woodman and Hardy's (2003) meta-analysis suggests that self-confidence is significantly more strongly related to performance than cognitive anxiety. They continue that overall results from research suggest some support for a threshold hypothesis, although more research is needed. However, Hays *et al.* (2009) criticise self-confidence research, proposing that the majority of this research has been correlational, meaning that drawing conclusions about the causes of fluctuations in confidence has been difficult. One model which may help us to understand the sources of self-confidence is Vealey's (2001) model of sport confidence.

Vealey's model of sport confidence

As we illustrated in Learning Activity 8.1, Vealey's (2001) model proposes that sports confidence will influence performance through its impact on how athletes think, feel and behave in the sporting environment. Figure 8.2 outlines the proposals of this model.

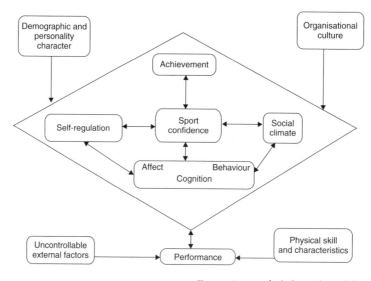

Figure 8.2 Vealey's (2001) model of sports confidence.

At the centre of the model is sports confidence. This includes confidence in decision-making skills, confidence in physical skills and training, and confidence in resiliency. There are three sources of sports confidence that will impact on the confidence level of the athlete. These are self-regulation, achievement and social climate.

- *Self-regulation* refers to the ability to control one's emotions, thoughts and feelings in order to plan and regulate our behaviour in the pursuit of goals. For example, the athlete who feels psychologically prepared for competition may be able to self-regulate, feel calmer, more relaxed, and consequently focus on their performance strategies and feel more self-confident. Bandura (1986) suggests that this is a significant source of self-confidence for athletes and as such is the central focus of interventions in sport psychology (Vealey, 2001).
- *Achievement* relates to the impact of our past accomplishments on levels of confidence. The athlete who has won his previous three matches has a number of past accomplishments and therefore may be more confident about his future performances. Vealey *et al.* (1998) suggest that mastering or improving personal skills is an important source of confidence.
- *Social climate* refers to the salient sources of confidence in the environment, including social support from the coach, from other athletes, or from friends and family, vicarious experiences (such as seeing another athlete with a similar level or ability complete the same skill), or feeling familiar in the sports environment (e.g. competing at your home venue). Rees and Freeman (2007) demonstrated the beneficial effect of social support on self-confidence, both directly and by reducing the negative effect of stress on self-confidence. Further, Horn and Weiss (1991) emphasised the importance of feedback on perceptions of competence in sport.

Each of these sources of sports confidence will impact on the behaviours, cognitions (thoughts) and affect (feelings/emotions) of the athlete which continuously interact to influence performance (Vealey, 2001). For further information on the impact of self-efficacy on performance and decision making see the further reading at the end of this chapter.

Practical application

Let's take the central portion of the model and look at how the sources of sports confidence might be evident in athletes who are high and low in confidence and how these sources influence their affect, behaviour and cognition.

Sophie is a springboard diver who has a high level of sport confidence. Her diving club provides a very supportive environment. She regularly trains with the same coach who is very supportive of her efforts and who praises her achievements. She is also part of an elite squad whose members congratulate each other's efforts and who regularly compete together as a team. Sophie is encouraged by her team-mates and feels more confident when she sees other divers performing the skills that she is learning (social climate). Because training is going well Sophie feels ready for the upcoming competition season, and is able to regulate her anxiety and interpret this as a positive sign of psychological readiness (self-regulation). Last season she achieved a podium position at the National Championships and so feels confident about the upcoming season (achievement). These sources have contributed to Sophie's high level of sport self-confidence. This is reflected in her affect (she experiences positive emotions while training), her behaviour (she is persistent when learning new skills), and her cognitions (she has a positive approach to training and attributes success to her own hard work).

In contrast, James is a footballer who has low levels of sports self-confidence. Last season his team was relegated a division in the local football league. Although their season had started well it ended in a series of defeats (achievement). Consequently James does not feel confident about the upcoming season. To add to this the relegation has caused a number of players to leave the club and James does not feel well supported by his coach (social climate). He is concerned about the upcoming season and is not able to regulate his emotions well (self-regulation). This lack of sport confidence is reflected in his affect (he experiences anxiety and general dissatisfaction with his training), his behaviour (he gives up easily when he finds training difficult as he can not see the point in persisting), and his cognitions (he lacks focus and can not see the value in playing in a lower division).

Overall these two examples demonstrate how the three sources will impact on sport confidence, and consequently on affect, behaviour and cognitions. They show that a social climate can be created in which team-mates support each other and work together.

We can use these examples to show how the sources of sports confidence could be used to help our gymnast Sam to improve his confidence. This could be developed within Sam's gymnastics club by encouraging a team ethos and setting team goals. These two examples also indicate the importance of achievement, both within training and competition. Sam's coach may choose to emphasise the achievements that he is making and remind him of these when he is trying new skills. Finally, Sophie is able to control her emotions and this may also be beneficial for Sam. A sport psychologist could work with Sam to enable him to interpret his anxiety more positively, thereby increasing his confidence when he is in anxiety provoking situations.

Sport self-confidence

Vealey's (2001) model also suggests that demographic and personality characteristics and the organisational culture will influence confidence development. Demographic and personality characteristics include characteristics, attitudes and values related to performance (e.g. goal orientation), as well as demographic variables such as age, gender and experience. An example of the impact of these factors is demonstrated in the finding that males exhibit higher levels of self-confidence than females (Lirgg, 1991; Vealey, 1988); although indications are that differences in self-confidence between males and females will relate to perceptions of the gender-appropriateness of the task (Clifton and Gill, 1994). While there is a tendency for females to have lower levels of self-confidence, this may be mediated by the nature of the task. When the task that is undertaken is gender-appropriate, females do not display lower self-confidence than males. Research has also demonstrated that females will identify different sources of self-confidence. For example, Vealey et al. (1998) found that females perceived social support and physical self-presentation as more important sources of confidence than did males. The organisational culture refers to the structural aspects of the sport subculture which influence the way in which confidence is developed. For example, training in a well-organised and well-supported environment may positively impact on the confidence levels of an athlete in comparison to training in a highly pressured environment with a number of distractions.

The final part of the model highlights that it is not only psychological factors that will impact on performance. Vealey et al. (1998) acknowledge that while sport confidence will impact on performance by influencing an athlete's affect, behaviour and cognitions, this is not the only variable that will influence performance. Therefore, the final section of the model proposes that performance will also be influenced by uncontrollable external factors and the physical skill and characteristics of the athlete. Thus part of the model highlights that high levels of confidence alone will not predict performance success and failure. In any sporting situation there will be external factors that are not under the control of the athlete (Dugdale *et al.*, 2002). For example, the referee may make an unfair decision against the player, or the weather may impact on the athlete's standard of performance. Further, Vealey *et al.* acknowledge that performance is also dependent on the physical skill and characteristics of the athlete. Thus the athlete should not only aim to have optimal levels of sports self-confidence, but also to gain physical skills within their sport.

Self-Efficacy Theory

Similar to the sport confidence model, Bandura's (1977) Self-Efficacy Theory is based on the principle that people learn by watching others and that the individual's environment, behaviour and cognition will all influence the development of self-efficacy.

Box 8.2 Definition: Self-efficacy

Self-efficacy refers to people's judgements of their capabilities to organise and execute courses of action required to attain designated types of performances (Bandura, 1977).

Whereas self-confidence is quite a global construct, self-efficacy is a more specific form of self-confidence. Thus self-efficacy refers to a performer's perception of his or her competence to succeed in a given task at a given time. Bandura (1977, page 205) emphasised the importance of self-efficacy:

Assuming that an individual is capable of a response (i.e. has the required skill level) and appropriate incentives for performance are available, then self-efficacy theory asserts that actual performance will be predicted by the individual's belief in their personal competence.

According to Self-Efficacy Theory there are six sources of efficacy information: performance accomplishments, vicarious experiences, verbal persuasion, physiological states, emotional states, and imaginal experiences.

Learning Activity 8.2

To check your understanding of each source, try to complete one example of how this may be achieved in sport. The first example is completed for you.

Self-efficacy source	Explanation
Performance accomplishments	This refers to an individual's mastery experiences. If an athlete has previous experiences of mastery/performing well this will influence their subsequent beliefs in their ability to complete the task. Example: If a javelin thrower has previously managed to throw the javelin a particular distance then their confidence in repeating this will be elevated.
Vicarious experiences	This refers to the self-efficacy that can be gained through watching others complete the same skill. Thus it is based on modelling behaviours and social comparison. Example:
Verbal persuasion	This refers to gaining self-efficacy through verbal encouragement from others, verbal feedback, or even from self-talk. Example:
Physiological states	This includes obtaining efficacy information from the individual's physiological state such as interpreting the arousal levels that are experienced prior to completing a difficult skill as a sign of readiness. Example:
Emotional states	This refers to efficacy information that is gained from positive (happiness, tranquillity) and negative (sadness, anxiety) affect successfully. Example:
Imaginal experiences	Efficacy beliefs can be changed by using imagery to imagine oneself completing a skill. Example:

You can check your examples with the techniques used to enhance self-efficacy in the next section.

Enhancing self-efficacy

Now that you have an understanding of the sources of efficacy information it is also important to examine how these sources can be used to make suggestions for enhancing self-efficacy. Some suggestions of strategies a sport psychologist or coach could use to enhance efficacy beliefs in an athlete are listed below:

Performance accomplishments:
- Physical practice
- Goal setting

Vicarious experiences:
- Previous success
- Role models

Verbal persuasion:
- Positive self-talk
- Encouragement

Physiological and emotional states:
- Centring
- Relaxation

Imaginal experiences:
- Positive imagery.

There are a number of techniques that could be used by a sports coach or sport psychologist to increase the efficacy beliefs of the athletes that they coach. First, they may focus on enhancing *performance accomplishments* by ensuring that the athlete has experience of mastery during their training sessions. This could involve training that is specifically devised so that athletes gain experience of success, or that includes training goals that are challenging but realistic enough to be achieved by the athlete. A sense of performance accomplishment is important as athlete perceptions of insufficient progress will have a negative effect on performance (Schmidt and De Shon, 2009). To encourage perceptions of success the coach may remind athletes of their previous successes during team talks or prior to competition. Marsh and Perry (2005) propose that individuals who perceive themselves to be more effective, confident and able can accomplish more than individuals with a less positive self-perception.

Second, the coach or sport psychologist may enhance the *vicarious experiences* of the athlete by using role models in the training environment. To do this the coach could use other athletes to demonstrate skills or encourage group learning of particular skills to facilitate positive social comparison. Ram *et al.* (2007) suggest that during modelling observers form beliefs about their own confidence in performing a task based on information they obtain from watching someone else perform the task. Similarly, individuals can increase their self-efficacy through imagery (McKenzie and Howe, 1997) by visualising themselves completing a task (*imaginal experiences*). Thus a combination of imagery and modelling could be used in the training environment (Atienza *et al.*, 1998).

Third, the coach may use constructive feedback to enhance *verbal persuasion*. In doing this they can reward effort and persistence from athletes, give recognition for achievement and encouragement for attempting skills. Research has demonstrated that both coaches and athletes perceive verbal persuasion as a highly used and effective coaching tool for increasing self-efficacy (Vargas-Tonsing *et al.*, 2004). The use of positive self-talk may also be encouraged, remembering that verbal persuasion does not have to stem from others but can also originate from the self. The use of self-talk has been well advocated in the research literature (e.g. Harvey *et al.*, 2002). Further, Hardy *et al.* (2005) and Hatzigeorgiadis *et al.* (2008) found that the use of self-talk could facilitate increases in self-efficacy.

Finally, the sport psychologist or coach could teach the athlete to use techniques that can help to regulate *physiological and emotional states*. For example, strategies such as centring (which involves breathing techniques; Haddad and Tremayne, 2009) and progressive muscular relaxation (which involves contracting and relaxing muscle groups; Jacobson, 1938) may help the athlete to regulate their emotional responses. The sport psychologist may also help the athlete to reinterpret their physiological and emotional symptoms of arousal as signs of readiness to perform rather than anxiety (Hanton and Jones, 1999).

Goal orientation and motivational climate

Earlier in this chapter we identified that demographic and personality characteristics influence sport confidence, and one such characteristic is the individual's goal orientation. According to Nicholls (1984) how the individual defines success influences the goals that they adopt in an achievement setting and how they evaluate their performances. Consider how you might judge success in your own sport. You might have answered that the meaning of success to you is winning an important competition or match. Alternatively, you might have answered that success is based on mastering skills or on personal improvement. An individual who evaluates if they have achieved success based on comparison with others has an *ego or outcome goal orientation*. In contrast, an individual who feels that they have achieved success through improving their own performance and their skills has a *task or mastery goal orientation*.

In a similar way, the environment can emphasise these different goal orientations, known as 'motivational climate'. An environment that emphasises competition, social comparison, punishes mistakes and only rewards success is known as an outcome motivational climate. In contrast, an environment that emphasises cooperation, values learning and effort and rewards these alongside personal improvement is known as a mastery motivational climate.

One study which demonstrates the detrimental effects of an ego orientation and an outcome climate in sport is examined below.

Research Focus

Krane *et al.* (1997) presented a case study of the motivational climate of one elite gymnast in their paper 'Reaching for gold and the price of glory'. The aim of this study was to understand the behaviours of an elite gymnast and her coach using the principles of achievement motivation theory.

The participant in this study was an American former elite level gymnast given the pseudonym Susan. Susan began gymnastics at a young age and quickly progressed to a high level. During her time in training she incurred a number of serious injuries and developed disordered eating. The study used interviews to gain information on Susan's gymnastics career and asked her to describe her experiences as a gymnast. In follow-up interviews Susan was also asked the question 'what drives an athlete to persist under such extreme circumstances?' At the end of the interviews the authors examined the themes that occurred in the data which included: motivational climate, evidence of an ego orientation, and correlates of ego involvement.

Krane *et al.* proposed that an individual's goal orientation will be strongly influenced by the motivational climate or the emphasis on mastery by significant individuals within the environment. Susan trained in an environment which emphasised winning, perfect performance and competing through pain. These were the only acceptable goals in this climate. Rewards were only given for perfection and complete compliance to instructions, whereas physical punishment was used when performance was poor. Both Susan and her parents were socialised into accepting this culture and these excessive training techniques, perceiving the ego involved environment as normal and acceptable.

Susan used social comparison as her primary source of information regarding her ability. She placed high importance on external feedback and rewards, seeing them as confirmation of her status as an athlete. Consequently, Susan had a great need to show superiority and to defeat others. She would also strive for perfection which was never obtainable. When she did finish in second or third place she would feel like a failure and her self-worth and self-confidence declined. This demonstrates the impact that an ego orientation may have on self-confidence. When an ego-orientated athlete is winning, their confidence will be high, but when they are not, their confidence often declines as this is how they define success. Susan consistently dwelt on mistakes, experienced negative cognitions, negative affect and adopted a pessimistic perspective. In her drive for perfection Susan practised excessively, trained through injury and engaged in unhealthy patterns of eating.

Krane *et al.* concluded that the intensely outcome-focused motivational climate surrounding Susan legitimised her unhealthy training behaviours. These behaviours were then positively reinforced by her coaches and her parents as methods of attaining her goals. They went on to propose that a number of changes could be made in order to make this a more task-focused environment through changing the goals, expectations and reinforcements in the environment.

Learning Activity 8.3

The article described above highlights that a more task-focused motivational climate could be attained if some changes were made within the gymnastics club. Consider the ego-focused environment that Susan described and try to suggest what changes could be made to this environment to make it more task focused. You may wish to consider the following subheadings:

- Goals: What currently defines success and how could this be changed?
- Expectations: What are Susan's, her parents' and her coach's expectations for Susan? How could these be changed?
- Reinforcements: What rewards or actions reinforce Susan's current behaviours? What could be used as reinforcement instead? What behaviours would you aim to reinforce?

Krane *et al.* make a number of suggestions to develop a more task-orientated motivational climate in the conclusion of their article. How do your answers compare with their suggestions?

They suggest that rather than focusing on outcome goals, instead the focus should be on personal improvement and on long-term, healthy training techniques. They suggest that coaches and parents should be educated about alternative training methods (e.g. those that do not include physical punishment) and the psychological implications of the training environment. Both coaches and parents should also support and reinforce task-orientated behaviours (e.g. setting goals towards personal achievement), which will encourage Susan to adopt these rather than her ego-orientated approach. The emphasis should be on development, effort, personal improvement and positive peer relations. Coaches should use positive and instructional feedback and include the athlete in decision making. Finally, evaluations should be based on how well an individual improves rather than on social comparison with others' levels of success. Together, these elements of a mastery climate are likely to lead to high levels of perceived competence.

The link between perceived competence and motivational climate is further emphasised by Boyce *et al.* (2009). Their study found that perceptions of a task-involving climate positively predicted perceived competence. Based on this they proposed that coaches should feel fairly confident that emphasising a mastery climate will promote adaptive motivational responses among their athletes. This will enhance their perceptions of competence and their use of adaptive practice strategies by enabling them to identify effective ways to improve skill development. As well as encouraging the individual to adopt a more task-focused approach, changes can be made to the training environment. One such approach is the TARGET approach.

Changing motivational climate using TARGET

Ames (1992) suggested that changes to the motivational climate could be made using the acronym TARGET, where each letter stands for a different aspect of the environment that could be changed.

- Task: The most motivating tasks are meaningful and moderately challenging. Tasks that are varied with different levels of difficulty will help athletes to monitor their own progress.
- Authority: In order to promote a task orientation the coach should aim to include athletes in decisions. This will encourage the athlete to take responsibility and to be independent.
- Recognition: Coaches should reward effort and progress in individuals rather than focusing on social comparisons.
- Grouping: Coaches should avoid ability groups, particularly where these may lead to competition between athletes. Instead groups should be varied with an emphasis on cooperation.
- Evaluation: Coaches should evaluate personal progress and encourage self-evaluation. Mistakes should be viewed as part of the learning process.
- Timing: Tasks should be meaningful and should give ample time for completion, especially when the task is complex.

The TARGET approach could be used to help Sam the gymnast. Sam and his coach have always focused on outcomes but are beginning to recognise that this may not be the most useful approach to Sam's training. Using the TARGET approach a more task-orientated climate could be encouraged. Tasks could be matched to the ability of the individual rather than setting a whole group task. Sam could take some authority for his own training and select the skills that he would like to practise in some of his training sessions. Sam's achievements should be recognised, so his coach may focus on praising Sam for achieving his personal goals. Groups could be varied, which would allow Sam to train with more and less able gymnasts. Evaluation sheets could be completed by Sam at regular intervals to assess his own progress. Finally timings could be set on the length of the session that will be spent practising particular skills.

Section summary: goal orientation and motivational climate

At the start of our section on motivational climate we proposed that the goal orientation of the individual may influence their perceptions of their own ability. Krane *et al.*'s paper further endorsed the link between these concepts, highlighting the possible negative effects of an outcome-orientated climate. The individual who trains in a task orientated climate may receive rewards for their effort and gain feedback based on their personal improvements. Consequently this reinforces the value of effort and perseverance and enhances perceptions of competence. In contrast, the individual who trains in an ego-orientated climate is only rewarded for defeating others and may be punished for making mistakes. Thus success is more difficult to achieve and so perceptions of ability may be lower.

Attention and training for competition

So far in this chapter we have looked at two factors that may influence the performance levels of the athlete who is training for competition: motivational climate and self-confidence/self-efficacy. In this final part of the chapter we consider our final individual factor, how attentional focus can impact on an athlete's performance in training.

It is important that athletes can perceive events quickly and accurately, however, for many athletes maintaining attention may be a problem. Think about when you have been performing in sport and there were distractions that disrupted your attention. These distractions may have been knowing that particular people were watching your match, for example friends and family, they may have been caused by a particular event, for example a photographer taking your photo while you were playing, or it may have been that you were distracted by events outside the sports context, for example thinking about needing to complete an essay while you were playing. All of these distractions may have distracted you from playing your sport and you may have noticed that your performance suffered.

Since there are so many distractions that may occur in the sporting context, we can categorise these based on the causes and the type of attentional shift that results from these distractions. There are four shifts that may occur (Nideffer, 1976) as illustrated in the example below.

Georgia is a tennis player who is playing in an important match. She begins the session by focusing on her opponent's match play as she tries to understand her competitive strategy (*external focus*). As she plays her attention constantly shifts from watching the ball to watching her opponent's return (*voluntary shift*). At one stage of the match just before she is about to serve a crowd member shouts some encouragement (*involuntary shift*). She continues to play but as she gets tired she starts thinking about how heavy her legs feel (*internal focus*).

You should notice from this example that there are two main considerations when we examine these shifts of attention. These are a shift between an external and an internal focus and the potential cause of this shift that may be voluntary or involuntary. So, for example, if Georgia were to slip and injure her ankle then she may incur an internal, involuntary shift in attention.

Nideffer (1993) expands on this perspective and suggests that rather than the focus of attention being internal or external there are four types of attentional focus as illustrated in Figure 8.3.

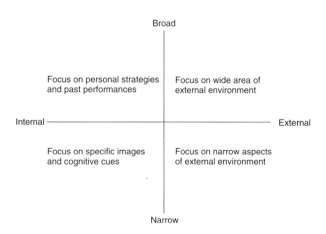

Figure 8.3 Attentional focus.

Learning Activity 8.4

Try to identify the types of attentional focus that these athletes are using:

- A golfer focuses on the ball just before she is about to putt
- A runner is planning his race strategy
- A netball player looks to see who is available to pass the ball to during the match
- A gymnast uses imagery to practise her routine prior to competition.

You should have identified that the golfer is using an external narrow focus by focusing on one object that is an external cue. The runner is using an internal broad focus by focusing on his own actions but this may include a broad range of cues or events in his race strategy. The netball player is using an external broad focus by looking for other players. Finally the gymnast is using an internal narrow focus to practise her own routine.

The concept of attentional focus has played an important role in research on endurance sport. An endurance runner may choose to adopt one of two strategies while they are running. First, they may have an internal focus, where attention is directed towards physical sensations, speed and pain. Second, they may choose to adopt an external focus in which attention is directed away from physical effort and sensations and is focused instead on external cues. These are also referred to as 'association' (most often associated with internal cues) and 'dissociation' (most often associated with external cues). The key research question when examining attention in endurance running has been which of these attentional strategies will be better for performance.

Which is better for endurance performance: an internal or external focus?

Before we introduce some of the research evidence that has examined this question, consider which attentional style you would find most helpful if you were to go running. Would you choose an associative or a dissociative style? Which would you expect to be associated with better performance?

Although research findings on attentional focus are not always consistent, Masters and Ogles (1998) proposed that an internal focus is associated with a faster running speed and an external focus with a slower running speed. The superior performance using an internal focus may be because monitoring bodily signals and adequately adjusting resources in response to these may be beneficial for the endurance athlete.

However, motor control research suggests that an external focus would usually be more beneficial. This is because of the disruption that may be caused to motor programmes (see Chapter 10, section on Choking and conscious processing). Schücker *et al.* (2009) conducted an experimental study to determine whether an internal or an external focus of attention would result in changes in physiological variables during endurance exercise. They examined whether the focus of attention could influence oxygen consumption at a set running speed (which produces an index of running economy). Trained runners were asked to focus their attention either on their movement (internal), their breathing (internal) or on their surroundings (external) while running on a treadmill. Results showed that running economy increased in the external focus condition. Consequently, their results supported the motor control hypothesis that an external focus may be better for performance, demonstrating that some disagreement exists about the optimal attentional strategy for running performance.

Tenenbaum (2001) suggests that the focus of an athlete's attention will also be dependent on the intensity of the workload. His model predicts that at low intensities, attention can be shifted voluntarily from an external to an internal focus. However, under high-intensity exercise voluntary control of the focus of attention is limited and the individual's focus becomes increasingly internal. Thus when training at low intensity an athlete may be able to voluntarily shift their attention, whereas at high intensity this becomes increasingly difficult.

Attention and anxiety

One issue that we also need to consider when examining attention is the possible difference in attentional strategy during conditions of high and low anxiety. You may have noticed that when you have been in an anxious situation, your focus of attention has changed. It may have been that you missed particular cues that you would usually pick up on or that you found it difficult to concentrate. This is because of the impact that anxiety has on attention. An example of this is demonstrated by Williams and Elliot's (1999) research into visual search strategy in karate. They examined the effects of cognitive anxiety on visual search by looking at the number of fixations (measured using eye tracking) made by karate performers. They proposed that the most efficient search pattern during sparring is one with fewer fixations of longer durations. They found that highly anxious individuals made a number of fixations and spent less time on each fixation.

Similarly, research such as that by Eubank *et al.* (2000) found that individuals high in trait anxiety and who viewed anxiety as debilitative, spent longer attending to and processing threatening stimuli. This indicates that in anxiety-provoking situations, individuals are more likely to pay attention to stimuli that are threatening. Eysenck (1992) calls this a processing bias. When we are faced with something which makes us anxious we are more likely to focus our attention on this stimulus.

Let us take the example of someone who is afraid of spiders. Imagine that while this person is watching television a spider crawls across the room and scuttles under the coffee table. The likelihood is that this person would subsequently pay less attention to the programme that they were watching on television and pay more attention to the spider. They may attempt to continue watching the television programme but may be constantly checking under the table because they are afraid that the spider may reappear. The spider is the fear stimulus, and the individual pays more attention to this stimulus because they are afraid.

Early psychology research used Stroop tests, which require individuals to read out words that are presented on a screen (Lester, 1932). Researchers can then time how long it takes for an individual to respond to the word that is shown. When the words used are highly emotional or threat related, individuals take longer to respond compared to their responses to words which are neutral or positive. Eysenck (1992) explains that anxiety reduces our attentional capacity for processing information and disrupts our working memory. To overcome this we invest more effort. Yet as a result of this increase in effort we become less efficient at processing information. This hypothesis can be used to explain why individuals take longer when asked to read out threatening words than neutral words. For further information on this see the further reading suggested at the end of this chapter.

Chapter Review

At the start of this chapter we defined self-confidence and considered how this influences feelings, cognitions and behaviours. This led us into a discussion of Vealey's model of sports confidence and the domains used to source confidence (Learning Objective 1). We then examined each of the domains (self-regulation, achievement and social climate) and how these may impact on sport confidence. Next we considered a more situation-specific form of confidence: self-efficacy. We first described Bandura's theory of self-efficacy and examined each of the six sources of self-efficacy. We then suggested how an athlete's level of self-efficacy could be improved using Bandura's theory (Learning Objective 2). We made suggestions that could be applied both by the sport psychologist working with the athlete, and by the coach during training sessions. This led us to our discussion on motivational climate and goal orientation. Vealey's model suggested that motivational climate will impact on the self-confidence level of the athlete.

Using Krane *et al.*'s article we then discussed the negative impact of an ego-orientated and outcome-orientated motivational climate (Learning Objective 3). The final individual factor that we considered was attentional strategy. First, we outlined the different types of attentional strategy (Learning Objective 4), suggesting that an athlete may adopt an internal–external or broad–narrow focus. It was also suggested that attention constantly shifts and that these shifts in attention are both voluntary and involuntary. We highlighted the impact that attention may have on performance, focusing on research that examined whether an associative or a dissociative attentional strategy may be more appropriate during endurance performance.

Finally, we examined the impact that anxiety can have on attention (Learning Objective 5), suggesting that an anxious individual may make more fixations of a shorter duration. We also suggested explanations for these effects, such as processing efficiency theory.

Learning Activity 8.5
Test your understanding

1. Using Vealey's model, describe the affect, behaviour and cognitions an athlete will display when they are high in self-confidence.
2. Explain how imagery could be used to increase levels of self-efficacy and discuss why this may be effective.
3. What might be the negative consequences of an ego orientation?
4. What are the factors that may determine the attentional strategy that best suits an individual athlete or sport?

Further Reading

Kingston, K, Lane, A and Thomas, O (2010) A temporal examination of elite performers sources of sport-confidence. *The Sport Psychologist*, 18: 313–332.
This paper examined temporal changes in sports confidence during the build-up to competition. It emphasises the sources of sports confidence as proposed by Vealey and demonstrates how these may change over time.

Boyce, BA, Gano-Overway, LA and Campbell, AL (2009) Perceived motivational climate's influence on goal orientations, perceived competence, and practice strategies across the athletic season. *Journal of Applied Sport Psychology*, 21: 381–394.
This paper provides a useful link between motivational climate and perceived ability.

Murray, NP and Janelle, CM (2007) Event-related potential evidence for the processing efficiency theory. *Journal of Sports Sciences*, 25: 161–171.
This paper provides further explanation on processing efficiency theory. It confirms that anxiety can result in a reduction in processing efficiency.

Stanley, CT, Pargman, D and Tenenbaum, G (2007) The effect of attentional coping strategies on perceived exertion in a cycling task. *Journal of Applied Sport Psychology*, 19: 352–363.
This study examined the effects of attentional intervention strategies on perceived exertion in female exercisers. It provides a useful example of how research has examined attention.

Chapter 9
Training for competition: social factors

This chapter is designed to help you be able to:

1. understand what is meant by the term 'expectancy effect bias' and how this may affect an athlete in an aesthetically judged sport;
2. describe how a self-fulfilling prophecy may occur in a sporting context;
3. suggest how schema theory may help to explain impression formation in sport;
4. identify why interpersonal skills may be important in sport;
5. suggest intervention techniques for improving communication and interpersonal skills in sport.

Introduction

Imagine that you are about to take part in a rugby match and are standing on the pitch waiting for the opposition to appear from the changing rooms. As you stand there you begin to imagine what the opposition will look like. Think about what aspects of their appearance would make you feel more confident about succeeding against this team. Try to imagine what a weaker team would look like. There may be a number of characteristics that you associate with a weaker team. These might include their physical build, the clothes that they are wearing and/or their body language. They may be physically small, wearing quite old shabby kit, and they may not maintain eye contact with you and look nervous and apprehensive. Now imagine that the players who walk out of the changing room are wearing the latest expensive kit, that they seem cohesive and take part in a group warm-up, that they maintain eye contact with you as they emerge from the changing room and that they appear strong and muscular. How might this impact on your perception of these players and the upcoming game?

The above example illustrates that how we perceive others may impact on our experiences of success, sometimes before we have even begun to compete. The aim of this chapter is to examine how these perceptions may impact on sporting performance. We start by examining expectation bias, which refers to the bias in our perception of others that may occur due to prior knowledge and expectations about a team or individual. Your prior knowledge and expectations of others may then impact on judgements you make and the way you behave and perform. In the next part of this chapter we examine the related topic of person perception. This refers to how we form perceptions of others, and we consider the visual cues that we may attend to and the factors that may impact on our judgements when developing these perceptions of others. In our introductory scenario we suggested that factors such as body language, clothing, and warm-up strategy may have an impact on our perceptions of others in sport. This part of the chapter discusses the impact of such factors and how they may affect our perceptions of future success or failure in sport.

We conclude by examining the importance of interpersonal skills in sport. In doing this we examine how we can assess an individual's interpersonal skills and how these skills may impact on our relationships with others. We end this section of the chapter by discussing how a sport psychologist or coach could deliver interventions to improve the interpersonal and communication skills of an individual or team.

Expectation bias and sports performance

When was the last time that you were influenced by your prior knowledge or expectations of something or someone? It may have been before an exam, in which you expected that the questions on the paper would be too difficult for you to answer. You may have formed this expectation based on your prior knowledge that your lecturer was quite strict in class and asked difficult questions in seminars. Alternatively, you may have experienced driving behind a sports car and expected it to speed off. This expectation may have been based on your knowledge of the potential of the car, or of the type of person who may be driving a sports car. If either of these examples are familiar then, like most of us, you have previously formed certain expectations based on your prior experiences and knowledge of a person or situation. You may have learned that lecturers who are strict in class are likely to set more difficult exams, or that owners of sports cars are more likely to break the speed limit. What becomes important is how you respond to such expectations.

Imagine that you have walked into an exam that you perceive will be impossible to pass. This evaluation may subsequently impact on your self-confidence and possibly even on your approach to the exam, even if you are capable of passing. Your behaviour when driving behind the sports car may not change but you may be surprised when the driver keeps to the speed limits. However, imagine you were a police officer monitoring drivers' speed: who would you be more likely to expect to have to stop, the driver of the sports car or a driver of a family saloon car? Most likely your decisions would be impacted by your prior knowledge and you would choose the sports car.

Having considered some examples from everyday life let us consider how our expectations may impact how we perform in the sporting context and research into this phenomenon. Much like a police officer, a referee in sport may have prior knowledge and expectations of individuals who are likely to break the rules. While the police officer may judge this by appearance or by the car being driven, the referee may be privy to even more prior knowledge based on previous performances by the teams that they are officiating. Thus there are many sources of information that may underpin their expectations, including position in the league and the reputations of players. A similar outcome of expectation bias exists for athletes in aesthetic sports, where appearance is important and the athletes are judged by a panel of judges who need to remain unbiased.

> ## Box 9.1 Definition: Expectancy effects
>
> Expectancy effects refer to the expectations that are formed concerning the potential of an individual (positive or negative) which may then be reflected in different behaviours towards that individual.

Origins of expectancy research

Early research into expectancy effects was often conducted in an educational setting. One of the most famous experiments of this kind was called 'Pygmalion in the classroom' (Rosenthal and Jacobson, 1968). This study suggested that if teachers were led to expect high levels of performance from a child, then that child would indeed perform highly. These social psychology experiments most often examined the impact of conveying false information to classroom teachers regarding the intelligence and potential of their students. Brophy and Good (1970) suggested that the different expectations that were formed of students would change the behaviour of the teachers towards those students. This change in behaviour would convey the type of response and achievement expected to the student, and as a consequence, over a period of time the students would then conform to these expectations. Rosenthal (1974) suggested that when a teacher had high expectations of a student they would alter their behaviour towards that student in four different ways. They would provide:

- a warmer socioemotional instructional climate;
- more instructional input;
- more performance feedback;
- more opportunities to respond and ask questions.

This is called a 'self-fulfilling prophecy'. Snyder *et al.* (1977) found further evidence for this self-fulfilling prophecy, proposing that our initial impressions of individuals can lead to self-fulfilling prophecies. Participants were led to believe that another individual who they were talking to on the phone was either physically attractive or unattractive. They found that those individuals who were presented as more attractive would also be judged as friendlier. People then acted in a more positive way towards these individuals, and as a consequence, those who were judged as friendly would then act in a more friendly manner themselves. Thus the friendly expectations that were held led to a change in behaviour, which in turn resulted in a self-fulfilling prophecy.

Learning Activity 9.1

Let us take this model above and apply it to a sporting context. Imagine that you are coaching a group of athletes in your own sport. You have been told by your head coach that he can see real talent in one particular child and that he believes they have great potential to become an elite athlete. He then also comments that another child in the group has no talent at all, in fact he believes that this child will drop out of the sport within the next year. See if you can complete the gaps in Figure 9.1 to show how a self-fulfilling prophecy may develop.

The flow charts in Figure 9.1 should have illustrated the differences in behaviour that may result from an individual's expectancies. On the one hand, one athlete receives more attention and feedback and because of this exerts more effort and enjoys taking part in sport. On the other hand the other athlete may feel like they are constantly receiving criticism and may be aware that they receive less attention than

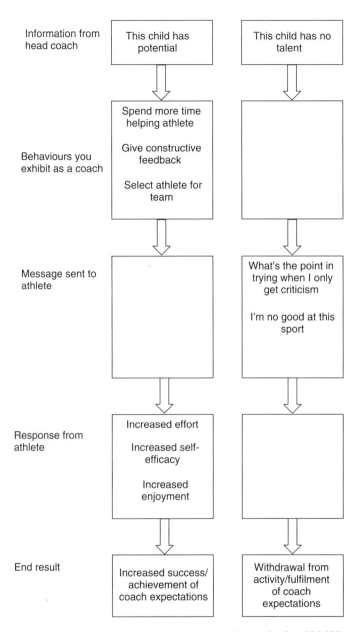

Figure 9.1 Example of a self-fulfilling prophecy in sport.

others. As a result of this they may then exert less effort and consequently fail to improve, leading them to eventually withdraw from the sport altogether.

Self-fulfilling prophecies in coaching

Learning activity 9.1 asked you to consider the potential consequences of forming expectations in sport. Expectancy theory has been used to explain the impact of these expectancies in the sporting context

(Horn *et al.*, 2001; Solomon, 2001). This is a four-stage cyclical model which examines how expectancies that are formed influence coaches and the subsequent behaviour of athletes. Figure 9.2 demonstrates the cyclic nature of this model, showing that as the athlete begins to conform to the coach's expectancies this reaffirms the coach's perceptions and expectations.

The model illustrates that the coach may change his or her coaching behaviours based on his or her expectancies in a similar way to the four changes in teacher behaviour outlined by Rosenthal (1974). Research supports these proposals by demonstrating that coaches will adapt the quality and/or quantity of feedback that they give. Based on their expectations they may give more praise and instruction to high expectancy athletes (Solomon *et al.*, 1998), as well as more practice time (Lacy and Martin, 1994).

The model also demonstrates how these expectancies may lead to a self-fulfilling prophecy since the behaviours of the coach will impact on the behaviours of the athlete. In addition to this, since the athlete will generally conform to the coach's expectations, this reinforces the coach's belief that they are able to accurately predict ability (Becker and Solomon, 2005). Further, Becker and Solomon (2005) proposed that differences in team success are more dependent on the coach's ability to communicate expectations rather than on the actual criteria (e.g. physique of player) used to form their expectations. As a consequence of this they suggest that coaches should learn to openly communicate their expectations. This will ensure that athletes know what to expect and can work towards common goals which can ultimately facilitate performance success.

How do coaches form their expectations?

The first stage of expectancy theory suggests that expectations are based on personal, performance, and psychological cues (see Figure 9.2 for examples). However, research has demonstrated that while coaches use these cues these are not significant predictors of athletic ability. Solomon (2001) asked coaches to

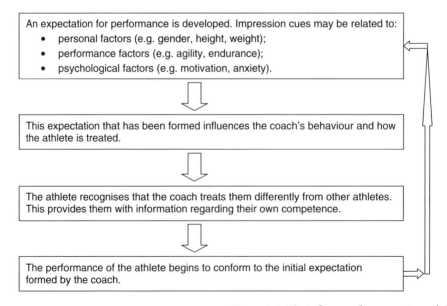

Figure 9.2 The influence of expectancies on behaviour.

evaluate athletic ability based on performance (physical ability) and psychological factors (confidence). However, results demonstrated that the only significant predictor of actual performance was coach perception of confidence. Thus while coaches may use these cues to evaluate athletic potential and form their expectancies, this study demonstrates that they do not necessarily provide accurate representations of ability. In addition to this, Becker and Solomon (2005) proposed that while it is understood that coaches use personal, performance and psychological cues to form their expectations, these may encompass a number of different dimensions. They therefore examined more specifically which sources of information were used by coaches to form expectancies. Using the Solomon Expectancy Source Scale (Solomon, 2003) they examined the criteria that head basketball coaches used to assess ability. Interestingly, psychological attributes were the most salient characteristics that coaches relied on to judge athletic ability. Physical components were not even rated among the top ten criteria used to assess athletes, possibly because at an elite level athletes vary very little in their physical characteristics.

Becker and Solomon also examined the differences in criteria used between more and less successful coaches based on the team's level of success. While there was no significant difference between the sources of information used by the coaches, mean trends indicated that successful coaches placed a higher degree of importance on psychological factors, while less successful coaches prioritised physical attributes. See the section on further reading at the end of this chapter to find out more about this study.

Adopting an alternative perspective, research has also attempted to categorise the cues that may be most influential when athletes form impressions of a coach. Manley *et al.* (2008) found that static cues (those that remain relatively stable during interaction such as gender and age) were relatively unimportant during impression formation. In contrast, dynamic cues (more changeable characteristics that may alter such as posture and body language) and third party reports (such as coaching qualifications or reputation) were more influential when forming expectancies.

Learning Activity 9.2

The Solomon Expectancy Source Scale is a 30-item instrument that was developed to determine the sources of information used by intercollegiate coaches to assess athlete ability. To create this questionnaire Solomon (2003) interviewed coaches from individual and team sports about the characteristics they used to assess athletic ability. From these interviews they established 30 factors that were considered important in assessing ability.

Imagine that you had been asked to take part in these interviews. What are the factors that you would deem to be important in assessing ability in the sport that you play? Take some time to produce a list of characteristics that you consider to be important, including both physical and psychological characteristics. Once you have made this list rank the characteristics from most to least important and think about why you have ranked the characteristics in this order.

Compare your list of characteristics to the list below which presents the characteristics rated by coaches in Becker and Solomon's (2005) study. ···▶

Learning Activity 9.2 continued

- Hard worker   Factors most used when assessing athletic ability
- Receptivity to coaching
- Willingness to learn
- Love of sport
- Willingness to listen
- Competitiveness
- Honesty
- Respect
- Self-discipline
- Integrity
- Team chemistry
- Trust
- Athleticism
- Coordination
- Courage
- High aspirations
- Communication
- Confidence
- Role acceptance
- Pressure
- Agility
- Leadership
- Speed
- Concentration
- Mental maturity
- Athletic experience
- Reaction time
- Strength
- Good strategy
- Complete assessments   Factors least used when assessing athletic ability

How do the characteristics that you use to judge athletic ability compare with those suggested by Becker and Solomon (2005)?

Are there any similarities between those characteristics that you perceive as important in judging ability and those listed above?

If your suggested characteristics are different from those presented above can you explain why?

Expectation bias and judging sports performance

In the sporting context it is not easy to remain unbiased by prior knowledge, particularly at an elite level. For every athlete a wealth of information may already be known by the officials and judges who need to remain objective in their judgements. One such sport which provides a good example of the importance of objective judging is artistic gymnastics. Gymnastics judging, similar to judging in other aesthetic sports, may be vulnerable to a number of non-performance based influences (Boen *et al.*, 2008). This is because in these sports performance is not judged by objective measures such as time or distance, but by the subjective evaluations of a panel of judges. Early research noted a change in judges' scores as competition progressed (e.g. Scheer, 1973), meaning that despite the random order of competitors, those competing in the last two-thirds of the competition were at an advantage in comparison to those competing in the first third. Further, Ansorge *et al.* (1978) suggested that the tendency of coaches to rank order their gymnasts for competition in each event created a naturally induced expectation that better gymnasts would compete last. Even when routines were taped and judged in a random order, those participants appearing at the end of the tape were deemed to be at a scoring advantage. However, Scheer *et al.* (1983) suggested that some judges were more resistant to the influence of expectation biases and attempts to manipulate their scoring. These judges were found to be high in levels of dominance, autonomy and had an internal locus of control.

In addition to the order effect bias, Boen *et al.* (2008) proposed that aesthetic sports may also present a conformity bias in which judges tend to adapt their scores to the scores of their surrounding judges. Boen *et al.* (2006) noted that in aesthetic sports the judges can often see and/or hear the scores that are given for the same performance by the judges surrounding them after each performance (open feedback). As a consequence they are provided with feedback on whether their score is higher, lower, or the same as the rest of their colleagues' scores. They proposed that this may lead to conformity among panels of judges which is not necessarily based on the performance of the athletes. This conformity is suggested to occur for two main reasons. Informational influencing suggests that individuals will conform to the group norm because they want to make a correct judgement and place more trust in the abilities of others than their own. Normative influencing suggests that individuals will conform to the group norm because they fear being rejected by others in the group. Boen *et al.* (2008) found less variation between the judges' scores on judging panels that received feedback after each performance than within panels that had not received any feedback. This therefore confirmed that the availability of feedback will elicit conformity.

Another type of bias may be created by the reputation of an athlete. Findlay and Ste-Marie (2004) examined whether expectations, assumed to be formed by an athlete's positive reputation, produced a bias in judging in figure skating. They proposed that using information based on the knowledge of prior behaviours or performances will be similar to having prior expectations of performance. Furthermore, in any social situation an individual will have some type of expectations or assumptions about the people and the characteristics involved in the situation. Thus such assumptions exist even when attempting to objectively judge a sport such as figure skating. Findlay and Ste-Marie (2004) examined whether the ordinal ranking of figure skaters would be better when skaters were evaluated by judges who knew their positive reputation, compared with when they were evaluated by judges who had not heard of them. Thus they were able to observe the potential impact of a skater's positive reputation and 'name' recognition. Results from this study indicated that ordinal rankings were higher when skaters were known by the judges compared with when they were unknown. While their artistic marks and deductions for errors did not differ, known skaters received significantly higher technical merit marks. The general finding was that a reputation bias does exist in figure skating judging. Thus the name of the skater, when associated with a positive reputation, led the judges to expect a more solid and aesthetically superior performance.

Why do expectancies occur? A schema theory explanation

One suggested explanation for the occurrence of expectancies in sport is the influence of schemas on social judgements.

Box 9.2 Definition: Schemas

Schemas are cognitive structures that represent a person's knowledge of a concept, including its attributes and the relationship between those attributes (Plessner, 1999: 132).

We all have schemas that underpin our expectations of individuals and of situations that we may encounter. These schemas may include expectations of how an individual should behave in a particular situation, or they may refer to certain social roles that are expected of an individual. We may also have schemas of how groups of people are expected to perform and we may have self-schemas (categories that you may use to judge yourself). These may be influenced by our past experiences, theories of the world and personal biases and will guide how we encode and integrate information. When we encode information this refers to how we may perceive a particular stimulus and individuals may interpret information obtained from the same stimulus differently, based on their schema knowledge. This is because our attention and information processing are shaped by the expectations we form on the basis of our schema.

For example, in a school PE lesson, one of the children turns up with a bandage on their ankle and informs the two teachers present that they will not be able to participate in today's netball lesson. One teacher who knows the child well knows that the child is reluctant to take part in any PE lessons and has missed a lot of previous classes. The other teacher, who does not know the child, has no prior information yet has expectancies that most children enjoy PE. Thus while both are presented with the same stimulus (the ankle bandage) their prior knowledge may lead them to make very different interpretations of the situation. Their decisions to allow the child to miss the lesson may therefore be based on the schemas that are held.

Fiedler (1996) suggests that individuals will have a tendency to confirm rather than disconfirm prior expectations. Thus schemas facilitate expectation congruent information. Using the example above, the teacher with prior knowledge may focus on behaviours that confirm her expectations rather than attempting to disprove them.

We can also manipulate individuals into forming schemas that are untrue about particular athletes or teams by providing them with false information. This manipulation has been used in research that has examined the impact of forming particular schemas on decision making. MV Jones *et al.* (2002) examined the impact of forming expectations of a team as 'aggressive' on the decisions made by association football referees. Participants were shown clips of incidents from football games and were asked to decide whether a foul had been committed and by which team. One group of participants received information prior to watching the tapes which informed them that the team in the blue strip had an aggressive reputation for foul play, whereas the other group of participants did not receive this information. Although there was no difference in the number of decisions made, those participants who had received the aggressive information awarded significantly more red and yellow cards against the blue team than those participants who had not received this information. This suggests that football referees who are informed that a team has an aggressive reputation will respond differently to identical incidents, in comparison with referees who have not received such information.

This study supports previous research that has examined a number of alternative cues that have also been found to impact on the decision making of referees. These have included the crowd noise (Nevill *et al.*, 2002), the colour of a player's kit (Tiryaki, 2005), the height of the player involved in the foul (van Quaquebeke and Giessner, 2010), and preceding foul judgements (Plessner and Betsch, 2001).

Plessner (1999) proposed two factors that influence the degree to which schemas impact on social judgements:

- individuals will become more accurate in their perceptions and encoding the longer they are exposed to a stimulus;
- their judgement strategies will depend on factors such as motivation, ability and task difficulty.

Individuals will use a more systematic judgement system if they have time to consider their judgements, and if their motivation and ability are high and the task undertaken is easy. The impact of expectations will be greatest when information and ability are low, the overall task is difficult, and time available to make decisions/judgements is limited. The sporting context provides the ideal situation in which to examine such proposals, since situations are regularly created in which individuals need to make difficult decisions under intense time pressures. Plessner (1999) suggested that this situation may often occur in gymnastics judging, which is a difficult task, presented at high speed. He examined the judgement of gymnastics judges who were asked to score videotaped routines of a men's competition appearing in team order. A placement effect was found (later routines were scored higher based on the expectation that better gymnasts will compete last) depending on the difficulty level of the task. Expectations were shown to bias the processing of information in a self-confirming way if the task difficulty exceeded abilities. Thus on fast apparatus (pommel horse, vault, horizontal bar) the gymnasts received significantly more points if their routines were presented fifth in the team order than if they were presented first. When the judges had longer to consider their judgements they were able to use a more systematic approach. However when they were judging the fast apparatus they had less time to make judgements and consequently the impact of their expectations was greater.

Warr and Knapper's model of person perception

Warr and Knapper's (1968) model suggests that when forming expectations about an individual three sources of information are used:

- information that is already held, either that has previously been formed about the individual or stored information based on a particular stimulus;

- information that is received at the time of the interaction;
- information that is determined by the context (for example, different behaviour may be expected from an individual depending on the situation that they are in).

A vast amount of information may be gained from these three sources which means that the individual will not be able to attend to all these sources. Instead the information attended to will be selected based on the current state of the individual (e.g. mood, goals) and their stable personal characteristics (e.g. personality, beliefs). This can be used to explain why highly anxious individuals may focus on threatening stimuli (Eysenck, 1992). In this example, the individual's anxiety levels may cause them to attend to particular information that is presented.

There are three interdependent consequences of any interaction with another individual.

- *An attributive response*: This involves judgements that are made about the goals and characteristics of the individual involved in the interaction. For example, a judgement may be made about the height of the individual or about their level of experience. These judgements may be episodic (about that person at that particular moment) or dispositional (about an enduring characteristic). For example, the information gained about an opponent before a 100 m race may be that as they walk out onto the track they have a muscular frame (dispositional judgement) and appear to be calm (episodic judgement).
- *An affective response*: This involves the emotional response that occurs as a result of the interaction. For example, the perception that an opponent is muscular and looks relaxed about competing may cause the perceiver to feel anxious. Other alternative emotions may include jealously, envy, anger, happiness, or fear.
- *An expectancy response*: Individuals will use the information received about others to form expectancies about how others are likely to behave and about the future progress of the interaction. For example, an athlete may perceive that they will easily be able to win the match and that little effort will be required.

Once a perception has been formed and responses have been experienced then further information will continue to be selected and perceived. Thus new information may be processed following our initial responses to the individual and the situation and so our perceptions may continue to change.

Research Focus

Individuals may hold schemas for what a good player will look like. At the start of this chapter you were asked to imagine a rugby team that you would be confident of playing well against. The schemas that you held regarding that rugby team may have included knowledge about the clothes the players would wear, their physique and what their body language may be like. These can be described as person schemas, that is, the attributes of a specific type of person (e.g. a good rugby player).

Greenlees *et al.* (2005) suggested that the body language and clothing of a tennis player may impact on the impressions that are formed of them by observers. Participants in their study were 40 male, competitive, club level tennis players. Each participant was asked to view videos of a tennis player warming up prior to a match. The footage included the player walking on court, removing a racket from his bag, completing a series of stretches and warm-up exercises, and approaching the court to begin play. For each of the videos the footage of the first and third player remained the same while the footage of the second player was manipulated. In this footage the player displayed a combination of either positive or negative body language, and was wearing either general sportswear or tennis-specific clothing. Positive body language included walking tall, head up, chin up and looking towards the camera, whereas negative body language included a hunched posture, head and chin down, eyes looking down and only briefly looking at the camera. For the clothing manipulation the player either wore a tracksuit made by a recognised tennis manufacturer (tennis-specific) or non-brand tracksuit bottoms and a t-shirt.

Participants viewed the footage and were then asked to rate their impressions of the likely outcome of the match. To examine episodic judgements participants rated the player on five dimensions reflecting his perceived readiness and mental state (e.g. focused/not focused). To examine dispositional judgements participants were asked to rate the player on five dimensions: aggressiveness, competitiveness, assertiveness, talent and mental fragility. Results supported the hypothesis that body language, but not clothing, would influence the judgements made by participants about mental state and readiness (episodic judgements). These results indicated that when positive body language was displayed the player was perceived to be in a more positive state. This supports Warr and Knapper's (1968) proposition that early information will lead an individual to form an impression. The model was further supported as both body language and clothing influenced dispositional judgements. When the player was viewed wearing sport-specific clothing and with positive body language he was rated more positively. On the dispositional characteristics assessed Warr and Knapper's contention that early information will be used to develop expectancies for later interactions was also supported by the finding that body language impacted on outcome expectations. Those participants who viewed positive body language also reported lower expectations of their own success.

Interpersonal skills in sport

Our final consideration in this chapter emerges from research that has discussed the impact that expectancies may have on the individual. Overall conclusions have suggested that positively manipulating the body language of an individual will lead to lower perceptions of success from an opponent (e.g. Greenlees et al., 2005). In addition to this we have also discussed the importance of ensuring good communication skills within a team which will allow coaches to vocalise their expectancies (e.g. Becker and Solomon, 2005). With this in mind the final part of this chapter focuses on research that has attempted to improve assertiveness and the interpersonal and communication skills of sports teams.

Early research suggested that effective communication is a crucial element in athletic performance (e.g. Martens, 1987). Further, Wang and Ramsey (1997) proposed that the ability to communicate is one of the most critical skills in becoming a coach. When we consider an individual's interpersonal skills we are likely to first think about how that individual communicates verbally with others. However, it is important to remember that communication skills are not only verbal but also non-verbal (Hargie and Dickson, 2004). It may be proposed that an individual's non-verbal communication may be just as important as their verbal communication. Further, as suggested by Haselwood et al. (2005) it is important that athletes and coaches become skilled in both sending and receiving messages in order to communicate effectively and achieve their goals. See the further reading at the end of this chapter for more information on non-verbal communication skills.

Hargie and Dickson (2004) suggested that there are five key features of skilled interpersonal interactions which form the acronym CLIPS. They suggest that successful interpersonal skills are:

- controlled by the individual;
- learned behaviours that improve with practice and feedback;
- integrated and interrelated verbal and non-verbal responses;
- purposive and goal directed;
- smooth in the manner in which they are directed.

We can use these principles to teach an athlete to master particular interpersonal skills that are valuable to them in their sport. Useful interpersonal skills may include improving communication skills within a team, improving communication from a coach, or learning advantageous methods of communicating with an opponent. Jowett (2003) suggests that if communication is effective then this will provide coaches and athletes with an opportunity to share one another's experiences and subsequently develop co-orientation. When we consider interpersonal communication in sport we may have a tendency to focus on positive aspects of communication that may be improved to help effective functioning in a team. Yet as Kerr and Grange (2009) proposed, within the sporting context there are also aspects of interpersonal communications in sport that may be negative, such as the verbal aggression that may occur between rivals. Consequently, in order to improve interpersonal skills in sport it may be necessary to remove negative interactions as well as promote positive communication.

Improving interpersonal skills in sport

While research has emphasised the importance of both verbal and non-verbal interpersonal skills (Hargie and Dickson, 2004), there are few studies that have examined interventions to improve these skills in the sporting context. Connelly and Rotella (1991) suggested that assertiveness will influence an individual's tendencies to respond to interpersonal situations with a degree of appropriate expression of personal thoughts and feelings. They continued that for some athletes the negative consequences associated with speaking out may be too great to risk, causing them to be perceived as uncooperative or as a troublemaker. Consequently, in order to improve communication within a team they proposed that assertiveness skills could be taught to athletes. To do so many of the skills included in mental skills training programmes can be used, including goal setting, cognitive restructuring and self-talk. These can help the athlete to reduce uncertainties about communicating within a team. It is also suggested that anticipatory coping is used, which involves teaching the athlete to anticipate how the assertive communication might be received and how the athlete would then cope. Importantly, athletes and coaches must accept responsibility to practise appropriate communication skills which may in turn help to prevent and deal with communication problems that may be encountered.

Further research has focused on the impact of the breakdown of communication skills in sport. Jowett (2003) examined the interpersonal conflicts present in an athlete–coach relationship and found marked differences in the coach's and athlete's perceptions about their relationship. She noted that there was a lack of communication and consequently a lack of understanding between the coach's and the athlete's needs, wants and desires, which then prevented the successful coach–athlete partnership. This is further supported by Camiré *et al.* (2009), who found that for some athletes, poor communication with coaches led to conflict and had a negative impact on sporting performance.

Trenholm and Jensen (1996) suggested that in order for communication to be effective a number of different competencies need to be fulfilled:

- *interpretive competence* – being able to pick out information that is important and disregard irrelevant cues;
- *role competence* – taking on appropriate roles and social behaviours;
- *self-competence* – choosing and presenting a desired image;
- *goal competence* – knowing the aims of communication and overcoming any barriers to achieve these aims;
- *message competence* – sending messages (verbally and non-verbally) that others can comprehend and responding to the messages of others.

Haselwood *et al.* (2005) examined female athletes' perceptions of their head coach's communication competence using Trenholm and Jensen's competencies. They first found that there were no significant differences in the perceived communication competencies of male and female coaches. Interestingly, their study revealed a significant difference between the perceptions of coaches and athletes regarding their communication competence. Findings suggested that in comparison to athletes, coaches had stronger perceptions that their messages were clear, easy to understand and that they had a good command of language.

Chapter Review

We started this chapter by encouraging you to consider your own personal expectancies in sport, based on the physical and psychological characteristics of your opponents. We then went on to discuss how forming similar expectations as a coach may impact on the athlete. We discussed expectancy theory, which can be used to explain why a self-fulfilling prophecy may occur in a sporting context (Learning Objective 2). You were asked to consider how expectancies could have both positive and negative effects on athletes. Following this, we examined expectancy effects and how these may affect an athlete, particularly someone taking part in an aesthetically judged sport (Learning Objective 1). We considered research on gymnastics judging and figure skating and how these may be impacted by expectancies. In order to explain how impressions and expectancies are formed we used schema theory and Warr and Knapper's model (Learning Objective 3). In our final section we identified why interpersonal skills may be important in sport (Learning Objective 4). Although there is limited research available which focuses on improving interpersonal skills in the sporting context, we examined research that suggested improvements in assertiveness and coach–athlete communication (Learning Objective 5).

Learning Activity 9.3
Test your understanding

1. How might the expectancies of a coach impact both positively and negatively on an athlete's performance?
2. Objectivity in high-level gymnastics judging is impossible – discuss.
3. What are the characteristics of an athlete that may cause a successful coach to have high expectations and why?
4. How might the appearance of an athlete influence their opponent's perception of future success of the athlete and why?
5. What are the factors suggested to be important in competent communication?

Further Reading

Buscombe, R, Greenlees, I, Holder, T, Thelwell, R and Rimmer, M (2006) Expectancy effects in tennis: The impact of opponents' pre-match non-verbal behaviour on male tennis players. *Journal of Sports Sciences,* 24: 1265–1272.
This study examined the impact of an opponent's body language and clothing on how performance was judged by an observer. It provides a good example of research into non-verbal behaviours and expectancies.

Hargie, O and Dickson, D (2004) *Skilled Interpersonal Communication*. East Sussex: Routledge.
This book provides information on the theory and practice of effective interpersonal communication. It includes a useful chapter on non-verbal communication (chapter 3).

Chapter 10
Coping with competition pressure

Learning Objectives

This chapter is designed to help you be able to:

1. define choking and understand when choking is likely to occur in sport;
2. outline theoretical explanations for choking in sport;
3. understand the role of dispositional self-consciousness in choking susceptibility;
4. understand what is meant by the term 'ironic mental process';
5. identify potential strategies for reducing choking in sport.

Introduction

When we think about sport we are often reminded of great sporting triumphs and successes. Young athletes who dream of sporting success may see themselves on the Olympic podium or hear the crowd roar as they score a winning goal in a cup final. Newspaper articles and media headlines frequently report the pride and happiness that are associated with sporting success. However, it is important to remember that to be successful in sport an athlete may often have to deal with adversity. On the other side of the success stories, we hear of athletes who 'choke' when it really matters. These may be individuals or teams who cannot cope with the pressure of a crucial moment in sport, such as a penalty kick or serving for the Wimbledon tennis final. They do not perform up to expectations and their performance often crumbles under the pressure of the occasion.

These negative experiences in sport are not uncommon. Evidently, some athletes are able to cope with adversity and achieve sporting success, whereas others choke under pressure and fail to achieve their sporting goals. In this chapter, we consider the psychological processes involved in coping with adversity in sporting competition. We examine theoretical explanations for why some athletes choke under pressure and we focus on two explanations of choking. First, we consider the catastrophe theory that links choking to increases in cognitive anxiety and physiological arousal. Second, we discuss the conscious processing hypothesis that suggests that choking is caused by an increase in pressure resulting in a change in attentional focus. Specifically, we examine the work of Masters and Baumeister, who offer two different perspectives on the role of dispositional self-consciousness in choking. Finally, since it is clear that some athletes are able to triumph despite adversity we examine how athletes may be taught to cope in high pressured or anxiety-provoking situations, using strategies such as music and pre-performance routines.

Stress and choking in sport

There are a number of situations in sport that we can identify as particularly highly pressured because they induce high levels of stress. Even as a spectator we may have felt the pressure that has built up in a specific match situation. Think back to the last time that you watched a sporting event that contained a high level of pressure. This may have been a penalty shoot out in football or an important event such as an Olympic final. Consider how you felt about that event even as a spectator. Maybe you felt that you were unable to watch the events that were about to unfold, or maybe you found yourself shouting at the television willing your team to succeed. Whatever your reaction you were probably aware of the high levels of stress that your team were under. As we saw in Chapter 8 there are a number of individual difference factors that may influence both behaviour and performance outcomes in sport. These can include the individual's levels of self-confidence, motivation and their focus of attention. In addition, for an athlete to be successful they must also be able to withstand the pressures of sporting competition. Thus to help any athlete to thrive under pressure it is important to understand and be able to apply the psychological theories that explain choking in sport.

Learning Activity 10.1

Imagine the following scenario:

You are working as a sport psychologist and are approached by the manager of your local football team. He tells you that his team are currently bottom of the league. Although they are a team of strong players whenever they are in a penalty situation they seem unable to score. Sometimes the shots that they take are so wide of the goal that the manager is embarrassed by their performance. Even the local press have branded the team as 'chokers'. He has tried to solve this performance problem by increasing the number of penalty practices in the team's training sessions, and has found that in training his players are quite capable of scoring. Now the manager is unsure how to help his team further and would like to enlist your assistance.

From the situation outlined above it can be suggested that the players are choking under pressure. Consider what knowledge or information you would need to be able to help in this situation. Discuss your ideas with a partner and check your responses with those suggested below.

- *Knowledge of the problem itself*: Before you could work with this team you would need to understand what is meant by the term 'choking'. The manager tells you that the team's problem has been branded as choking by the press but you would need further knowledge of how choking is defined before you could conclude that this is a problem of choking and not something else such as a lack of skill.
- *Knowledge of when choking may be likely to occur*: The manager has explained that choking occurs during penalty shootouts – but what is it about this situation that makes the players more prone to choking under pressure? Are there particular situations that may be more likely to make a player choke?
- *Knowledge of the theoretical explanations of choking*: This would help you to understand why the team may be choking. It is important to understand the causes of the team's inability to score penalties. This may also tell you whether some individuals are more prone to choking under pressure than others and if this is related to a particular personality type.
- *Knowledge of strategies that may help to prevent choking*: These strategies may include ways of preventing choking or interventions that may help a player who is already prone to choking. Consequently if you were going to work with this team to try and solve the problem you would need to have some awareness of interventions that may be effective.

What is choking?

We often read newspaper articles or hear broadcasters refer to athletes as 'chokers', but what does this term mean? Although researchers do not always agree on an operational definition Baumeister and Showers (1986, page 361) define choking as, 'the occurrence of inferior performance despite striving and incentives for superior performance.'

This definition indicates that there are two main features that help us to define choking. First, choking will always be indicated by inferior performance. Thus someone who is not good at sport can not be labelled a choker; this term is only relevant to an athlete who usually achieves higher performance standards. Second, this definition implies that the athlete is motivated to achieve. This means that an athlete who lacks motivation and therefore gives up in a high pressured situation cannot be labelled a choker. Wallace *et al.* (2005) further emphasised that individuals will feel performance pressure when they care deeply about the outcome of an event and when they perceive that their performance is instrumental in the attainment of a personal goal or outcome.

When does choking occur?

We know from the example in Learning Activity 10.1 that choking can occur in situations such as penalty shootouts, but are there particular situations in which athletes are more likely to choke? There are thought to be three likely situations in which choking occurs:

- *Performing well in training but not in competition*: This type of choking may be more likely to occur in athletes who are sub-elite. This is because if they are able to perform well in training but not in competition they are unlikely to have reached an elite level. An elite athlete has had to compete well to have achieved this level of performance. This means that we might hear athletes who have suffered from this type of choking say, 'I could have made it but I just couldn't handle the pressure of competing.'
- *Performing well in competition until the 'big match'*: This type of choking will occur in athletes who are able to play well in less important events such as qualifying rounds yet who choke under pressure when it really counts. Examples of this kind of choking occur in players who play really well up until the finals of a competition or match and then choke in the final. We might expect an athlete who chokes in this kind of situation to say, 'I play really well until it really counts and then I can't hold it together.'
- *Performing well, even in 'big matches' until critical points in the match*: This type of choking will occur when athletes are able to play well, even in an important match, but when it comes to a critical moment in competition they choke under pressure. Examples of this might be a tennis player who chokes on the final point of a match or a golfer who misses the final short putt of the competition. We could also include the example outlined in Learning Activity 10.1 of the local football team that is unable to score penalties. In this situation we would be likely to hear a player say, 'I play very well, even under pressure, but when it comes to the most critical point in the match, such as penalties, then I lose it.'

Theoretical explanations of choking

You may be able to find a number of examples in the media of athletes who have choked under pressure. There are a number of theoretical explanations that help us to understand the causes of choking. The two main explanations are *catastrophe theory* and the *conscious processing hypothesis*.

Catastrophe theory

Catastrophe theory (Hardy and Fazey, 1987; Figure 10.1) suggests that if an athlete who is anxious experiences continual increases in arousal then this will lead to a sudden and dramatic decline in performance levels. To explain this decline in performance, catastrophe theory examines the relationship between cognitive anxiety, physiological arousal and performance. Cognitive anxiety refers to the thought component of anxiety and is characterised by worry and apprehension. Physiological arousal refers to the athlete's level of physiological activation such as heart and respiration rate.

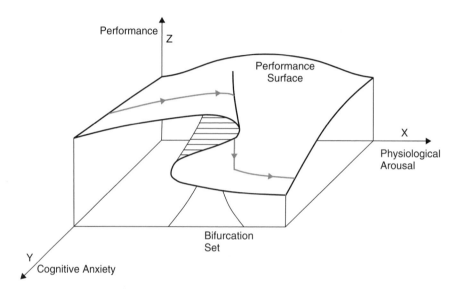

Figure 10.1 Catastrophe theory.

To understand this theory, imagine that you are playing in the Wimbledon tennis final. In the opening sets of the match you have moderate levels of cognitive anxiety and physiological arousal. Since it is an important match we would expect you to experience elevated levels of cognitive anxiety and physiological arousal. As the match progresses and you take the lead you realise that you could be on your way to winning the title. As you start to win more points you feel your levels of cognitive anxiety and physiological arousal increase further. As this happens, initially your performance starts to improve slightly. However, the closer you get to winning the final set the higher your levels of cognitive anxiety and physiological arousal. As these levels start to increase, you reach what is termed the 'cusp' of the catastrophe model. This part of the model is similar to the crest of a wave. At this point, any increase in physiological arousal will lead to a sudden and dramatic decline in performance. The top surface of the model is the performance surface. We can see that as an athlete reaches the cusp of the performance surface then performance deterioration is sudden and the athlete chokes.

> ## Learning Activity 10.2
>
> What you may also notice about this model is the relationship between physiological arousal and cognitive anxiety. Look at the performance surface of the model. Try to answer the following questions:
>
> 1. What would happen to performance if an individual had high levels of physiological arousal and a low level of cognitive anxiety? Is choking likely to occur?
> 2. What would happen to performance if an individual had high levels of cognitive anxiety and a low level of physiological arousal? Is choking likely to occur?
> 3. Is there an optimum level of cognitive anxiety and physiological arousal for performance?

Consider your answers in relation to the explanation that follows. The first question suggests that if cognitive anxiety is very low then choking will not occur. However, the slope of the performance surface indicates that performance will still deteriorate, although not as rapidly as the deterioration that is associated with choking. It is also worth noting that choking can still occur, even with moderate levels of cognitive anxiety and high levels of physiological arousal. The second question highlights that even if cognitive anxiety is very high choking will not occur without high physiological arousal. Finally, the third question asked you to identify the point on the model where performance was highest. You can see from the model that this occurs with moderate levels of cognitive anxiety and physiological arousal.

One final presupposition of the catastrophe model that you may have noticed is that once choking has occurred it becomes very difficult to regain previous performance levels. Even if the individual is able to lower their levels of cognitive anxiety and physiological arousal then they do not return to the same level of performance they had achieved previously. This means that once an athlete has choked they will find it difficult to recover and to regain their previous level of performance.

Conscious processing hypothesis

The catastrophe theory explains choking by focusing on the relationship between anxiety and arousal. In contrast, the conscious processing hypothesis posits that it is an increase in performance pressure that leads to choking. This increase in pressure may result when an individual is highly motivated to achieve in an important situation.

When an individual cares deeply about the outcome of their performance they may try to do everything possible to ensure that they execute each element well. Unfortunately, these extra efforts can ironically sometimes cause them to fail. This is because they begin to consciously control aspects of their performance which previously they did not think about. When we try to consciously control performance our attention shifts from a more external focus (e.g. watching where the next player is that you will pass to) to a more internal focus (e.g. thinking about where to position your foot when striking the ball). This switch to conscious processing may then result in choking.

The effects of conscious processing can be seen in the very simple children's nursery rhyme called the Centipedes Dilemma that is outlined below.

A centipede was happy quite,
Until a frog in fun
Said, 'Pray which leg comes after which?'
This raised her mind to such a pitch,
She lay distracted in the ditch
Considering how to run.

This rhyme shows us the essence of conscious processing, that when we are put under pressure our attention is drawn inward and we are unable to perform the task successfully. Consider an activity that you are able to do quite easily (or automatically) without having to think about it, such as driving a car. Once we have learned to drive a car we very rarely need to think about the actions of our feet in order to change gear or to pull out at a junction. But consider what would happen if someone asked you to explain exactly how to drive a car as you were trying to do this. The likelihood is that once you are asked to consider this it would slow down your actions as you would be forced to revert back to thinking about how you perform this task. Similarly, when faced with a high pressure situation individuals will often revert back to conscious processing. A simplified explanation of what happens to an individual when there is an increase in performance pressure is as follows: when we have no pressure we perform skills automatically, but an increase in performance pressure causes anxiety, which causes us to focus on ourselves and what we are doing. By thinking about what we are doing we start to consciously control the skill and we don't perform as well (choked performance).

This explanation illustrates that important competitions or important moments in competition can increase arousal. In turn, this results in an attentional focus on oneself and disruption of well-learned skills.

Liao and Masters (2002) examined the role of self-focused attention in novice basketball players and demonstrated that self-focused attention increased levels of anxiety. Basketball players were asked to perform a basketball free throw shot. When focusing on the mechanics of shooting the ball their performance suffered significant decrements. This research supports the conscious processing hypothesis, illustrating the deterioration in performance when attention was focused inward. The further reading section at the end of this chapter includes a paper by Mullen and Hardy (2000) which describes a study into conscious processing in relation to motor performance.

Reflection Point

Try to think of a time when you knew that someone was assessing you or when you knew that you were being watched in your sport. Think about how it influenced your thoughts and your performance: Did you make mistakes, if so what were these? This increase in pressure may have made you much more conscious of the skills that you were performing.

One method of increasing pressure in a laboratory setting has been to include an audience. Butler and Baumeister (1995) systematically manipulated audience support in laboratory experiments and found that participants did not perform as well in front of supportive as opposed to unsupportive audiences. This may not be what we would intuitively expect but often a supportive audience can increase the amount of performance pressure on the individual. This may have strong implications for athletes who are playing competitive matches in front of a home crowd. Wallace *et al.* (2005) proposed that the so-called home advantage might be better titled the 'home disadvantage'. They highlight that audience support actually magnifies performance pressure and induces performers to avoid failure rather than to strive to achieve success. In front of a home crowd Wallace *et al.* suggest that an individual would be more likely to have an increased self-focus, which in turn may then disrupt the execution of skilled performance and lead to choking.

Individual differences in choking: the role of dispositional self-consciousness

Although the conscious processing hypothesis explains what happens when an individual chokes, this cannot answer the question of why some individuals thrive under performance pressure whereas others are more susceptible to choking. We can all probably think of examples of athletes who have been able to overcome the greatest amounts of performance pressure and triumphed. So what makes these individuals able to cope with pressure whereas others may choke in the same situations? Research has considered individual differences in susceptibility to choking by examining differences in the tendency to become self-focused (referred to as trait or dispositional self-consciousness) and in the propensity to reinvest conscious control (referred to as reinvestment).

Box 10.1 Definitions: Trait self-consciousness and high reinvestment

- An athlete with high levels of *trait self-consciousness* will show a high level of self-awareness and self-focus.
- An athlete who is a *high reinvestor* will show a propensity to consciously control their movements.

Research has investigated these individual differences by examining individuals who are high and low in reinvestment and self-consciousness in high and low pressured situations. The measure most frequently used in sport psychology research to assess these variables (e.g. Masters *et al.*, 1993) is the reinvestment scale (Fenigstein *et al.*, 1975). This measure contains 20 items drawn from three scales that are used to predict individual propensity for reinvestment of controlled processing. It includes 12 questions from the self-consciousness scale and asks participants to rate themselves on questions such as:

- I reflect about myself a lot;
- I am alert to changes in my mood;
- I am concerned about the way I present myself;
- I'm self-conscious about the way that I look;
- I'm always trying to figure myself out;
- One of the last things I do before leaving my house is look in the mirror.

Research has proposed that both the self-consciousness scale and the reinvestment scale can be used to identify individuals who are more likely to choke under pressure. We now examine two opposing approaches to self-consciousness and choking which have used these scales.

Self-consciousness and choking: Baumeister's approach

There are two conflicting approaches to the role of self-consciousness in choking. According to Baumeister (1984) those individuals who are habitually self-conscious should find it easier to cope with situations that engender self-consciousness because they are accustomed to performing in these situations. This means that an individual who has high levels of self-consciousness would be less likely to choke. According to Baumeister this is because even in situations with no performance pressure the habitually self-conscious individual will still have to perform skills well while highly self-conscious. Consequently, when there is an increase in performance pressure the highly self-conscious individual is already accustomed to performing skills when their attention is turned inward. On the other hand, the individual who is habitually low in self-consciousness is not accustomed to performing with a high level of self-consciousness. Thus when the low self-conscious athlete is placed in a pressured situation, they are not familiar with performing skills with such levels of self-consciousness and are therefore more likely to choke.

Baumeister (1984) conducted six experimental studies to examine the conscious processing hypothesis and the role of self-consciousness in choking. The task that was used for experiments one to five was a 'roll up' game in which two rods were attached to a vertical board at one end and the participant was instructed to hold the other end with his or her hands. A metal ball was used and the participant was instructed to score points by moving the rods apart so that the ball dropped into the platform beneath the rods. The results of these experiments are summarised below.

Experiment 1
- *Method*: Participants were divided into two groups. Group 1 were instructed to focus on hand position (internal focus), group 2 were instructed to focus on the ball (external focus).
- *Result*: Group 1 (internal focus) performed worse than group 2 (external focus).

Experiment 2
- *Method*: Group 1 were instructed to focus on hand position (internal focus), group 2 were given no focusing instructions.
- *Result*: Group 1 (internal) performed worse although this was not significant.

Experiment 3
- *Method*: Group 1 were instructed to focus on hand position (internal focus). Group 2 were given no focusing instructions. Dispositional self-consciousness was measured.
- *Result*: Performance disrupted in low self-conscious individuals in group 1.

Experiment 5
- *Method*: Participants were offered a monetary incentive to perform at a target level.

- *Results*: Participants high and low in self-consciousness showed signs of choking, although the effect was stronger for those low in self-consciousness.

Experiment 6

- *Method*: Participants were customers playing 'Pac-man' at a video arcade. Previous score was recorded and participants were then offered a free game and asked to achieve the best possible score.
- *Result*: Average change was a 25 per cent drop in performance.

Experiment 4

Experiment 4 highlights the essence of Baumeister's theory. Participants performed with a confederate (a researcher pretending to be another participant; this allows their performance on the task to be manipulated). There were three experimental conditions: high pressure in which the confederate performed better than the participant, and low pressure in which the confederate performed worse than the participant, and a control condition. Table 10.1 presents the results from this study for individuals who were high and low in self-consciousness. Higher scores on the game indicated higher levels of performance.

	High pressure	Low pressure	Control
High self-conscious	74.0	80.1	67.2
Low self-conscious	65.1	83.3	81.2

Table 10.1 Experiment 4

The table shows that both the high and low self-conscious participants performed best in the low pressure condition. However, the decrease in performance between the low and high pressure conditions was significantly greater for the low compared with the high self-conscious participants. Results from these experiments therefore support Baumeister's assertions that highly self-conscious individuals will be less likely to choke under pressure.

Self-consciousness and choking: Masters' approach

Masters (1992) offers an alternative explanation for the role of self-consciousness in choking. He proposes instead that it is the highly self-conscious individual who is more likely to choke under pressure. According to Masters' theory, the more self-conscious we are the more likely the execution of the skill will be disrupted. In general, sport psychology research has shown more support for Masters' explanation than for Baumeister's. One such study that has supported Masters' theory was conducted by Chell *et al.* (2003). This study looked at performance under pressure in high versus low reinvestors. Participants were asked to perform a wall volley task in two conditions: alone (no pressure) and with an audience (high pressure). As expected, performance deteriorated in the high pressure condition in comparison to the low pressure condition. Chell *et al.* found the greatest reduction in performance in the high reinvestor group. This supports the assertions of Masters, demonstrating that high reinvestors exhibited greater performance reduction under pressure than low reinvestors.

Research Focus

In order to understand choking in sport it is important to appreciate the research methodology that is typically used to investigate this phenomenon. The study by Jackson *et al.* (2006) is illustrative of research that has examined the role of self-consciousness in sport performance. Jackson *et al.* undertook two experiments, the first of which is outlined below.

The aim of this study was to understand how attentional demands interact with situational pressure and dispositional reinvestment to influence skilled performance. To do so the study examined the performance levels of both high and low reinvestors when asked to focus on different aspects of performance in both low and high pressure conditions.

In their first experiment field hockey players were asked to perform a dribbling task in three experimental conditions. In the first condition (single task) participants were instructed to complete the dribbling task as quickly and accurately as possible. In the second task (skill focus) participants completed the same dribbling task but were asked to pay attention to the position of their hands throughout the trial. Every 6 seconds, on the sound of a tone, participants were instructed to identify whether their hand position was up or down. In the final condition (dual task) participants were instructed to generate a random letter of the alphabet on the sound of a tone every 6 seconds. Participants performed the single task, skill focus task and dual task in both high and low pressure conditions. To induce pressure in the high pressure condition participants were told that they were being filmed for a governing body film on field hockey. Reinvestment was measured using the reinvestment scale.

Results showed that in the low pressure condition performance was best on the dual task in which participants generated random letters of the alphabet. In the high pressure condition high reinvestors slowed (an indication of performance deterioration) significantly more than low reinvestors, showing support for Masters' theory. Further, performance deterioration in the skill-focused condition was compounded by the high pressure condition. This suggests that a combined skill focus and pressure condition may have additive effects, resulting in an even poorer performance.

Learning Activity 10.3

The study outlined above is from Jackson, RC, Ashford, KJ and Norsworthy, G (2006) Attentional focus, dispositional reinvestment, and skilled motor performance under pressure. *Journal of Sport and Exercise Psychology*, 28, 49–68. Read through the second experiment reported in this paper and try to write a similar outline to the one provided for experiment one. It may help you to use the following subheadings: aims, method, results and conclusions.

Sport-specific examples of choking

Some researchers have suggested that there are sport-specific forms of choking that can have more long-term implications for performance. These sport-specific examples have included 'dartitis' (darts), in which the player is unable to release the dart, 'the yips' (golf and cricket), in which the golfer is unable to sink even simple putts and the cricket bowler is unable to bowl, often either completely losing his or her technique or being unable to release the ball, and 'lost move syndrome' (acrobatic sports such as diving, gymnastics and trampolining), in which previously learnt and often simple skills can not be performed.

Bawden and Maynard (2001) examined the yips in cricket, concluding that the mechanisms associated with this condition represent an extreme form of choking which is constantly reinforced by poor performance and thus becomes a chronic performance problem. Similarly, Day *et al.* (2006) examined lost move syndrome in trampolinists, finding that the loss of skill in competitive trampolinists was often linked to an over-analysis of the skill, an increase in negative cognitions and a switch in attentional focus. Consequently, although choking most often occurs during a crucial match or at a crucial moment, there is some evidence to suggest that specific sporting movements may suffer from a long-term switch to conscious processing, resulting in a more chronic form of choking.

Is it possible to prevent choking?

Now that we have gained an understanding of why choking may occur it is also important to consider whether there any strategies that can be put in place to prevent an individual from choking. Here we focus on three main strategies: the type of learning, distractions and pre-performance routines.

Skill acquisition: implicit versus explicit learning

First, let us go back to the conscious processing hypothesis to examine whether it is possible to prevent choking. According to Masters, skill disruption will be less likely if the skill has been learned implicitly. Implicit learning means that skills have been gained using very few instruction or rules. Thus the gymnast using implicit learning to perform a handstand is able to develop this skill without being instructed on where to place his or her hands or how much force with which to kick up his or her legs. Instead they are able to learn by trial and error, experiencing what works and what does not until they are able to master the skill. On the other hand, explicit learning uses instructions and rules to teach an individual how to perform the skill. Thus the same gymnast may be shown the precise hand position for a handstand and taught how to kick up to a straight position. The explicit learner would be aware of facts and rules of how to perform the skill and would be able to articulate these. The implicit learner would 'know' how to perform the skill but would be less aware of the mechanics by which this is done and would therefore be less able to articulate these. Try to think back to how you learnt the skills of your sport; was this explicit or implicit learning? Masters suggests that we learn skills by following the basic rules of skill execution and as we progress these skills become more automatic. Increased pressure, however, makes us become more conscious of skill execution and we revert back to the rules by which we originally learnt the skill. The more rules we used to learn the skill the more chance we have of choking. Masters' suggestions about the role of implicit versus explicit knowledge when placed under performance pressure demonstrates that as we become well practised at a skill we become more autonomous at performing that skill.

When the skill is well-learned we do not need to focus on the mechanics of carrying out the skill and are able to perform the skill with very little conscious attention. We have therefore progressed from a cognitive through to an autonomous stage (Fitts and Posner, 1967). However, an increase in performance pressure causes us to revert back to conscious processing. Masters (1992) suggests that skills that have been learned implicitly will be more robust under pressure, whereas skills that have been learned explicitly will be more vulnerable to the effects of pressure and may therefore suffer performance decrements. This is because under pressure the individual will begin to think about how he or she is executing the skill and will attempt to perform the skill with his or her explicit knowledge of its mechanics. Masters suggests that if explicit learning is minimised in the skill acquisition phases when progressing from novice to expert then the athlete will have less conscious knowledge of the rules for executing the skill and therefore will not be able to reinvest this knowledge when put under pressure. Consequently the athlete will be less likely to choke in high pressure situations. Further reading on this idea can be found at the end of the chapter.

Ironic mental processes

Research has clearly demonstrated that focusing on the skill mechanics while performing a skill is detrimental to performance, suggesting that we should encourage an athlete to adopt an external focus in all high pressured situations. However, ironic mental processing suggests that this may not be such a simple solution. Wegner (1989) suggested that controlling thought processes is often more difficult than it seems. The act of exerting mental control may occasionally cause the athlete to dwell on the very thought or action that she or he was trying to avoid. Thus the footballer who consistently misses penalty kicks may try not to dwell on previous performance mistakes, yet find himself inextricably obsessed with the possibility that the next penalty may also be missed. Thus the term 'ironic mental processes' refers to the tendency to feel, act and think in a way that is opposite to the intended direction of emotion, behaviour and cognition. This means that telling our footballer not to concentrate on the position of his foot when taking a penalty may lead to an increased focus on the very thought that he was trying to avoid. Further suggested reading on this process can be found at the end of the chapter.

Reducing choking: distractions and pre-performance routines

Within choking studies, researchers have generally found that using a dual task reduces the likelihood of self-focusing and improves performance under pressure. Such tasks have included random alphabet letter generation every 6 seconds (Jackson *et al.*, 2006) and counting backwards in multiples of two (Lewis and Linder, 1997). Completing such tasks is proposed to distract the athlete from self-focusing by providing them with an alternative task. Given results from these studies it could be proposed that asking athletes to complete similar tasks at crucial moments of performance would limit the risk of choking. However, in actual competition it is unrealistic to expect athletes to verbalise the alphabet or count backwards.

Instead, Mesagno *et al.* (2008) suggest that using a pre-performance routine could alleviate the effects of choking. Using a ten pin bowling task, participants were trained in a pre-performance routine that involved a series of physiological, psychological and behavioural steps. This training included modifying optimal arousal levels, behavioural steps, attention control and cue words. During a high pressure condition participants improved in accuracy when using the pre-performance routine. Qualitative results also indicated that participants were able to reduce self-awareness and decrease conscious processing when using the pre-performance routine. Mesagno *et al.* (2009) published a similar experiment in which a music intervention was used instead of a pre-performance routine. Again, participants improved their performance with the use of the music intervention. These studies demonstrate that both pre-performance routines and music can be used as intervention techniques to reduce self-focus and to minimise explicit monitoring, which may in turn reduce the likelihood of choking.

Chapter Review

At the start of this chapter we defined the term choking under pressure (Learning Objective 1) categorising it using two main factors: the occurrence of inferior performance and the striving of the individual to achieve a personally significant goal. We also outlined three potential situations in which choking is most likely to occur in sport (Learning Objective 1). Following this we identified two main theoretical explanations for choking: the conscious processing hypothesis and the catastrophe theory (Learning Objective 2). We outlined that catastrophe theory explains choking by examining the relationship between cognitive anxiety and physiological arousal. In contrast, the conscious processing hypothesis posits that choking is caused by an increase in performance pressure that may cause the individual to revert to consciously monitoring their movements while performing the skill. We discussed two approaches to the role of dispositional levels of self-consciousness in choking (Learning Objective 3). After reviewing the research evidence we acknowledged that although Baumeister's experiments indicated that low self-conscious individuals will be more likely to choke, the sport psychology literature has shown more support for Masters' proposal that high self-conscious individuals will be more susceptible to choking. Finally, we examined how we might be able to prevent choking under pressure. In discussing this we outlined what is meant by ironic mental processes and explicit learning and why these may cause difficulties for an individual who is choking under pressure (Learning Objective 4). Nevertheless we were able to identify potential strategies for reducing the likelihood of choking in sport such as pre-performance routines and the use of music (Learning Objective 5).

Learning Activity 10.4
Test your understanding

1. Explain what is meant by the term choking under pressure and identify when this is most likely to occur in sport.
2. Outline why choking occurs in sport using two theoretical perspectives.
3. Identify why some individuals may be more susceptible to choking than others.
4. Outline possible methods of reducing the likelihood of choking and identify possible barriers to their effectiveness.

Further Reading

Janelle, CM (1999) Ironic mental processes in sport: Implications for sport psychologists. *The Sport Psychologist*, 13: 201–220.
This paper provides a clear outline of theory on ironic mental processes in sport.

Masters, RSW (1992) Knowledge, knerves and knowhow: The role of explicit versus implicit knowledge in the breakdown of a complex motor skill under pressure. *British Journal of Psychology*, 83: 343–358.
This paper details Masters' experiment in which participants developed a golf putting skill either explicitly or implicitly and were then tested in stressful conditions.

Mullen, R and Hardy, L (2000) State anxiety and motor performance: Testing the conscious processing hypothesis. *Journal of Sports Sciences*, 18: 785–799.
This paper extends Masters' earlier experiment by also examining Eysenck's (1992) processing efficiency theory.

Chapter 11
Coping with adversity: injury and burnout

Learning Objectives

This chapter is designed to help you be able to:

1. explain key models outlining psychological causes of sports injury and athletes' responses to injury;
2. explain key psychosocial models of burnout and related research;
3. identify interventions to help athletes to cope with injury and burnout.

Introduction

At some point in their career, most athletes will be faced with adversity or challenges to overcome such as a serious injury or a period of burnout. In this chapter we consider key models that have been offered to understand these challenges from a psychosocial perspective (incorporating psychological and social factors), and discuss research that has examined these models. We also consider the practical interventions that can be used to help athletes to deal with these challenges.

Sports injury

> ### Reflection Point
>
> Think back to a time when you incurred a relatively serious sporting injury (i.e. one that occurred because of training or competing in sport and prevented you from taking part for at least 2–3 weeks). Describe how and when your injury occurred, including the stage of the competitive season and your athletic career, whether you were experiencing any key life events at the time and anything else you think is important in explaining why your injury occurred. If you are fortunate never to have experienced an injury, talk to someone who has and try to obtain answers to the questions above to allow you to describe their injury occurrence.

Psychological causes of sports injury

Although the majority of sporting injuries are caused by physical factors (e.g. collision with another player) or repetition of movement patterns leading to overuse injuries (Andersen and Williams, 1988), psychological factors are also thought to influence whether or not an athlete sustains a sporting injury. Williams and Andersen (1998) posited a model to explain how psychological factors may play a role in the occurrence of acute sports injury. A brief explanation of this model follows and then a hypothetical case study is presented to illustrate this model in more detail.

Central to this model is the suggestion that an athlete is more likely to sustain an injury when they are stressed. An athlete's response to stress may include psychological and physiological elements which can be detrimental to performance, such as attention disruption (distractability or a narrowed attentional field), increased muscle tension or poor audition detection. An athlete interprets an event as stressful if it has important consequences for them, such as team selection, and if they feel that the demands of the situation outweigh the resources they have to deal with these demands, such as being played out of position during team trials. The likelihood of an athlete interpreting a sporting event or situation as stressful is influenced by a number of psychological factors:

- the athlete's personality (low self-esteem, high competitive trait anxiety, an external locus of control, high achievement motivation and a low level of coherence and hardiness, where the athlete approaches events as threats and not challenges, and, less stable personal factors such as a negative mood state and the absence of a positive state of mind);
- the athlete's history of stressors (previous injury possibly causing fear of re-injury, a high level of daily hassles or experiencing a stressful life event such as a divorce);
- the athlete's coping resources (their use of adaptive coping behaviours, social support, stress management strategies and mental skills).

The final element of the model proposes that psychological interventions (such as imagery, relaxation and cognitive restructuring) can be used to help athletes to modify their responses to stress (such as increased muscular tension) and their stress appraisals to reinterpret potentially stressful sporting situations as challenges and not threats.

Return to your personal example of injury and consider if any of these factors in Williams and Andersen's (1998) model contributed to the occurrence of your own injury.

Case Study 11.1
Psychological causes of sports injury

John is a 20-year-old university student who has recently been invited for the first time to national Under 21 squad trials. Unlike some of his team-mates who have been invited and who relish this challenge, John becomes highly anxious about the trials. He is worried that if he isn't selected, he will let his parents and his coach down and that he might blow his chance of gaining a place on a national squad. To prepare for the trials he increases his training volume, supplementing club fitness, weights and technical training sessions with his own sessions in the weights room and on the pitch each week. As John is a final year student with an ambition of achieving a good degree, his extra training is eating into the time he has available to study and he is beginning to fall behind with his university work. His parents are currently working abroad and while he can talk to them and gain their support remotely, he misses the reassurance he gets from being with them in person. John has little knowledge or experience of sport psychology and is unaware of the best strategies he could use to help him to deal with the stress he is experiencing.

*With squad trials two weeks away and an important assignment deadline looming John's old
shoulder injury begins to niggle in one of his extra weight training sessions. During club training
that week John is tired from trying to combine his extra training with studying and is not paying full
attention to the coach's instructions about the training drill. His mind is preoccupied with avoiding
a full blown shoulder injury and with the work he needs to do on his assignment after training. As a
result he takes a wrong turn during the drill and collides with a team-mate who is charging in the
opposite direction, dislocating his previously injured shoulder.*

Research examining psychological causes of sports injury

Some evidence supports the role of psychological risk factors for sports injury proposed by Williams and
Andersen (1998). A prospective study of 845 elite athletes from a range of sports indicated that 67 per
cent sustained an injury over a 12-month period. These athletes reported significantly greater life stress and
mood state disturbance than those who did not sustain an injury during this time (Galambos *et al.*, 2005).
In another study, 1430 female football players were surveyed concerning their injuries in the two months
prior to the competitive season, and during this period, a similar percentage (70 per cent) sustained an
injury (Steffen *et al.*, 2009). They also reported their goal orientation, perceived motivational climate, life
stresses, sport performance trait anxiety and the coping strategies they used. Of these, a perceived mastery
climate and life stresses were significant risk factors for injury, and, as Williams and Andersen's model
predicts, players with a previous injury to the same site or region injured during the study period presented
twice the risk of being injured as players without a similar injury history.

Psychological and emotional responses to sports injury

Reflection Point

Return once more to your personal experience of injury. You have considered the potential
psychological causes of your injury, now consider your response to the injury. Think about how and
why your injury affected you:

- socially (e.g. your relationships with others);
- personally (e.g. your view of yourself);
- emotionally (did your emotions change? How and why?);
- in other areas of your life (e.g. work or academic studies).

Did you seek or receive any help or use any strategies to help you to deal with the effects of your injury? Did
any of your responses to your injury change over time? If so, can you identify any reasons why? Make a note
of your responses to these questions as we'll revisit them later.

Researchers in sport psychology are also interested in the answers to these questions and, in doing so,
have developed or applied models from other areas of psychology to attempt to explain and understand

psychological and emotional responses to sports injury. The most widely used and empirically supported of these is Wiese-Bjornstal *et al.*'s (1998) Integrated Response Model (e.g. Anderson *et al.*, 2004; Figure 11.1).

You may recognise the top portion of this model as this is Williams and Andersen's (1998) stress-based model of psychological predictors of injury. Wiese-Bjornstal and her colleagues have integrated this model, along with two other key approaches that have been used to understand psychological responses to injury: grief and cognitive appraisal. The cognitive appraisal approach is explained in relation to the Integrated Response Model below. Briefly, Kübler-Ross' (1969) model of the grief response describes how people respond when bereaved or suffering from terminal illness. They progress (and often regress) through different stages in their response: denial and isolation, anger, depression and acceptance. As you can see in Figure 11.1, this grief response is viewed as one of a number of emotional responses to sports injury in the Integrated Response Model. We do not have the space to consider this model in detail in this chapter but you can find out more about it in Walker *et al.* (2007) listed in the further reading at the end of the chapter.

Before we discuss the Integrated Response Model, let us return to our case study, John.

Case Study 11.2
More about John . . .

Initially, John is emotionally devastated by his injury and experiences a range of negative emotions: anger at himself for not paying attention in training; anger at his team-mate for training so aggressively; frustration at his bad luck at being injured at such a crucial time; and feeling hopeless as his injury cannot be rehabilitated in time for the trials. He feels depressed and, with his family abroad, misses the social support that he needs from them.

John cannot bring himself to attend training sessions and although his coach and team-mates visited him to check on his wellbeing at first, they are now busy with their own lives. He sought help from a sports therapist who provided him with a clear diagnosis of his injury and a rehabilitation programme to follow. He lacks motivation, however, to complete his rehabilitation exercises and despairs at the amount of time it will take him to recover fully and compete again. He feels lost as prior to his injury his days revolved around training and although he now has more time to work on his university assignments he is struggling to find the motivation to do so. The pain he experiences in his shoulder often prevents him from sleeping, meaning that he has difficulty concentrating when he does attempt to study. His thoughts are preoccupied with his injury; he constantly blames himself and worries about his loss of form and fitness, experiencing regret over a perceived pivotal opportunity in his rugby career.

As this is a non-normative transition, not all athletes will experience injury and not all will respond as John has but athletes will typically experience some negative cognitions, emotions or behaviours following a sports injury. John's response provides a good illustration of the proposals made in the Integrated Response Model as we can see in Figure 11.1.

Following sports injury, which, as we have seen, is often underpinned by stress, the athlete's response to his or her injury is influenced by personal and situational factors related to the athlete and their injury. Figure 11.1 lists a whole host of personal factors that could influence the athlete's response. In John's case, the most relevant of these might be: perceived cause, coping skills and athletic identity. Of the situational factors listed in Figure 11.1, the most relevant might be: time in season, practice versus

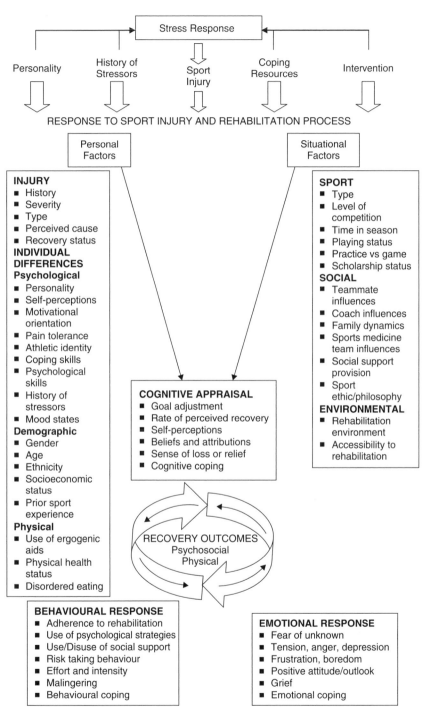

Figure 11.1 Integrated Response Model to sports injury. Reprinted with permission from Taylor & Francis from Wiese-Bjornstal, DM, Smith, AM, Shaffer, SM and Morrey, MA (1998) An integrated model of response to sport injury: psychological and social dynamics. Journal of Applied Sport Psychology, *10: 46–69.*

game, social support provision and/or family dynamics. Combined, these personal and situational factors influence the first of the three types of responses included in the Integrated Response Model: the athlete's cognitive appraisal of the injury. In John's case, these include: a sense of loss, attributing blame for the injury to himself, and to some degree, his team-mate, lack of cognitive coping (e.g. preoccupation with the injury) and a slow rate of perceived recovery. His cognitive appraisals are therefore maladaptive, partially because of influencing personal and situational factors (such as a strong athletic identity as a rugby player leading to a sense of loss, blaming himself for the injury, an inability to deal with stress, sustaining the injury in an inconsequential training session prior to important trials, and lacking social support from his coach, team-mates and family). These cognitive appraisals influence both his emotional and behavioural responses to his injury: feeling anger at himself and others for causing the injury, grief at his sense of loss, frustration and depression about his recovery rate and therefore not adhering to his rehabilitation.

Cognitive appraisals, emotional and behavioural responses interact to influence the athlete's recovery, represented as a dynamic process in the centre of the model as outcomes can be positive such as coping with the injury and negative (e.g. lack of coping). These can change over time, if, for instance, a setback occurs in the athlete's rehabilitation, and take both psychosocial and physical forms. These do not necessarily progress at the same rate, hence, an athlete may be recovered physically but not psychologically (e.g. they may fear re-injury on their return to competition).

Some research lends support for this model but these studies do have their limitations (e.g. failure to explore the full injury experience; Walker *et al.*, 2007). As such, more research is needed to verify its proposals, but at present the Integrated Response Model offers the most complete picture of the athlete's psychological, emotional and behavioural response to sports injury (Walker *et al.*, 2007).

Reflection Point

Think back to your responses to your own sports injury. How do these compare with those identified in the Integrated Response Model? Use this model to explain your responses and their relationships to a partner.

Coping with injury: psychological strategy use during rehabilitation

In their Integrated Response Model, Wiese-Bjornstal *et al.* (1998) suggest that athletes can use psychological skills training strategies to modify cognitive appraisals of their injury and thus help to manage their emotional and behavioural responses. Many athletes consult with a sport psychologist to do so, such as the injured female footballer discussed in a consultancy case study presented by Walker *et al.* (2004). She sustained a head injury while heading the ball in competition and although physically recovered she experienced re-injury anxiety. To help her to overcome this anxiety they used a technique known as systematic desensitisation, where the athlete learnt to replace her anxiety response with a more appropriate response, in this case, using a form of progressive muscular relaxation (Jacobson, 1938). This involves relaxing and tensing muscle groups so that the athlete becomes aware of these two different physical states. They are then able to recognise and relax tense muscles to get rid of unwanted muscle tension in the future. She progressed in stages from relatively anxiety-free situations (i.e. heading the ball she had fed to herself) to a situation that provoked maximum anxiety (i.e. heading the ball in competition against the opposition player who caused the injury). She used imagery (see Chapter 13) to recreate each situation safely in her head until the situation no longer provoked anxiety, then practised coping with anxiety-provoking scenarios in training and eventually competition.

Despite their inclusion in the Integrated Response Model and use in applied real life examples, research in the use of psychological skills to help athletes to cope with the repercussions of and recovery from sports injury is still limited. Some research does exist, however, and here we consider two studies which both investigated the use of imagery during rehabilitation from sports injury but with very different methodologies and purposes.

Christakou *et al.* (2007) conducted an experimental study involving 20 injured athletes undergoing physical therapy, half of whom also attended 12 individual imagery sessions. In these sessions the athletes imaged themselves performing the rehabilitation exercises they had performed in their physical therapy session immediately prior to this. The focus of the study was on physical recovery indices (functional use, stability and dynamic balance). Although the imagery group only showed significantly greater post-intervention performance on one of the functional use tests (muscular endurance) these results provide some support for the use of imagery as an adjunctive (additional) intervention for aiding athletes' physical recovery from injury.

Imagery can also be used to help athletes' psychological recovery from injury, as shown in a case study involving multiple interviews throughout the rehabilitation of an elite injured athlete (Hare *et al.*, 2008). Changes in the focus and function of the athlete's imagery as he progressed through his rehabilitation are illustrated below.

Early rehabilitation	Rehearsal of rehabilitation exercises	Functions of this imagery were to boost confidence of eventual return to competition and to cope with pain
Mid rehabilitation	Rehearsal of sport-specific movements	Functions of this imagery were to maintain confidence of eventual return to competition and motivation to adhere to rehabilitation
End of rehabilitation	Rehearsal of performing in the competitive environment including all its salient characteristics (e.g. spectators)	The function of this imagery was to facilitate excitement at the return to competition
Return to training and competition	Rehearsal of competitive routine	The function of this imagery was to feel relaxed and confident about competing again

Learning Activity 11.1

Read through John's response to his injury as described in the case study above. Highlight the key psychological, emotional and behavioural problems that John might benefit from addressing to help him cope with this non-normative transition. Produce a table and list these in the first column. In the second column briefly identify any strategies that you think might help John to cope with these specific problems. Draw on your own and others' experiences of coping with injury and any strategies that we have discussed in this or other chapters that you think may be of help. The table on page 202 gives some possible responses you may have identified; these strategies are not discussed in detail here as they are explored in more depth in the other sport psychology chapters. Obviously we would not implement all of these strategies at once but at different stages of John's rehabilitation depending on which problem is in most need of attention at that time.

Athlete burnout

Learning Activity 11.2

Using newspaper, magazine or internet sources, find two examples of athletes or teams who have been said to have burnt out or have been suggested as being in danger of burnout. Locate as much information as you can about the athletes and record the following information from your case studies:

- how burnout has been defined in the article;
- the suggested symptoms of the athlete's/team's burnt out (or potentially burnt out) state;
- the reasons suggested for the athlete's/team's burnt out (or potentially burnt out) state.

What is burnout?

It is likely that your case studies of burnt out athletes referred to the athletes' physical and mental exhaustion, their loss of enthusiasm and motivation for their sport and performing below their usual standard in competition. These are the three key components of athlete burnout (Raedeke, 1997). These components are discussed below and items from the Athlete Burnout Questionnaire (Raedeke and Smith, 2001, page 306) are included with each description to illustrate how each component is measured.

- *Sport devaluation*: In contrast with previously, the athlete no longer sees their sport as their main priority and concern, measured using items such as: 'I don't care as much about my [athlete's sport] performance as I used to.' This may lead to feelings of frustration and disillusionment.
- *Reduced sense of accomplishment*: The athlete's competitive performance deteriorates below previously

achieved levels causing resentment as the athlete sees others still achieving. This component is measured using items such as: 'I am not performing up to my ability in [athlete's sport].'

- *Physical and emotional exhaustion*: The athlete has no energy and is extremely tired, both physically and mentally, due to intense training and competition schedules, depicted in the following item: 'I am exhausted by the mental and physical demands of [athlete's sport].'

Evidence from the field has confirmed that these are elements of athlete burnout (e.g. Gustafsson *et al.*, 2008). Raedeke *et al.* (2002) interviewed coaches of young swimmers in the United States who suggested that these were all signs that they used to spot burnout in the athletes they coached, in addition to the athlete's withdrawal from the sport both mentally (e.g. interacting less with team-mates) and physically (e.g. missing training sessions). Similarly, male professional rugby union players in New Zealand discussed suffering from these elements of burnout, proposing that reduced personal accomplishment and the low professional efficacy that results from this are key elements of their experiences of burnout (Cresswell and Eklund, 2006). Incidentally, athletes are not the only sports people who can experience burnout; coaches, officials and trainers are all susceptible to burnout and studies have found evidence of burnout in these individuals (for instance, see Kelley *et al.*'s (1999) research with head tennis coaches in the United States). Here though we focus on athletes, as discussing burnout in all these different individuals is beyond the scope of this chapter.

Why do athletes burn out?

Before considering models that have been used to understand and explain why athletes burn out from sport, let us examine some of the research into athlete burnout to start to build up a picture of how these might look.

Athlete stress and burnout

In early research, young golfers discussed stress caused either by excessive or insufficient challenge and demands as potential causes of burnout (Cohn, 1990). Similarly, young tennis players who were burnt out described the physical strain from too much training and competing and social psychological strain, deriving from pressure from others and pressure placed on themselves, as some of the key reasons for their burnt out state (Gould *et al.*, 1996). Athletes who place undue pressure on themselves to perform well are often perfectionists, and this personality characteristic, along with high ego and low task orientation, low perceived ability, a high performance and low mastery climate (see Chapter 8) is part of a maladaptive profile that has been associated with higher levels of burnout in Olympic squad and elite junior athletes (Lemyre *et al.*, 2008).

Athlete entrapment and burnout

Another key theme evident in research that has investigated athlete burnout has been labelled 'entrapment'. To illustrate this idea, consider the usual characteristics of an elite athlete's sporting career, and possibly your own career in sport. The athlete trains and competes for long hours from an early age, leaving no time for other interests or alternative activities, often with substantial emotional, financial and time investment from significant others such as parents and coaches. The majority of athletes who are not burnt out enjoy training and competing in their sport and perceive that the costs of doing so (e.g. time and sacrificing other experiences) are outweighed by the benefits (e.g. achievement, self-esteem, enjoyment).

Entrapment has been suggested as one of the factors leading to the burnout of elite athletes from a range of sports. Their entrapment was characterised by high levels of investment, a persisting desire to achieve, social constraints, such as feeling in debt to their parents, and restraints such as having to train and potential loss of friends or moving schools if they quit the sport (Gustaffson *et al.*, 2008). Weiss and Weiss (2003, 2006) conducted studies with adolescent female gymnasts which examined entrapment and offer an initial longitudinal perspective on burnout. Using a range of questionnaire measures their first study revealed three groups of gymnasts:

- *Attracted gymnasts* ($n = 66$) who enjoyed their sport, perceived benefits as high and costs as low and reported high levels of investment and few more attractive alternatives to being an athlete and participating in gymnastics.
- *Entrapped athletes* ($n = 14$) who did not enjoy their sport, perceived benefits as low and costs as high and reported moderate levels of investment, high levels of social constraints and a perception that a number of alternative activities were more attractive than their sport.
- *Vulnerable athletes* ($n = 44$) who, in relation to the attracted and entrapped athletes, reported moderate levels of all these factors with the exceptions of high social constraints and low levels of investment.

The following year, 86 per cent of these athletes were still competing in gymnastics, with most of the drop-outs coming from the entrapped group and those confirming their status as 'vulnerable'. Although 50 per cent of this group had moved into the attracted group, 50 per cent had moved into the entrapped group (Weiss and Weiss, 2006).

Similar athlete profiles were identified in an earlier study of young swimmers, in addition to a fourth group who reported low levels of burnout and commitment to their sport and were therefore more likely to drop out than burn out from swimming (Raedeke, 1997). Enthusiastic swimmers (analogous to the attracted gymnasts in Weiss and Weiss, 2003) displayed high levels of enjoyment and commitment to swimming and low levels of burnout. Obligated swimmers (analogous to the vulnerable group in Weiss and Weiss) reported moderate levels of burnout, swim identity and personal investment in swimming, along with low personal control and high social constraints. Malcontented swimmers (analogous to entrapped swimmers in Weiss and Weiss) reported high levels of burnout and social constraints but low levels of personal control, investment and attractive alternatives other than participating in swimming.

In addition to the entrapment characteristics we noted at the start of this section, in Raedeke's (1997) results, we begin to see evidence of other factors that may lead to burnout: the athlete's perceived personal control and their athletic identity. We consider these in the following section.

Athlete empowerment, identity and burnout

During interviews, adolescent athletes who identified themselves as burnt out discussed a perceived lack of control, or empowerment, over their lives and their sporting participation. This was largely attributed to the organisation of sport which determined, for instance, their training and competition intensities and schedules and even their lifestyles (Coakley, 1992). Related to this, they felt they had missed out on opportunities their peers had had to gain a range of different experiences. Think of all the different things that you and your friends do and the different activities you tried and maybe decided you did not like, such as playing in a band, conservation work or joining a photography club. These athletes suggested that because all their time and energy had been focused on their sport, they missed out on opportunities to develop in ways other than as an athlete. Thus, their self-concept, the way they and others viewed the athlete, centred solely on them as an athlete, resulting in a unidimensional self-concept (see Chapter 3). They also felt in debt to others, like their coach and their parents, who had invested a great deal in the athlete's sporting career. Thus they felt obliged to remain in their sport to show their gratitude for the sacrifices made by others.

More recent research supports these qualitative data; adolescent athletes who had been involved in their sport since 6 years of age and who reported higher levels of all three components of burnout had less positive personal identities (Strachan *et al.*, 2009). In addition, athletes who reported higher levels of reduced personal accomplishment felt less empowered to take personal control over their lives and those who reported higher levels of sport devaluation felt they received less support from significant others.

Models of burnout

Based on the research discussed above and the athlete case studies you identified at the start of the chapter we can compile a summary of the factors that contribute to athlete burnout (see Box 11.1). Have a go at compiling your own list and compare the factors you have identified with the key factors presented below.

Box 11.1 Key factors contributing to burnout

Excessive pressure/stress	Insufficient challenge	Physical strain
Psychosocial strain	Perfectionism	Limited identity development
Organisational and social constraints	Lack of empowerment	Perfectionism
Low enjoyment and perceived benefits of sport	High costs and moderate–high levels of investment	High ego orientation/performance climate and low task orientation/mastery climate

---

These factors reflect the key elements of the three main models that have been employed to attempt to explain and understand athlete burnout: the Cognitive–Affective Stress Model, the Empowerment Model and the Investment Model.

Cognitive–Affective Stress Model of burnout (Smith, 1986)

In Smith's (1986) model, stress is at the heart of burnout. Smith (1986) proposed that, as burnout is underpinned by stress, which is considered a process, burnout should also be viewed as a process and one which includes comparable elements to the stress process. Figure 11.2 depicts this model of burnout with

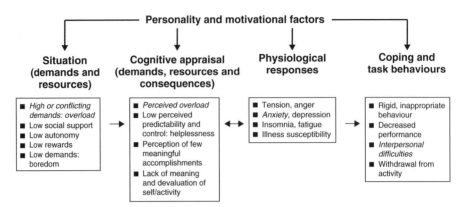

Figure 11.2   Cognitive–Affective Stress Model of burnout (Reprinted with permission from Human Kinetics from Smith, RE (1986) Toward a cognitive-affective model of athletic burnout. Journal of Sport Psychology, 8: 36–50.)

basic elements of the stress process in bold and factors highlighted in italics which we use to illustrate the process of burnout.

If the sporting situation places a high demand or overload on the athlete, he or she appraises this situation as a perceived overload, for instance an athlete who feels they cannot meet their coach's expectations. This may result in anxiety and interpersonal difficulties (e.g. resenting the coach). Each stage of this burnout process is influenced by the athlete's motivation and personality, so unlike an athlete with low competitive trait anxiety an athlete who is high in competitive trait anxiety will perceive a high demand as overload, and will therefore be more likely to experience burnout.

An important point made by Smith (1986) is that burnout results from a chronic build up of stress, that is, over a long period of time, and does not just happen overnight as a result of an acute, short-term stressor. This was emphasised by the swimming coaches who were interviewed by Raedeke and his colleagues (2002) who suggested that without a long-term commitment to sport, dropout and not burnout occurs.

Empowerment Model

In his Empowerment Model Coakley (1992) views burnout as stemming not from the stress created by competitive sport and the individual's inability to deal with this stress but from the way in which sport, in particular youth sport, is organised. As we noted above when we considered his research findings on which this model is based, this model describes two key interrelated elements that are related to burnout in young athletes:

- *Social organisation of sport*: The athlete has no control over what they do (or, low autonomy), to try out new activities, to develop in ways unrelated to sport and to do the things their peers do. These restrictions are influenced by the power relationships that predicate in youth sport where adults make important decisions about what the athlete does and does not do, with the athlete's life and lifestyle focused on achieving the goal of becoming an elite athlete.
- *Restricted identity development*: Burnt out athletes have had no opportunity to develop anything other than an identity as an athlete because of their constrained set of life experiences. It is important that we

explore different identities as we develop to prevent this phenomenon known as identity foreclosure. Not surprisingly athletes with a unidimensional identity may start to doubt themselves and the future value of their hard earned athletic skills and competencies, and are less able to deal with the stress that accompanies athletic competition.

Investment Model

The third model of burnout we consider is Schmidt and Stein's (1991) Investment Model. Similar to Coakley (1992), these authors do not deny that stress plays a role in burnout but argue that stress is not the sole cause. Most athletes experience stress at one time or another but, as we saw in Weiss and Weiss' (2003) study of adolescent gymnasts, the number of individuals who do not experience burnout far outweighs the number who do. Schmidt and Stein propose that there are three different types of athletes who display different profiles. They identify athletes who are:

- committed to their sport because they enjoy it as they perceive that their sport offers low costs, high or increasing rewards, they gain high levels of satisfaction, have made high levels of investment in their sport and perceive few attractive alternatives to their sporting involvement;
- committed to their sport but are burnt out as they perceive that their sport offers increasing costs, decreasing rewards and satisfaction, they are decreasing their investment in the sport and gain high levels of satisfaction, have made high levels of investment in their sport and perceive that there are increasing attractive alternatives to their sporting involvement;
- likely to drop out of their sport as they perceive that their sport offers increasing costs, decreasing rewards and satisfaction, their investment in their sport is high or increasing and they perceive that there are few attractive alternatives to their sporting involvement.

The critical differences, according to Schmidt and Stein, between potential drop outs and burnt out athletes who remain committed to their sport, are their levels of investment and attractive alternatives to their sporting involvement. The burnt out athlete feels entrapped in their sport and that they have no other choice but to continue their involvement.

Although we have considered the proposals of these different models of burnout in isolation from each other, in reality, it is likely that the different factors within each model overlap and combine with each other to influence whether or not an athlete develops burnout. The example below is a hypothetical case study which illustrates how this might be the case.

Case Study 11.3
Sarah

Sarah is a 17-year-old elite junior high jumper who trains 6 days a week with a day off to catch up on her college work. She used to love training and used to feel a real sense of accomplishment after every session. Over the past 4 or 5 months, however, Sarah feels like she's going through the motions: training is rigorous but undemanding. She is also gaining decreasing satisfaction from the competitions she enters; these are dictated to her largely by her athletics club and it feels like she's been there before: the same venues, the same competitors, the same outcomes, since she started competing seriously at 13. Consequently, she finds it difficult to get excited about

*competing and winning and feels like she's losing out on opportunities to do normal things, like go
to the cinema with friends or develop interests other than athletics. She's beginning to get down
about her high jumping and is starting to feel tense in training and competitions. She has regularly
started to miss training, which can be partly, but not completely, attributed to the increased
number of colds and infections she seems to have picked up lately. She doesn't want to leave
athletics as she has spent so many years training to reach her current level and being an athlete is
how she and others see her.*

Preventing burnout

Based on the models of burnout and supporting research that we have considered we can suggest a number
of ways to try to prevent burnout in athletes. These strategies could be athlete-focused, helping them to
develop a task orientation, stress management skills or recognising and reducing maladaptive perfectionist
tendencies that may lead to self-imposed pressure. We could focus our attention on the social environment,
helping coaches to emphasise a mastery oriented climate, increase athlete autonomy and offer opportunities
for the athlete to have similar experiences to their peers and develop aspects of themselves not centred on
their athletic identity. We could also attempt to ensure that the athlete gains satisfaction and some of the
rewards they value from their sporting involvement, and parents and coaches could de-emphasise their
personal costs of the athlete's involvement in sport.

Although founded in theory, these suggestions have not been tested empirically as there is a dearth
of research examining ways to prevent and help athletes to cope with burnout. A study by Cresswell and
Eklund (2007) with male professional rugby players in New Zealand provides some insight into strategies
that may be helpful in preventing burnout, at the same time, supporting some of these theoretically based
proposals. Although some of the players who were interviewed had experienced burnout others had not
and, based on their positive experiences, some suggestions of how to prevent burnout can be made:

- open and honest communication with management and coaches;
- trust and confidence in the support team;
- fair treatment for all players and availability of appropriate opportunities in rugby;
- a perception of low playing demands;
- a perception of progress in one's rugby career;
- social support (within and outside rugby);
- positive momentum in activities outside rugby;
- flexible responsibilities outside rugby.

Learning Activity 11.3

Revisit the case studies you located at the start of this section of famous athletes who have or are
said to have burnt out. Use the three models of burnout we have examined to interpret your case
studies. Which model best explains why the athletes burned out? Are different elements from the
three models supported by your case studies?

Chapter Review

We first discussed Williams and Andersen's (1998) stress-based model to explain how psychological factors may increase the athlete's risk of sustaining a sports injury and Wiese-Bjornstal *et al.*'s (1998) model to explain how emotional, behavioural and cognitive responses to injury interact to influence psychosocial and physical recovery from injury (Learning Objective 1). Next we considered burnout, first examining research that has been conducted into athlete burnout and from this identified key explanations for burnout as stress, entrapment and restricted identity development (Learning Objective 2). Theoretical models which propose these as key underpinning factors were then discussed: Smith's (1986) Cognitive–Affective Stress Model, Coakley's (1992) Empowerment Model, and Schmidt and Stein's (1991) Investment Model (Learning Objective 2). Throughout the chapter we discussed interventions to help athletes to cope with injury, such as imagery (Learning Objective 3). There are really no studies to speak of that have examined interventions to prevent or treat burnout. We therefore discussed suggested strategies for preventing burnout, such as social support and open communication within teams that are based on players' positive experiences in sport and theoretical predictions (Learning Objective 3).

Learning Activity 11.4
Test your understanding

1. Identify the four psychological factors that Williams and Andersen (1998) proposed can increase the risk of sustaining a sports injury through increased stress. Provide two examples of each factor.
2. From memory, try to reproduce Wiese-Bjornstal *et al.*'s (1998) model of responses to injury, including as many influencing factors and responses that you can.
3. For each of the models of burnout that we have discussed, describe one study that lends support for its proposals.
4. Identify similarities and differences between the three models of burnout that we have discussed.

Further Reading

- For further discussion on models of sports injury:

Walker, N, Thatcher, J and Lavallee, D (2007) Psychological responses to injury in competitive sport: A critical review. *Journal of the Royal Society for the Promotion of Health*, 127: 174–180.
In addition to reviewing grief, cognitive appraisal and the integrated response models of sports injury, Walker *et al.* (2007) present a critical discussion, based on their own longitudinal research with injured athletes (2004), of the Integrated Response Model and the proposed relationships between the different

responses in the model. They speculate on modifications and developments of the model that stem from their research observations but that clearly require further empirical examination.

- For a discussion of the use of Self-Determination Theory to understand the precursors of burnout:

Lonsdale, C, Hodge, K, and Rose, E (2009) Athlete burnout in elite sport: A self-determination perspective. *Journal of Sports Sciences*, 27: 785–795.

In this chapter we have examined models developed specifically to explain why burnout occurs; however, researchers have begun to examine if theories in other areas can offer a different perspective on understanding the causes of burnout. This paper applies Self-Determination Theory to examine the relationships between need satisfaction, self-determination and athlete burnout.

Chapter 12
Achieving peak performance and excellence in competition

Learning Objectives

This chapter is designed to help you be able to:

1. describe the psychological characteristics associated with excellence and peak performance in sport;
2. explain what is meant by 'mental toughness';
3. discuss, using supporting research, whether mental toughness is innate or whether it is learned;
4. understand the psychological concept of flow.

Introduction

The aim of this chapter is to discuss the key concepts of peak performance and excellence in sport. At the height of peak performance and excellence we would expect that an athlete has refined their technique, achieved optimal strength and conditioning, is fully fit, and that they would be psychologically prepared for competition. Throughout this chapter we will consider what it means to be psychologically prepared for elite level competition, and how sport psychology may be used to help an athlete achieve this.

Most of us will have watched the Olympic Games on television. This is an event that may be considered the pinnacle of many athletes' careers and a central goal and focus for those involved in many elite sports. Many young athletes grow up dreaming of an Olympic medal or imagining standing on the top of the podium while their national anthem rings out. Yet when we watch these athletes live on television, stepping out into the Olympic stadium, we may begin to ask ourselves some key questions about peak performance and excellence. First, what is it about those athletes who achieve Olympic glory that separates them from those who don't quite make it? For every athlete who has achieved Olympic success there are many more who achieved reserve places, who took part in Olympic trials, who represented their county or region, or who have played at club level. So just what is it about that Olympic level athlete that has taken them all the way to the top of their sport? Olusoga *et al.* (2009) further suggest that coaches' expectations for those who are selected to represent their country are to win medals; therefore it is not only about qualifying for an Olympics but achieving optimal performance at the Olympics. To answer these questions about peak performance and excellence there are three main themes in this chapter:

- excellence/peak performance;
- mental toughness;
- flow.

We begin by examining what is meant by excellence and peak performance. We examine research that has sought to identify the psychological constructs and characteristics that will lead to peak performance. It has been frequently cited that mental toughness is a core quality of success in sport (e.g. Bull *et al.*, 2005; Thelwell *et al.*, 2005, 2010a). In this chapter we explore the research evidence that suggests whether mental toughness is innate, or whether this is something that can be learned. If mental toughness can be learned then this suggests that as sport psychologists and coaches we will be able to enhance the mental toughness of the athletes that we work with.

The final section of this chapter examines the literature on the concept of flow. In sport, flow is often described as a time when an individual is completely involved in what they are doing, when they lose self-consciousness and find themselves able to perform optimally. We consider the psychological explanation for flow and examine research that has demonstrated how the flow state may impact on performance.

Understanding peak performance and excellence

Research into peak performance and excellence has sought to uncover those psychological characteristics which are found in the very best elite athletes that enable them to perform and succeed at this level (Krane and Williams, 2006). It has been consistently acknowledged that these psychological characteristics may separate those athletes who truly excel in their sport from those who achieve at an elite level (e.g. Durand-Bush and Samela, 2002; Gould *et al.*, 2002). Maynard (2010) makes an interesting point that: 'for me "elite" is often better defined by attitudes rather than ranking' (page 63). Thus he suggests that being an elite athlete is not only about having the appropriate skills and technique to be able to succeed. In addition to having these skills, he proposes that having the appropriate attitude required for success may be more important to the elite athlete.

Learning Activity 12.1

Before we discuss the research evidence into peak performance and excellence we can make some suggestions about which characteristics may be important.

Pick out at least four elite level athletes from a variety of sports who you perceive to have excelled in their chosen sport. Try to list as many psychological characteristics that you would associate with these athletes. Are there any common characteristics between these athletes? Produce a table to record your thoughts. In the first column write the characteristic, in the second column try to provide an explanation or definition of this characteristic. In the third column write the name of at least one elite athlete who you feel has exhibited this characteristic. An example is completed below for you; see how many more you can think of.

Characteristic	Explanation	Demonstrated by ...
Bouncing back after adversity	Being able to suffer defeat/injury and yet come back stronger	Kelly Holmes

You should have been able to pick out a number of characteristics that are exhibited by elite level athletes. These may have included their emotional responses, their ability to cope, their overall outlook, attitude or expectations and their psychological skills (e.g. imagery, goal setting). The next section examines the research findings that have aimed to establish exactly what these characteristics are.

Researching peak performance and excellence

Consider the research question: What are the main psychological characteristics of elite level performance and how might you go about finding out what these characteristics are?

In general, research has tended to use qualitative methods or mixed methods to answer this question. This has often involved conducting semi-structured interviews with elite level athletes. Initially you may have answered that the proposed research question could be answered by interviewing elite athletes about the characteristics that they possess. However, you may already have noticed a flaw in this approach. It may be suggested that elite athletes may not be aware of which characteristics have led to their success. Consequently an alternative strategy has been to examine differences between more and less successful athletes at high level events.

Early research by Mahoney and Avener (1977) demonstrated that certain psychological characteristics differentiated Olympic male gymnasts from those who failed to make the Olympic team. Mahoney and Avener assessed the patterns and level of arousal of finalists at the 1976 US Men's Olympic gymnastics team trials. Their results demonstrated that qualifiers had higher arousal levels which peaked prior to warm-up whereas non-qualifiers had lower arousal levels and lower overall perceptions of control. The content of pre-competition thoughts was more task specific (a 'self-coaching' emphasis) for the qualifiers, while non-qualifiers used negative statements and had self-doubts. This early research demonstrates some trends emerging, with those who made the Olympic team using different cognitive strategies in their approach to competition in comparison with those who did not make the team.

More recent research has examined personal factors and characteristics of athletes that may influence their preparation and approach to competition, as well as situational or environmental factors that may also impact on success. It is important to recognise that while an athlete may have the optimal psychological characteristics for elite performance there are also external factors that may influence their level of success. For example, factors such as being drawn in a particular lane for a sprinter, a poor decision made by the referee for a football player, or other unexpected and unpredictable stressors may impact on performance (Dugdale *et al.*, 2002; Gould *et al.*, 1999). However, despite the influence of external factors, a number of studies have distinguished elite athletes from non-elite by their psychological qualities (Golby and Sheard, 2004). Further, Holland *et al.* (2010) propose that that elite youth athletes will have perceptions of particular qualities (e.g. adaptability, awareness, determination) that are important to their future sport participation (see further reading at the end of this chapter for more information).

In their review of psychological preparation for Olympic Games performance, Gould and Maynard (2009) present a list of psychological factors that may be associated with Olympic success. They divide these into psychological/emotional states or attributes, cognitive and behavioural strategies, and personal dispositions. Consider these factors in relation to the answers that you have given in Learning Activity 12.1.

- *Psychological/emotional state or attribute*: confidence/self-belief, concentration, determination/motivation/commitment, optimal level of emotions/arousal/anxiety, emotional control, automaticity, motivation-commitment, body awareness, pain management and self-awareness.

- *Cognitive and behavioural strategies*: self-talk, imagery, goal setting, competitive simulations, competitive plans/routines, distraction preparation strategies, mistake management plans, success management plans, enjoyment strategies and emotional control.
- *Personal disposition*: optimism, goal orientation, adaptive perfectionism, competitiveness, sport intelligence, trait hope, locus of control and intrinsic/extrinsic motivation orientation.

Are there any factors in common with those that you identified as important for elite performance? Are there any factors that you did not expect? There are a number of common themes that can be identified in the factors associated with Olympic success outlined by Gould and Maynard.

- *Self-regulation*: Many of the psychological/emotional states are characteristic of an athlete who is able to regulate their emotions such as anxiety and anger.
- *Psychological skills*: These include cognitive and behavioural strategies to enhance performance (we discuss some of these in Chapter 13). Common strategies used by successful Olympians include setting goals, imagery, self-talk, and planning coping strategies for all eventualities (both positive and negative).
- *Personal dispositions*: These include the type and levels of motivation, and the individual's approach to competition (optimistic, hopeful).

While Gould and Maynard present a useful overview of the psychological factors associated with Olympic success they also propose that research needs to identify the interactions between the three factors. For example, how does the athlete's personal disposition influence their use of cognitive and behavioural strategies and how do these then impact on the athlete's psychological/emotional state. More specific questions might be: how does an athlete who is highly optimistic use goal setting and preparation strategies and how might these strategies then impact on that athlete's levels of motivation and commitment.

Orlick (2000) suggests that there are seven key elements that will lead to performance excellence. He depicts these seven elements as a 'wheel of excellence'. According to Orlick each of these elements are important in achieving peak performance and excellence. He explains that the individual must be committed to self-development and achieving their goals. They must be fully focused on the task at hand, and confident in their own potential. They should have positive images of flawless execution as well as feeling mentally ready and fully planned and prepared for their performance. Finally, they should be able to control distractions while performing and be committed to continually reflecting and learning.

Research has most frequently focused on the general psychological characteristics of elite or more successful athletes; however, an alternative approach has been to examine the psychological characteristics required for elite performance in a particular sport. This has included professional golfers (Hellström, 2009), gymnasts (Mahoney and Avener, 1977), wrestlers (Highlen and Bennett, 1979), and cricketers (Sanctuary *et al.*, 2010). While it is accepted that there may be general psychological characteristics that are essential for all elite athletes, there may be more specific characteristics that are deemed particularly relevant for certain sports. For example, Hellström (2009) suggests that a skilled golfer will score highly on positive mood, will consistently evaluate their performance, and will plan and make strategies for all eventualities. For cricketers, however, concentration and flow were highlighted as key psychological aspects of performance (Sanctuary *et al.*, 2010).

Introducing mental toughness

> ## Learning Activity 12.2
>
> Before we being this section on mental toughness, take a few minutes to consider what may be meant by this concept. Mental toughness is a term that we may often use to describe the psychological attributes of certain athletes in sport. You may have used this term when describing one of the qualities of peak performance in the earlier learning activities, but just what do we mean by mental toughness? It may help for you to start by thinking about those athletes who you would consider to be mentally tough. Try to list some examples of athletes who you would deem to be high in mental toughness and others you would deem to be low in mental toughness.
>
> Have a look at the list of athletes who you would deem to be mentally tough. Are there any commonalities between these athletes? Using these commonalities now try to write out your own definition of the term mental toughness

Defining mental toughness

It is somewhat surprising that prior to the last ten years there had been little scientific study of mental toughness. In fact in 2002, Jones *et al.* proposed that mental toughness was probably one of the most used but least understood terms in sport psychology. This is highlighted in a study by Gould *et al.* (1987) which reported that 82 per cent of coaches rated mental toughness as the most important psychological attribute in determining wrestling success. Despite the proposed importance of this construct, just 9 per cent of the coaches in Gould *et al.*'s study deemed that they had been successful in developing or enhancing the mental toughness of the athletes with whom they were working.

In 1995 Loehr published a book on training for mental toughness in sport which included psychological techniques to enhance mental toughness. He suggested that mental toughness was the ability to perform in the upper range of your talent and skill regardless of the circumstances. His book suggested four emotional characteristics of mental toughness:

- flexibility;
- responsiveness;
- psychological strength;
- resilience.

Despite being able to propose such characteristics, early suggestions for enhancing mental toughness generally lacked the necessary scientific rigour and conceptual clarity.

A more recent surge of interest, using both qualitative and quantitative methods, has led to increased clarity of the concept of mental toughness. Jones *et al.* (2002) suggested that mental toughness could be defined as a natural or developed psychological edge that enables mentally tough performers to generally cope better than their opponents with the demands and related pressures that occur at the highest level in sport. Similarly, Gucciardi *et al.* (2009a) suggested that mental toughness is made up of multiple key components, including values, attitudes, cognitions, emotions and behaviours. These components refer to an individual's ability to thrive through challenges, pressures and adversities. Training in mental toughness may therefore aim to increase work ethic, regulate emotions, enhance team cohesion, and encourage tough attitudes and receptivity to criticism (Gucciardi *et al.*, 2009b). The common feature of these definitions of mental toughness is that mental toughness includes the ability to thrive even in adverse situations. Consequently the mentally tough athlete is able to cope better with situations such as defeat, injury, poor calls from a referee, or facing tough opposition than an athlete who is not mentally tough.

Consider the example of our gymnast Sam (introduced in Chapter 8). In order to cope with the pressures associated with being an elite gymnast he will need to be mentally tough. As he begins to compete at a high level he will need to be able to cope with defeat, especially as he increases the ability level of the competitions that he enters. For Sam, being mentally tough may include perceiving difficult competitions as a challenge. As he also has a strict training schedule Sam may need to be able to cope with potential injuries that he may incur. This may include taking a positive attitude towards his rehabilitation and working hard on rehabilitation exercises.

Research Focus

In order to examine mental toughness it was first important to identify the attributes that may contribute to this construct to develop a clear conceptualisation of mental toughness. To do this, Jones *et al.* (2002) conducted one-to-one interviews and focus groups with ten international athletes that discussed the attributes of a mentally tough athlete. Overall, participants identified 12 attributes which were then ranked in order of importance (Table 12.1).

Attribute	Rank
An unshakeable self-belief in your ability to achieve your competition goals	1
Bouncing back from performance set-backs as a result of increased determination	2
An unshakeable self-belief that you possess unique qualities and abilities that make you better than your opponents	3
An insatiable desire and internalised motives to succeed	4=
Remaining fully focused on the task at hand in the face of competition-specific distractions	4=
Regaining psychological control following unexpected, uncontrollable events	6
Pushing back the boundaries of physical and emotional pain while still maintaining technique and effort under distress	7
Accepting that competition anxiety is inevitable and knowing that you can cope with it	8
Thriving on the pressure of competition	9=
Not being adversely affected by others' good and bad performances	9=
Remaining fully focused in the face of personal life distractions	11
Switching a sport focus on and off as required	12

Table 12.1 Twelve attributes of a mentally tough athlete identified in the study by Jones et al. *(2002)*

This research points out that while all of the attributes are an important part of being mentally tough, the ranking procedure suggests that some are clearly more important than others. Self-belief emerged as being most crucial to mental toughness, including the belief in your ability to achieve your goals (ranked first) and the belief in your ability to be better than your opponents (ranked third). Jones *et al.* suggested that the mental toughness attributes that emerged could be placed into the following categories: self-belief, desire and motivation, focus (performance-related), focus (lifestyle-related), dealing with competition pressure (external), and anxiety (internal), and dealing with physical and emotional pain.

The 4 Cs Model

Clough *et al.* (2002) developed the 4Cs model of mental toughness:

- *Control* – (emotional and life) this includes feeling in control of what you are doing and of your environment, being able to handle many things at the same time, and being able to control your emotions.
- *Commitment* – this involves a deep commitment to what you are doing, being able to carry out tasks successfully despite any problems or obstacles that may arise.
- *Challenge* – this includes seeing problems as opportunities, thriving in continually changing environments, and seeking out opportunities for personal development.
- *Confidence* – (in abilities and interpersonal) this includes assertiveness, self-belief, and an unshakeable belief in having the ability to achieve success.

Measuring mental toughness

One of the key tools used to measure mental toughness is the Mental Toughness Questionnaire 48 (MTQ48; Clough *et al.*, 2002). This scale includes 48 items rated using a five-point Likert scale ranging from (1) strongly disagree to (5) strongly agree. These items are structured so that they measure each of the 4Cs. There is research evidence that supports the validity and reliability of the MTQ48. For example, Clough *et al.* (2002) found that participants with high and low levels of mental toughness (using the MTQ48) had a similar perception of the physical demands of a low intensity workload, but when this workload was increased those low in mental toughness perceived significantly higher physical demands than those high in mental toughness. Further, Nicholls *et al.* (2008) found significant relationships between MTQ48 scores, optimism and coping skills. In particular, high levels of mental toughness were associated with more problem- or approach-focused coping strategies (taking action to change the stressor) and less use of avoidance coping (blocking out or avoiding the stressor).

A further, multidimensional measure of mental toughness was developed by Sheard *et al.* (2009), titled the Sports Mental Toughness Questionnaire (SMTQ). Items for the SMTQ were developed by using the raw data themes and quotes that had emerged from previous qualitative research on mental toughness. The SMTQ measures global mental toughness using three subscales: confidence, constancy and control. *Confidence* refers to beliefs in one's ability to achieve personal goals and be better than opponents. *Constancy* reflects the individual's personal responsibility, their determination, their unyielding attitude, and their ability to concentrate. Finally, *control* indicates the perception of being influential and the ability to bring about desired outcomes and control emotions.

In addition to these general measures of mental toughness in sport, some researchers have developed questionnaires that examine mental toughness in specific sports. For example Gucciardi *et al.* (2009a) developed a mental toughness questionnaire for use in Australian football, similarly, Gucciardi and Gordon (2009) developed a specific questionnaire for use in cricket. The development of such questionnaires provides sport-specific measures for mental toughness, however their development also suggests that there will be specific attributes of mental toughness that are important in particular sports. For example, Gucciardi and Gordon (2009) proposed five subscales of mental toughness in cricket: affective intelligence, attentional control, resilience, self-belief and desire to achieve. For Australian football four subscales were proposed: thrive through challenge, sport awareness, tough attitude and desire success (Gucciardi *et al.*, 2009a).

Despite the development of such sport-specific measures, research contends that there are attributes of mental toughness that will be common to all sports. See the further reading at the end of this chapter for further research on measuring mental toughness.

Mental toughness: born or developed?

One of the key debates within the literature on mental toughness is whether mental toughness is born or developed. This is a common theme in psychology and you may have previously read about the nature–nurture debate. Before we present these arguments on the development of mental toughness in more detail consider your own views on this topic. Do you believe that mental toughness is a trait (similar to other personality traits) and so this is an innate characteristic? Or do you believe that mental toughness is something which develops, meaning that as we gain experiences in life we can learn to develop mental toughness? You may wish to consider your own sporting experiences. If you consider yourself to be someone who has a high level of mental toughness then have you always been this way, or were there any life experiences that led you to become more mentally tough? If you consider yourself to have low levels of mental toughness why do you think this is? Have you ever attempted to develop your levels of mental toughness?

When we initially defined mental toughness at the start of this section we referred to Jones *et al.*'s (2002) definition which suggested that mental toughness could be defined as a natural or developed psychological edge. While this indicates the potential importance of both nature and nurture, the research literature on mental toughness continues to present two perspectives to this argument.

The suggestion that mental toughness can be acquired has led to an increase in research investigating how this construct can be developed in athletes. Connaughton *et al.* (2010) propose that there are a number of factors that may influence the development of mental toughness. These factors include: skill mastery, competitiveness, successes, international competitive experience, education and advice, the use of psychological skills, access to an understanding social support network, and reflective practice. Consequently an athlete may develop their mental toughness by gaining competitive experience, by mastering complex skill and by achieving in their sport. Their study also supports the proposition that experiencing critical incidents (positive and negative) can act as a catalyst to mental toughness. Positive critical incidents (such as talent recognition) were found to enhance self-belief and motivation. On the other hand, negative critical incidents (such as being involved in an accident) prompted the individual to reappraise their priorities and consequently increased their mental toughness. Findings from this study not only support the assertion that mental toughness can be developed, but also that it can fluctuate and therefore needs to be maintained.

The other side to this argument proposes that mental toughness is a trait characteristic which is innate. To explain this stance, mental toughness has been linked to the concept of hardiness (Kobasa, 1979). The two concepts share many similarities, since hardiness is described as a trait which acts as a buffer between stressful situations and an individual's reactions to these. Thus hardiness may determine the way in which an individual perceives situations and the actions that they choose to take. It is proposed that mental toughness is a similar trait to hardiness, yet also includes confidence relating to sports performance (Clough *et al.*, 2002). Consequently, Clough *et al.*'s (2002) MTQ48 measures mental toughness as a trait, asking how athletes generally feel and respond to situations rather than assessing mental toughness in specific situations (state measure).

Recent research by Horsburgh *et al.* (2009) was the first behavioural genetic study in this area to examine mental toughness in adult twins. They used the study of twins to determine the extent to which genes and/or environmental factors contributed to individual differences in mental toughness and to determine the genetic and/or environmental basis of any relationship between mental toughness and personality. Their findings demonstrated that individual differences in mental toughness were largely attributable to genetic and non-shared environmental factors. Their study reported support for the factor structure of the MTQ48 and proposed that mental toughness behaves in the same manner to other personality traits that have been investigated in behavioural genetics research.

Research Focus

The aim of this study by Gucciardi *et al.* (2009a) was to evaluate the effectiveness of two different psychological skills training (PST) packages in enhancing the mental toughness of athletes. The authors suggest PST packages (see Chapter 13) may be adapted and used to develop the mental toughness of athletes.

Participants were three under-15 male youth Australian football teams. Each team was randomly assigned to one experimental condition:

1. *Control group*: participants took part in physical training and did not receive any psychological skills training or contact from the researchers.
2. *PST group*: participants followed a programme of traditional sport psychology based educational and experiential group sessions. This included six 2-hour sessions on arousal regulation, mental rehearsal, attention control, self-efficacy and achieving the ideal performance state.
3. *Mental toughness training group*: participants in this group followed a programme of psychology-based educational and experiential group sessions that directly targeted characteristics of mental toughness. This included six 2-hour sessions on resilience, emotional intelligence, tough attitudes, physical toughness and motivation.

Results supported the overall effectiveness of multimodal PST packages with youth athletes. Both programmes resulted in more positive changes in subjective ratings of mental toughness, resilience and flow in comparison with the control group. In both training groups further increases were found in participants' perceptions of their ability to thrive through challenge, and in their perceptions of their tough attitude. However, no increases were reported in their desire for success or their sport awareness. Overall conclusions were made that neither programme was more effective in enhancing mental toughness, suggesting that the common components of a PST programme could be used to enhance mental toughness.

Flow in sport

The final part of this chapter examines a further construct which is often discussed in the literature on peak performance and excellence: the concept of flow.

Imagine a time in your own sport when you were totally involved in the moment, where you forgot all about anything else that may have been going on and where you were only concentrating on the competition. You may have felt confident, as if you had the ability to succeed in whatever you were doing. You may have overcome any feelings of anxiety and were not worried about failing.

This type of description is often used to describe the psychological state of flow. According to Csikszentmihalyi (1975) flow occurs when the actions and awareness of an individual merge, thus they are no longer consciously aware of their movements and actions. In a state of flow an individual's goals will seem clear and they will be striving to reach these. This sense of deep concentration and loss of self-consciousness are thought to underpin the experience of flow.

> ## Reflection Point
>
> You may be able to recognise the description of the psychological state of flow, but you may not have always used this term or recognised it as such. Give yourself three or four minutes to try and write down at least ten words or phrases you can think of that you may have used as alternative descriptions for the flow state.

You should have been able to come up with a number of different phrases that describe this state. Some examples might include: being in the zone, in the bubble, immersed, focused, on autopilot, when everything clicks, tuned in, easy speed, runner's high, switched on and in the groove. You may have thought of many more.

Although each of these phrases (and many more) may be words used by individuals to describe the state of flow, a clear operational definition is important.

Defining flow

As stated by Williams and Krane (1993) flow can be described as a magic moment that occurs when psychological and physical preparation fit together and so the flow state is often associated with above average and exceptional performance. The term 'flow' was introduced by Csikszentmihalyi (1975, 1985) and has been described as the ultimate autotelic experience. This means that it reflects an experience carried out purely for its own ends and own benefit. Jackson and Csikszentmihalyi (1999) noted that this is in contrast to much of what may happen in everyday life. In contrast to many other life experiences (such as going to work or studying for a qualification), sport can offer a state of being that is so rewarding that the value in sport is the experience of just being part of it. This means that the flow state may be more easily achieved in sport.

Learning Activity 12.3

Jackson and Csikszentmihalyi (1999) include quotations in their book from athletes who have experienced the flow state. Below is one such example:

> *I felt really in control, just felt terrific the whole way, and I didn't feel the pain that I would normally feel in that run . . . [I] just really enjoyed the experience of running and really had probably the most successful race ever of my life . . . It wasn't as painful as the others. I felt very in control, I felt very strong. I was able to run as I had planned . . . I felt really focused. I just felt like, you know, like athletes say 'it clicked' it felt great the whole way.*

(page 4)

Now that you have read this athlete's description of flow, try to write down one of your own flow experiences. Think about the situation when this happened, who you were with, what led up to this. As you recall your experience think about how you felt physically and emotionally, what kind of words you would use to describe this experience. Note down what kind of thoughts you may have had during this experience and anything else that you may remember.

Now have a look through the paragraph that you have written. Does it have any similarities with the athlete's experience quoted in Jackson and Csikszentmihalyi? What were the key parts of this experience for you?

There may have been a number of key components that all fit into our description of the flow state. These include:

- focus/absorption;
- enjoyable experience;
- often successful performance (although flow will not always depend on success).

The fundamental dimensions of flow

Jackson and Csikszentmihalyi (1999) propose that there are nine fundamental components or dimensions that best describe the flow mind-set. These are:

- challenge-skills balance;
- action-awareness merging;
- clear goals;
- unambiguous feedback;

- concentration on the task at hand;
- sense of control;
- loss of self-consciousness;
- transformation of time;
- autotelic experience.

The balance between challenge and skill

According to Csikszentmihalyi (1975) flow occurs when an individual is completely immersed in the task at hand. Further to this, flow occurs when an individual is faced with a high level of challenge but also has a high level of skill to match this challenge. This is called the challenge-skills balance. Let's use our case study example to explain this balance.

When Sam first took up the sport of gymnastics, he initially had a low skill level. At first he felt anxious at joining the gymnastics class because he could see those around him performing complex skills. He was worried that he would not be able to complete such difficult skills and so he anticipated a high level of challenge. However, as his class started he realised that he would need to grasp the basics first before he would be allowed to progress to the more difficult skills. As the next few weeks progressed Sam spent his time in the gym perfecting his forward rolls and handstands (basic skills). However, as time started to pass he no longer found this challenging and instead began to feel apathy. As Sam's skill level continued to increase each week he found that he was easily the best in his beginners group. He was able to master and perfect skills before the others in his group. Yet because of this he felt held back by his group and although he felt relaxed in the gym environment he started to become bored. Luckily for Sam his coach noticed his potential and suggested that he should move up to a competitive squad. While Sam's skill level remains high he has also become increasingly challenged by his new coach and his new squad. He now enjoys mastering complex skills and sometimes time just seems to disappear while he is training. He is now able to achieve the flow state.

The model in Figure 12.1 depicts the flow state and it is possible to identify the different states that Sam goes through as he begins to improve his gymnastics.

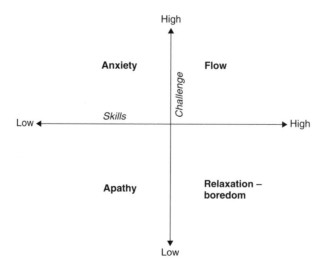

Figure 12.1 Model of the flow state.

Have a look at the model of the flow state and see if you have ever identified any of these states in your own sporting experiences. If you have felt bored during training was this because there was a low level of challenge in the environment? If you have felt anxious in the past was this because you did not have the required skill level to meet the challenge of the sport?

Research Focus

Partington *et al.* (2009) present a different account of the flow experience. While most research depicts flow as a positive experience, these authors suggest that there may also be negative consequences of flow.

To examine the negative consequences of flow, Partington *et al.* used a sample of 15 of the world's top big wave surfers from Hawaii, Australia and South Africa. Participants took part in semi-structured interviews which focused on perception of risk, experiences of flow and motives for participation. The authors then examined themes that had emerged from the data to examine the potential consequences of the flow experience.

Although Partington *et al.* acknowledge that it is difficult to measure directly whether these surfers had experienced the flow state (see further reading at the end of this chapter on measuring flow), their comments during interview reflected many of the nine components of flow. Findings from this study demonstrated that many of the surfers discussed a dependence on the flow state. Many also described a tolerance to flow and therefore needed to go higher or faster in order to continue to experience the feelings of the flow state. For some, the flow state became even more important than other incentives such as monetary reward. Further, others described social impairment as they felt that the pleasure of the flow state gained while surfing outweighed other social aspects of their lives. For one participant, this search for the flow state even outweighed his health or any pain and/or suffering that may be caused in the process. The authors concluded that while the flow state has often been positively associated with enjoyment, for some participants the enjoyment and emotions experienced were almost like a drug, with some even experiencing withdrawal symptoms when not able to surf. Thus there may be an association between the experience of flow and the compulsion to engage in an activity (see Chapter 7 for more discussion of exercise compulsion).

Chapter Review

At the start of this chapter we identified three key areas of research that have examined peak performance in sport. These are: peak performance and excellence, mental toughness and flow. First, we examined the psychological characteristics associated with excellence and peak performance in sport (Learning Objective 1). In doing this we discussed trends in the research literature that focused on comparing successful performances with unsuccessful performances. We examined the constructs that are considered important for successful performance such as adequate planning and the use of mental skills. We then discussed what is meant by the term 'mental toughness' (Learning Objective 2). To do this we examined a number of different definitions that have been used to describe this construct and the qualities that a mentally tough athlete may possess. We also discussed the opposing suggestions that mental toughness is an innate or that it is a learned characteristic (Learning Objective 3). Finally, we discussed the psychological concept of flow and how a flow state may be defined (Learning Objective 4). In doing this we examined when a flow state may occur and the nine dimensions that may be used to classify flow.

> ## Learning Activity 12.4
> **Test your understanding**
>
> 1. What psychological constructs may be associated with peak performance?
> 2. Mental toughness is developed through an individual's interactions with the environment. Discuss this statement with reference to relevant research.
> 3. What is the difference between achieving a flow state and performing well?

Further Reading

Clough, P, Earle, K and Sewell, D (2002) Mental toughness: The concept and its measurement, in Cockerill, I (ed.) *Solutions in Sport Psychology*. London: Thomson, pp. 32–43.
This chapter provides a useful insight into the development of the MTQ48 and the link between mental toughness and hardiness.

Jackson, S, Martin, AJ and Eklund, RC (2008) Long and short measures of flow: The construct validity of the FSS-2, DFS-2, and new brief counterparts. *Journal of Sport and Exercise Psychology*, 30: 561–587.
This paper provides an insight into how flow can be measured, examining both long and short flow scales. This will be useful reading if you are interested in measuring flow for a research project.

MacNamara, A, Button, A and Collins, D (2010) The role of psychological characteristics in facilitating the pathway to elite performance. Part 2: Examining environmental and stage related differences in skills and behaviours. *The Sport Psychologist*, 24: 74–96.
This paper is recommended because it introduces a different approach to peak performance, proposing that different skills will be needed at different stages of development. Twenty-four participants from a variety of sports were interviewed on their own pathways to excellence.

Chapter 13
Putting it all together: applying sport psychology

Learning Objectives

This chapter is designed to help you be able to:

1. understand what is meant by psychological skills training;
2. critically review the research evidence on the efficacy of goal setting as a psychological intervention;
3. describe the different types and functions of imagery and discuss whether these are effective;
4. make suggestions for using imagery based on the PETTLEP approach;
5. critically review the research evidence on the efficacy of psychological skills training packages;
6. suggest criticisms of the current psychological skills training research literature.

Introduction

Throughout the previous chapters of this book we have examined a number of potential factors that may impact on performance in sport. These include coping with adversity, managing impressions, building mental toughness and coping with career transitions. In this chapter we focus on psychological techniques that may be used to enhance performance. There are a number of techniques and strategies that can be taught to athletes or used to enhance their existing psychological skills. In turn the use of these psychological skills may then facilitate performance and encourage a positive approach to sports competition.

Psychological skills are generally considered to be an important part of preparing for competition (Thompson *et al.*, 1998). We might expect an elite athlete has the necessary psychological skills to cope with the pressures of high level competition, that they can maintain their focus despite media and audience presence and that they are motivated to achieve. This seems logical given that to achieve elite status an athlete must have performed and succeeded under such high pressure situations. This suggestion is further endorsed by research that has identified that the use of psychological skills may facilitate excellent performance (MacNamara *et al.*, 2010a, 2010b). Yet even as an elite athlete it is also possible to learn and enhance all of these skills through psychological skills training (PST).

In this chapter we first discuss the application of PST techniques in the sporting context, and then review the literature on the efficacy of these techniques. We focus on two such techniques: imagery and goal setting, as two of the most frequently used and applied techniques in this context. It is essential that sport psychologists ensure that they engage in evidence-based practice; therefore before using these techniques it is important to conduct research to establish their efficacy. Although both imagery and goal setting can be used individually, often they are combined into a PST package along with other techniques such as attention control and relaxation training. Thus we discuss the efficacy of PST packages and key considerations when developing a PST package for an athlete.

Although research evidence mostly supports the use of PST packages, there are also alternative approaches to applied sport psychology that are gradually gaining an increased focus in the research literature. Therefore we end the chapter by examining the argument that the use of PST packages is too prescriptive and examine some alternative approaches that could be adopted.

What are psychological skills?

It is important to first clarify what we mean by psychological skills and psychological skills training. Psychological skills are often used automatically in sport. If you think about your own experiences of sport then you will probably already use a number of psychological skills without being consciously aware that you are using them. Psychological skills can be defined as learned behaviours that are used by athletes and which, when practised, may help them in the pursuit of sporting excellence (Kremer and Moran, 2008). In the sport setting this means that psychological skills can be used, for instance, to enhance motivation, regulate anxiety and enhance self-confidence.

Consider the psychological skills that you use when playing sport. You may be able to recognise that you already use a number of psychological skills without having been taught these by a sport psychologist. Some of these skills will naturally occur in sport, some will be learned from role models or elite athletes and some may have been taught by a coach. McCarthy et al. (2010b) examined young athletes' (ages 10–15 years) understanding of four basic psychological skills: goal setting, mental imagery, self-talk and relaxation. To do this they asked each athlete to explain the meaning of each psychological skill, for example 'what do you think imagery means?' The athletes had some understanding of these skills, although the younger athletes were less able to explain the meaning of each psychological skill (for example, they were less able to explain what was meant by imagery or to describe how they used this skill). Overall, goal setting and mental imagery were better understood by all the young athletes than were self-talk and relaxation. Based on these findings, McCarthy et al. (2010b) suggested that young athletes could benefit from psychological skills training, and that this could be adapted to be appropriate for their age. They further suggested that these psychological skills were not only useful in sport, but were transferable skills that could be used in other life domains. For example, goal setting may not only be useful in sport but may also enhance an individual's academic performance.

Psychological skills training in sport

Over the past decade there has been an increase in the number of experimental studies that have examined the efficacy of psychological skills training. In general research has followed one of two pathways:

- *Pathway 1*: Efficacy of single psychological skills (e.g. McCarthy et al., 2010b; Shambrook and Bull, 1996; Wanlin et al., 1997).

- *Pathway 2*: Efficacy of multimodal packages (e.g. Hanton and Jones, 1999; Patrick and Hrycaiko 1998; Thelwell *et al.*, 2006; von Guenthner *et al.*, 2010).

Research that has examined single psychological skills has tested the efficacy of a number of different skills, most including imagery, pre-performance routines, goal setting and self-talk. Research that takes a multimodal approach has examined combinations of a number of mental skills, delivered as a package to athletes. For example, using this approach a sport psychologist might first provide athletes with sessions on positive self-talk, followed by sessions on imagery and then goal setting. These types of packages can be tailored to the specific needs and requirements of the sport and the athlete. Recently there has been an increase in the number of studies that have identified an enhancement in performance following a programme of psychological skills training (e.g. Thelwell *et al.*, 2010b). We first examine two individual psychological skills that are among the most frequently used in both research and practice (goal setting and imagery), followed by an examination of PST packages. When discussing these skills and packages we examine both their efficacy and their effectiveness.

Box 13.1 Definitions: Efficacy and effectiveness

- *Efficacy* refers to the capacity to produce an effect.
- *Effectiveness* refers to whether something produces change under real life conditions.

Goal setting

Often an athlete's main motive for engaging in sport is to demonstrate their ability and to feel competent (Harwood, 2005). To achieve these aims an individual may decide on particular outcomes that they would like to achieve and devise a plan that will help them to achieve these. Thus they may use goal setting to establish specific and measurable ways to achieve success. Goal setting has been a widely used technique in business and industrial settings, with research demonstrating that it can enhance both productivity and motivation (Latham and Locke, 1991). In the sports context it is a technique that has been used frequently and with high levels of perceived effectiveness by practitioners, coaches and athletes. Weinberg *et al.* (2001a) reported that goal setting was used extensively by the high school sports coaches who took part in their study. Almost all of the coaches who were interviewed set team goals, individual goals and personal coaching goals. Similarly, Weinberg *et al.* (2000) examined the perceived goal-setting practices of Olympic athletes using a questionnaire to assess the frequency, perceived effectiveness, goal preference and goal difficulty of the goals set by 338 Olympic athletes. All of the athletes used some type of goal setting and rated their goals as highly effective. Further, the athletes preferred goals that were difficult to attain and somewhat above their usual performance level, indicating that challenging goals were preferable to easily attainable goals.

Although the research by Weinberg *et al.* (2000, 2001b) provides some useful information on the goal-setting practices of both athletes and coaches, it can only give us an indication of the perception of effectiveness, rather than if goal setting actually improved performance. To assess the effectiveness of goal setting we need to examine the research evidence obtained when a goal-setting intervention has been employed. Before we examine this evidence it is important to consider the methodology employed to measure and evaluate the efficacy of goal setting. The activity below asks you to consider how you might design an experimental study to examine the efficacy of goal setting.

Learning Activity 13.1

You have been given the following hypothesis: 'Setting a goal prior to a basketball free throw will enhance performance more than setting no goals at all.' Consider how you would conduct an experiment to test this hypothesis using the headings below.

- *Participants* (Hint: how many participants will you include, what ability will they be, will they be grouped? If so how will you group them?)
- *Procedure* (Hint: what will you ask your participants to do during your experiment, if you have more than one group of participants what will be required of each group, what goals will you set for your participants?)
- *Measures* (Hint: how will you measure performance to determine the efficacy of the goal-setting intervention?)

Now consider whether the experiment that you have designed has any similarities with the following suggestions outlined below.

There have been a number of methods used to evaluate the effectiveness and efficacy of goal setting. Some studies have used randomised control trials whereas others have used case study, multiple baseline designs. The suggestion below outlines how you may have chosen to test this hypothesis using a randomised control trial. For an example of an alternative approach you could consult O'Brien *et al.*'s study (2009) which describes a multiple-baseline across-individuals single-subject design with three elite and three non-elite boxers to examine the effects of goal setting on performance.

Participants

You may have chosen any level of basketball players, from complete novice players to those at an elite level. However you may wish to consider the findings of O'Brien *et al.* (2009) who reported that while elite participants displayed consistent performance improvements during and after the goal-setting programme, non-elite participants revealed inconsistent patterns. When examining an intervention it may also be beneficial to use a homogenous group of participants with a similar level of ability. By doing this you might expect similar levels of performance gains from your participants.

Box 13.2 Definition: Homogenous

The term homogenous refers to using participants who are similar or who have certain commonalities. For example, you may use female, novice level, university students.

Once you have chosen your participants you may have allocated these randomly to one of two groups, one group that receives the intervention and one a control group that does not.

Procedure

Before examining the efficacy of goal setting you need to obtain a baseline measure of performance to assess the ability of the participants prior to the intervention to test whether they have improved afterwards. So your first step might be to ask each group of players to complete 20 free throws while you measure the number of throws that are successful.

The goal-setting group would then receive the goal-setting intervention. When devising this research you may have considered the types of goals that players could set. There are three main types of goals that you could choose from: performance, outcome and process (Burton, 1989; Kingston and Hardy, 1997). You may have chosen to give your participants a target to achieve that is slightly higher than their baseline performance. For example, the goal may be to improve performance by three successful shots, so a player who scored 10 successful free throws may have the goal to score 13 in the next test. This is a performance goal or, you could employ outcome goals such as trying to achieve the highest number of successful free throws in the group. Finally you could employ process goals. This type of goal is based on the process of performance and technique. It may include a goal such as focusing on wrist action when releasing the ball. Whichever type of goal you employ, based on recommendations by Weinberg *et al.* (2000) as discussed earlier, you will need to make sure that your goal is challenging for your participants.

After the intervention you could then ask each group to complete another 20 free throws. You would ask the goal-setting group to repeat their goal out loud prior to each free throw; this would help to ensure that they are focused on their goal prior to each performance.

Measures

Since our hypothesis is based on performance then this would be the main measure of the study. A successful intervention would mean that individuals in the goal-setting group would score more free throws after the intervention than before the intervention. We would also analyse whether performance in the control group improved in the post-intervention free throws. If their performance did improve then this may indicate that any performance increase may not have been due to the intervention but may have another cause instead, for example this may be due to a learning effect. This effect might be expected and so we need to examine if the experimental group improved more than the control group, which would still provide an indication of intervention efficacy.

Although the rationale for designing this research was to examine the impact of goal setting on performance, previous research has also demonstrated positive effects of goal setting on psychological variables such as anxiety, motivation, positive affect, perceptions of team cohesion and self-confidence (e.g. Locke and Latham, 2002, 2006; McCarthy *et al.*, 2010a; Senécal *et al.*, 2008; Weinberg *et al.*, 1997).

Limitations in researching the efficacy of goal setting

The example above demonstrates a simple method of testing the efficacy of goal setting yet you may have noticed a number of potential limitations of this design. First, there could be a range of variables that impact on the efficacy of the intervention. These include goal type, specificity and difficulty. If goals are too easy or too difficult, and/or goals are not specifically tailored to the task in question this may lessen their efficacy. Similarly, the types of goals that are set will also impact on the efficacy of a goal-setting intervention. Research has demonstrated that process goals are more effective for performance enhancement than performance goals (Kingston and Hardy, 1997). Further, the goal-setting literature advocates that athletes should have an active role in setting their own targets to maximise commitment to achieving their goals (Burton et al., 2001).

Another difficulty with testing the efficacy of goal setting is that often the control group may spontaneously set their own goals without being consciously aware of doing so. Individuals generally have the desire for self-improvement and may set themselves goals based on their first performance on the task, even when asked not to. Finally, although it may have been easier to use novice participants, the commitment, experience and skill level of elite athletes may help to increase understanding of goal setting (Burton et al., 2010).

Efficacy of goal setting

While in general, sport psychology research has demonstrated support for the use of goal setting and its positive impacts on performance, not all authors agree with this assertion. Burton et al. (2001) offer support for the use of goal setting and draw the 'unmistakable conclusion' that goal setting is an effective strategy for enhancing performance (page 521). Case study research such as that by Swain and Jones (1995) has also demonstrated the efficacy of a goal-setting intervention over 16 weeks, with three out of their four participants improving in their targeted area of performance. Despite these positive results there have been inconsistent findings in goal-setting research. Gardner and Moore (2006) presented an overview of research findings on goal-setting, highlighting 13 studies that contradict the positive relationship between goal setting and performance. However, as noted previously, further research has suggested that goal setting may not only impact on performance but may also enhance other psychological factors. For example, McCarthy et al. (2010a) found that goal setting may enhance positive affect among junior multi-event athletes. Further, Senécal et al. (2008) suggested that goal setting could be used to enhance team cohesion, reporting that athletes who had taken part in a goal-setting intervention programme during the season reported higher perceptions of cohesion than a control group. Thus, although research examining the relationship between goal setting and performance has produced mixed findings, further research that examined alternative outcome measures has found that goal setting can be used to enhance a number of psychological factors.

Mental imagery

Imagery has generally been referred to as a method of recreating an experience in the mind. Although a number of terms have been used to describe various forms of imagery (e.g. visualisation, mental practice, mental rehearsal), Hale et al. (2005) suggested that most practitioners will use the broader term mental imagery. Mental imagery describes the structured mental practice techniques that use the senses to recreate sporting performance with the aim of enhancing performance (Holmes and Collins, 2001). Mental imagery may have been one of the skills that you identified that you had used in your own sport at the start of this chapter. You may have imaged scoring the winning penalty in an important match or you may have imaged how it would feel to hold the FA Cup.

These different types of imagery are represented in the five different functions of imagery suggested by Martin *et al.* (1999). Their applied model of imagery use proposes that each of these functions of imagery will be related to a different outcome. Therefore rather than examining the efficacy of imagery on performance outcome alone it is important to consider the efficacy of imagery in relation to different outcomes based on its different functions. Martin *et al.* (1999) describe this approach as what you see (image) is what you get (outcome), suggesting that the function and outcome of the imagery will be dependent on the type of imagery that is used by the athlete. If you image scoring a winning penalty the outcome of the imagery may be skill improvement; alternatively if you imagine holding the FA Cup then the outcome may be increased motivation.

The five types of imagery outlined by Martin *et al.* (1999) in their applied model of imagery are described in Table 13.1.

Case Study 13.1
Adrian

Imagery type	Imagery purpose/function	Example
Cognitive specific (CS)	Rehearsal of specific sports skills	Penalty kick Back flip
Cognitive general (CG)	Rehearsal of general strategies or routines	Corner-taking strategy Balance beam routine
Motivation specific (MS)	Image-specific goals or strategies to achieve them	National selection Winning Wimbledon
Motivation general mastery (MG-M)	Being in control, mentally tough and self-confident	Imaging feeling mentally tough and strong
Motivation general arousal (MG-A)	Imagery of stressful, anxiety and arousal provoking situations	Imaging feeling anxious but overcoming this and performing well

Table 13.1 Five types of imagery outlined by Martin et al. *(1999)*

Adrian used to enjoy playing football but has recently been relegated to the substitute's bench on his local football team. His new job means that he has to work long hours and because of this he has sometimes missed practice sessions. Although he has been told by his coach that he has natural talent he lacks confidence in his abilities, particularly when taking penalties. Since he has been dropped from the starting line-up he has lacked the motivation and enthusiasm for the sport that he once loved.

Imagery could be used to help Adrian in a number of ways. First, when Adrian has missed practice sessions he could use imagery to practise and refine his skills. He could use cognitive-specific (CS) imagery to image his penalty taking and cognitive-general (CG) imagery to practise team strategies such as defending a corner. Although imagery is not a substitute for physical training, it may be helpful when he cannot attend training. To improve his self-confidence he could use motivation general mastery (MG-M) imagery by imagining feeling in control and competent, particularly when taking penalties. To improve his motivation he could use motivation-specific (MS) imagery to see himself as part of the team as they win the football league.

Examining the applied model of imagery

Nordin and Cumming (2008) examined the five different types of imagery proposed in Martin *et al.*'s applied model (1999). Athletes were asked whether they felt that the five imagery types fulfilled ten different functions (some imagery types fulfil more than one function, such as enhancing motivation and confidence). In support of the model, athletes reported that CS and CG imagery were used for skill learning and practice. However for the motivational types of imagery (MS, MG-A, MG-M) results offered less support for the predictions of the applied model. All motivational types of imagery were reported to be equally effective for enhancing motivation whereas Martin *et al.*'s model purported that MS imagery would be most effective. Further, MG-M and MG-A imagery were used for similar purposes and were indistinguishable from each other. This demonstrated that athletes may use more than one type of imagery for a variety of purposes as well as using several imagery types for a single purpose. Overall, the athletes perceived MG-M imagery to be the most effective type of imagery, both in general, and for specific motivational functions.

These findings extend previous work by Weinberg *et al.* (2003) and Short *et al.* (2004) who also examined the applied model of imagery. The overall conclusion of Nordin and Cumming's research is that what you see is not necessarily what you get, at least with regard to the motivational types of imagery. As a result, the authors suggest that imagery type should be verified with the athlete to ensure a match between the imagery intervention and the goals that the athlete is aiming to achieve by using imagery.

In their applied model of imagery, Martin *et al.* (1999) also suggest that imagery perspective and imagery ability will influence how effective imagery is. Nordin and Cumming (2008) examined this proposed moderating effect of imagery perspective and imagery ability. This proposal is based on previous suggestions that the effectiveness of imagery may depend on whether the individual uses an *internal* (seeing the image as if you were completing the skill) or an *external* (seeing the image as if watching someone else complete the skill) perspective, and how well an athlete is able to perform imagery (Mahoney and Avener, 1977). Imagery perspective was not found to moderate the relationship between imagery function and outcome.

With regards to imagery ability, Nordin and Cumming suggest that MG-M and CS images are easier to image than the other types of imagery and that this may impact on the frequency with which they are used by athletes. If an athlete finds a particular type of imagery easier to use then they are more likely to engage in this type of imagery more often. Think about the imagery that you have used in the past. Consider whether you imaged particular skills such as a penalty kick, a succession of skills such as team strategy, or winning the league. Identify which type of imagery you used most frequently and consider whether you continued to use this type of imagery more frequently because it was easier for you to image than other types.

The PETTLEP approach to mental imagery

So far we have examined the suggested effectiveness of different types of imagery for achieving different outcomes or functions. However, research on mental imagery can often be criticised for its lack of theoretical underpinning (Martin *et al.*, 1999). In response to this criticism, Holmes and Collins (2001) developed the PETTLEP model. Early neuroscience research found that the same neurophysiological processes underpin imagery and actual movement (Decety and Jeannerod, 1996). Thus when an individual images completing a particular skill there is a 'functional equivalence' to the movement when the skill is performed physically (Jeannerod, 1995). The aim of the PETTLEP model of imagery is to enhance this functional equivalence by making the imagery represent real movement as closely as possible. This should lead to more effective imagery and enhanced sports performance.

PETTLEP is an acronym which relates to seven aspects that help the athlete to recreate their experiences of sport using imagery and in doing so, increase the functional equivalence of the imagined movement. Each letter represents a different component of the imagery that needs to be considered to achieve this.

- *Physical*: This is related to recreating the physical responses that would be experienced in the sporting environment. If the athlete usually experiences tightness in their legs or the feeling of their heart pounding then this should be incorporated into the imagery.
- *Environment*: This is related to the physical environment in which the athlete usually performs. This should be specific to the individual and may include imaging aspects of the training environment or the competition venue.
- *Task*: This refers to the match that is needed between the imagery that is being performed and the movement that is being imaged. Thus the same thoughts and actions need to be included in the imagery.
- *Timing*: The imagined movement needs to be carried out at the same pace as the actual performance.
- *Learning*: This refers to the adaptation that needs to occur in the imagined skill as the athlete improves their level of performance on the actual skill. As the athlete moves from a cognitive stage of learning (when the athlete is aware of and needs to focus on each movement pattern needed) to a more autonomous stage (automatic performance) the imagery needs to be adapted to accommodate this.
- *Emotion*: This refers to the emotions that the individual should try to recreate that are associated with the particular sport or performance. For example, this might include feeling excitement before performing or happiness after being successful.
- *Perspective*: This factor suggests that athletes may wish to use a combination of both internal and external imagery perspectives.

Learning Activity 13.2

The explanation above details all of the components that are suggested to increase the functional equivalence of imagery and consequently to enhance sporting performance. To try and gain a full understanding of approaches to using psychological skills in sport psychology it can often be helpful to apply their suggestions to your own experiences in sport. List the components of the PETTLEP model and alongside each component suggest how you could apply each one to your own sport. It may be useful to pick an isolated skill such as a penalty kick or a golf putt.

Research Focus

Smith *et al.* (2007) conducted two studies to examine the effects of PETTLEP-based imagery compared with more traditional imagery interventions. In study one, 48 university hockey players were recruited who were inexperienced in the use of imagery. They were randomly assigned to one of four groups: sport-specific imagery, clothing imagery, traditional imagery and a control group.

The task used was a hockey penalty flick into an empty goal with no goal keeper. Points awarded on the task were dependent on the part of the goal the ball was flicked into. The most points were awarded if the ball was flicked into the top or bottom corners of the goal to make the task more challenging for participants.

Participants were allowed five practice shots and then completed ten penalty flicks as a pre-test measure. Following the pre-test, the imagery interventions were introduced to all the participants, with the exception of the control group. These were individualised for each participant to include relevant stimulus and response propositions (Lang *et al.*, 1980). The task component of the PETTLEP model suggests that the imagined task should be closely matched to the actual task. Thus, the imagery involved both stimulus and response propositions as discussed in Lang's Bioinformational Model of Imagery. Stimulus propositions refer to environmental cues, such as the sight of the hockey ball or the sound of the strike, while response propositions refer to physical and psychological responses, such as feeling the hands on the hockey stick, or the sensation of striking the ball. The sport-specific imagery group most closely followed the PETTLEP model and performed the imagery wearing their hockey kit while standing on the hockey pitch. The clothing imagery group performed the imagery at home but while wearing their kit (still following some aspects of the PETTLEP model), and the traditional imagery group performed their imagery at home while seated and in normal clothes. The control group spent an equal amount of time reading hockey-related literature as was spent practising imagery in the imagery groups.

Each participant performed his or her task (control group) or imagery (other three groups) for six weeks. Following this, post-intervention testing was carried out during which participants completed five practice flicks and ten measured flicks.

Results indicated that all forms of imagery were effective for enhancing performance. The most effective imagery interventions were found to be the PETTLEP interventions rather than the traditional imagery, as these resulted in the largest percentage improvements between pre- and post-intervention.

Further, the sport-specific intervention which was the intervention that most closely followed the PETTLEP model was found to be more effective than the other PETTLEP-based intervention used in the clothing imagery group. Thus, participants who performed the most functionally equivalent imagery were found to experience the greatest gains in performance, supporting the use of the PETTLEP model of imagery over a traditional imagery intervention.

Learning Activity 13.3

Smith *et al.* (2007) continue to discuss a second study that used a gymnastics balance beam task. Smith, D, Wright, C, Allsopp, A and Westhead, H (2007) It's all in the mind: PETTLEP-based imagery and sports performance. *Journal of Applied Sport Psychology*, 19: 80–92. Read this second part of the study and answer the following questions:

1. What were the hypotheses of this second study?
2. What were the components of the PETTLEP approach that were tested?
3. What do the results tell us about the effectiveness of the PETTLEP approach?

Answers to this activity are provided at the end of the book.

Research conclusions: imagery

While there are some studies that demonstrate support for the use of imagery as a performance-enhancing technique, Gardner and Moore (2006) suggest in their overview of imagery research that there is no empirical evidence to suggest that imagery is an effective intervention for performance enhancement and that instead it should be characterised as an experimental intervention. Support has been shown for the use of the PETTLEP approach in experimental research (e.g. Smith and Holmes, 2004) in particular using mental imagery, which has been examined in comparison to traditional imagery and has been shown to be more effective for enhancing performance. Consequently it may be concluded that while there is not strong support for the performance-enhancing effects of traditional imagery, the PETTLEP approach is well supported by the sport psychology literature. Research has illustrated that imagery interventions should be functionally equivalent to the actual skill being performed.

The psychological skills training package

In this chapter we have examined two psychological skills that may be effective for enhancing sporting performance. Although we have focused on just two – imagery and goal setting – a range of different psychological skills exist that athletes can use. The growing literature in this area has highlighted some of the most commonly researched strategies such as self-talk, arousal regulation strategies, relaxation strategies and pre-performance routines. As suggested earlier, often sport psychologists will use more than one intervention with an athlete. In doing this the sport psychologist is able to integrate several different techniques into an intervention which may target a specific outcome, for example, improving performance consistency or improving concentration. Therefore, as well as examining the efficacy of individual psychological skills, research has also recognised that frequently these will not be used in isolation and that it is also important to examine the efficacy of the PST package, or, the multimodal approach.

In their review of 20 articles on PST packages, Greenspan and Feltz (1998) suggested that imagery, self-talk, mental routines, concentration training and anxiety management were the most common skills to be combined in such packages. They also proposed that relaxation-based interventions and cognitive restructuring were the most effective skills for performance enhancement. Over the past decade, research on PST packages has continued to increase. In general, this research has examined the impact of PST packages on closed skills, subcomponents of sport skills, and endurance tasks, as discussed using illustrative examples in the following section.

Research into psychological skills training packages

Closed skills can be defined as those which take place in a stable, predictable environment, and in which the movement follows a specific pattern with a definitive beginning and end. For example, closed skills may include a javelin throw, a basketball free throw or a tennis serve. Pates *et al.* (2002) examined the use of hypnosis as a multimodal intervention which incorporated imagery, relaxation and self-talk triggers. This was found to be effective in enhancing performance of a basketball free throw.

Whereas research on closed skills has focused on performing an isolated skill, it is important to recognise that for many sports this will form only a small part of the overall performance. For example, although it is valuable to understand that particular multimodal approaches can enhance performance of the basketball free throw, this forms only a small part of the overall game for the basketball player. Therefore, it is important not only to focus on closed skills that are more easily researched because of their easily defined outcomes, but also to examine performance subcomponents of different sports skills.

Thelwell *et al.* (2006) designed a PST package to improve the specific skills required by a soccer midfielder which were identified as ball control, tackling and passing. Five university level players took part in three one-day workshops which taught them how to use relaxation, imagery and self-talk. Following these workshops, Thelwell *et al.* found varying levels of performance improvement. Overall, small improvements were made on each of the skills that were targeted, although only some participants demonstrated more consistency in their performance of the skills. All participants also rated the intervention as appropriate and successful.

Research has also documented that PST packages can be used to improve endurance performance. Patrick and Hrycaiko (1998) and Thelwell and Greenlees (2001) both examined PST packages that incorporated relaxation, imagery, self-talk and goal setting. While Patrick and Hrycaiko's study included endurance runners, the participants in Thelwell and Greenlees' study were triathletes. Both studies concluded that the PST package was successful for enhancing performance. Further, Thelwell and Greenlees found an increase in the use of psychological skills, perceptions of success and increased enjoyment of the sport following the intervention.

Implementing psychological skills training packages

The use of PST packages has been well documented and the overall conclusion from research is that their systematic use can enhance performance. In addition, there are a number of factors to consider prior to delivering PST programmes.

Imagine that as a sport psychologist you have been approached by a local hockey club to work with their team. Although the research literature has demonstrated the effectiveness of PST packages, how will you decide which skills to include in your PST package? Are there any factors that will influence your decisions?

There are a number of factors that you need to consider before you can plan your PST programme:

- *time available* – number of weeks of programme delivery and the length of sessions within the programme;
- *timing in the competitive season* – competitive season or rest phase;
- *needs of individual/team* – needs assessment should be carried out prior to a PST programme;
- *efficacy of psychological skills* – sufficient efficacy should have been demonstrated for the psychological skills that you will use in your PST package.

These contextual factors illustrate that in practice, the sport psychologist needs to be able to tailor the PST programme to the specific needs of the individual or team. PST programmes should also be periodised to match the phases in the athlete's annual training programme (Lidor *et al.*, 2007). Thus different skills could be taught in the preparation, competition and transition phases. For example, psychological skills may be learned in the preparation phase and then used in the competition phase.

Criticisms of research on psychological skills training packages

Although research has demonstrated that PST packages may have a performance-enhancing effect, there are a number of general criticisms of this research area (e.g. Blakeslee and Gough, 2007).

1. Limited participant numbers: Often research on PST packages includes only small numbers of participants because of the time and commitment required from athletes taking part in this research. This means that we must be cautious when making generalisations from research with limited numbers of participants.
2. Most studies measure change from baseline to intervention but do not check the maintenance of psychological skills use post-intervention. This means that while research often measures the effectiveness of the intervention, at the end of the intervention period there is no measure of continued adherence to the psychological skills or of sustained levels of performance post-intervention. Consequently, although research is able to demonstrate that PST packages are effective in enhancing performance the long-term effect of such interventions is mostly unknown.
3. Research does not include any measure of the 'art' of delivery. This refers to the possibility that the success of the PST programme may depend, in part, on the qualities of the sport psychology practitioner who delivers the sessions.

It can be proposed that while psychological skills training offers a useful intervention there is a limit to its effectiveness. As Petitpas *et al.* (1999) suggest, many athletes will require something that goes beyond traditional mental skills training as they struggle to manage emotions, make decisions or cope with career transitions. Consequently the 'one size fits all' approach of the PST package may, in reality, not fit the needs of all individuals since it lacks the capacity to deal with the more 'human' side of athlete needs. Nesti (2004) suggested that sport psychology practitioners should also develop counselling skills. He proposed that often PST techniques are merely sticking plasters, when much more is actually needed. Interestingly, however, the majority of research in sport and exercise psychology has focused on PST interventions rather than the art of practice or on service delivery. Thus further research is needed to examine the alternatives to using PST.

Chapter Review

The aim at the start of this chapter was to understand what is meant by psychological skills training (Learning Objective 1). To do this you reflected on the psychological skills that you may have developed through playing sport and those which you may have been taught. We then examined two psychological skills in detail: goal setting and mental imagery. First we critically reviewed the research evidence on the efficacy of goal setting (Learning Objective 2). We outlined how research could examine the efficacy of goal setting using a randomised control trial. Next we highlighted the different types and functions of imagery and discussed whether these were effective (Learning Objective 3). In doing this we examined the applied model of imagery and the cognitive and motivational types of imagery. As research has offered strong support for the PETTLEP model we focused on Smith and colleagues' (2007) study that demonstrated the use of a functional equivalence model. In Learning Activity 13.2 you were asked to make suggestions for using imagery based on the PETTLEP approach (Learning Objective 4). Having examined two psychological skills in detail we took a broader approach and focused on PST packages. We discussed that these have been useful for improving the performance of closed skills, subcomponents of sports performance and endurance tasks (Learning Objective 5). Finally, after reviewing the literature supporting the use of PST packages we examined limitations of PST packages and of using these packages with athletes (Learning Objective 6).

Learning Activity 13.4
Test your understanding

1. Define what is meant by the term psychological skills training.
2. Describe what is meant by a randomised control trial and discuss why this may be a useful method of examining psychological interventions.
3. Outline the PETTLEP approach to imagery and explain why this may be more effective than traditional imagery.
4. Suggest two general criticisms of research that has examined PST packages.

Further Reading

Kavussanu, M, Morris, RL and Ring, C (2009) The effects of achievement goals on performance, enjoyment, and practice of a novel motor task. *Journal of Sports Sciences*, 27: 1281–1292.
This study examines the responses of participants who were asked to take part in a golf putting task after being randomly assigned to one of three different goal conditions (mastery, performance-approach and performance-avoidance). This will add to your understanding of goal setting by considering three additional types of goals not discussed in this chapter.

Thelwell, RC, Greenlees, IA and Weston, NJV (2010b) Examining the use of psychological skills throughout soccer performance. *Journal of Sport Behavior*, 33: 109–127.
The main purpose of this study was to examine the effectiveness of a psychological skills training intervention on role-specific performance subcomponents during different stages of competition. It is one of the first studies to examine the extent to which psychological skills influence performance during competition.

Wright, C and Smith, D (2009) The effect of PETTLEP imagery on strength performance. *International Journal of Sport and Exercise Psychology*, 7: 18–31.
This article will be useful if you are interested in examining further research that has tested the effectiveness of the PETTLEP model of imagery on performance.

Answers to Learning Activities

Chapter 2

Answer to Learning Activity 2.2

Questionnaires are often used to measure personality traits, mood states and health conditions. They provide a quick and efficient way of gathering information from a large group of people without the need for time-consuming interviews or observation. However, it is important that researchers are sure that these questionnaires effectively measure what they are supposed to measure. In order to do this, researchers spend a considerable amount of time developing questionnaires and evaluating them to determine if they are valid and reliable. This involves checking that the wording of questions or items is effective (face validity), that the responses that participants provide to their questionnaire can be replicated over time (external reliability) and match the responses that the participants would give on a different questionnaire measuring the same construct (criterion validity). Once questionnaires have been subjected to these procedures they are said to be 'standardised questionnaires'. Researchers using unstandardised questionnaires cannot be sure that their results are valid because they cannot be sure that their questionnaire has measured what it purports to measure.

A number of questionnaires use a self-report methodology, which asks respondents to reflect on their own personality or behaviour. This can be effective, because who knows more about their behaviour or personality than themselves? However, one limitation of this type of response is that participants do not always answer honestly. Sometimes they might want to appear in a more positive light and so might answer more favourably than is in fact the case. Other times, they might genuinely not have a true perception of themselves, for example they might believe that they are moderately active when in fact what they consider to be moderately active is much less than is actually the case.

One way in which researchers can overcome these types of methodological problems is to use standardised questionnaires where possible, but also to consider using other methods such as observations or physiological and behavioural measures (e.g. pedometers to measure step count) to support and validate the participant's questionnaire responses.

Chapter 3

Example answers for Learning Activity 3.3

A number of studies have shown that physical activity declines significantly during adolescence, especially for girls. For example, Strauss *et al.* (2001) demonstrated that pre-teens spend approximately 35 per cent more time in low and high level activity than teenagers.

In addition, individuals in this age group are undergoing numerous physical changes to their bodies as a result of puberty which are likely to impact on their physical self-perceptions.

You might also recall how earlier in the chapter we discussed a study by Clay *et al.* (2005) who demonstrated that body dissatisfaction increased with age among adolescents and that this was linked to an increased awareness of societal views on attractiveness and comparisons made with models.

Given the relationship between physical activity and physical self-perceptions, this is an important age group to target in order to enhance physical activity levels, self-worth and therefore in turn, psychological and physiological health.

Chapter 4

Answers to Learning Activity 4.1

Hena – preparation stage; Tamsin – maintenance stage; Altab – contemplation stage.

Answers to Learning Activity 4.2

- *Intervention 1*: This advert will use a degree of gathering information by highlighting the fact that inactivity has consequences for obesity and cardiovascular health. It mainly plays on moving people emotionally by trying to distress the viewer into an emotional reaction of concern for the little boy. It also uses the message of being a role model by forcing parents to consider the consequences of their unhealthy behaviour for their children.
- *Intervention 2*: The leaflet mainly focuses on gathering information by documenting some of the risks of inactivity. The intervention itself, which provides counselling, works on the basis of providing social support for individuals to change their behaviour. Using the real life success stories and before and after pictures also provides individuals with an opportunity to consider their own self-image and develop their alternative healthy self-image.

Suggested responses to Learning Activity 4.3

- *Autonomy*: An interview with the exercise leader before starting the programme, to highlight the benefits of exercise and address any questions that the participant has, might encourage individuals to make their own decision to start the programme and not feel coerced by others. The intervention itself might offer a choice of activities.
- *Competence*: Offering the participants regular positive feedback on their progress will help to increase their perceptions of self-efficacy and competence to exercise. This could also be achieved by using diaries so that participants can look back and track their progress for themselves.
- *Relatedness*: Support for the participant could be offered by regular meetings or telephone contact from the exercise leader. Implementing a buddy system between the participants would also provide the opportunity for support from each other.

Chapter 6

Answers to Learning Activity 6.2

Small sample size; Sample only included recreationally active men; Laboratory setting does not include aspects of real-life exercise such as social interaction or competition; No control group; Post-exercise measures only taken up to 15 min post-exercise.

Chapter 11

Suggested responses to Learning Activity 11.1

Problems faced by John	Potential strategies
Anger, depression, frustration	Help John to understand that his emotions are a normal response to his injury and offer the opportunity to vent his emotions and possibly rationalise them (e.g. questioning his anger at his team-mate).
Attributing the injury to himself and his team-mate	Encourage re-attribution to reduce his self-blame and help manage his anger towards himself and his team-mate.
Perception of a single missed opportunity	Discuss role models of famous athletes who have achieved after sustaining a serious injury.
Isolation and lack of social support	Encourage John to attend training to feel part of the team and to complete lower body workouts.
Lack of motivation for rehabilitation exercises	Develop a structured rehabilitation routine with clear daily and weekly goals. Encourage John to record his achievements and to use imagery to see himself performing the exercises successfully.
Concentration problems	Encourage John to learn attention control strategies such as parking or thought stopping.
Sense of loss and lack of a strong identity	Encourage John to use the time away from rugby to start to develop other aspects of his identity and new interests which may also help him to cope better with such setbacks in the future.

Chapter 13

Suggested responses to Learning Activity 13.3

1. *What were the hypotheses of this second study?* That the physical practice intervention would be more effective for performance than the PETTLEP imagery intervention. The PETTLEP intervention would be more effective for performance than the stimulus imagery and control interventions.
2. *What were the components of the PETTLEP approach that were tested?* All of the components were tested.
3. *What do the results tell us about the effectiveness of the PETTLEP approach?* There was a significantly greater improvement in the PETTLEP group compared to the stimulus imagery only group. This supports the use of the PETTLEP model of imagery in comparison to stimulus only imagery. There was no significant difference between the PETTLEP group and the physical practice group. Therefore PETTLEP imagery appeared to be as effective as physically performing the task.

References

Adkin, EC and Keel, PK (2005) Does 'excessive' or 'compulsive' best describe exercise as a symptom of bulimia nervosa? *International Journal of Eating Disorders*, 38: 24–29.

Ajzen, I (1985) From intentions to actions: A theory of planned behavior, in Kuhl, J and Beckmann, J (eds) *Action Control: From Cognition to Behavior*. Berlin, Heidelberg, New York: Springer-Verlag.

Ajzen, I (1991) The theory of planned behaviour. *Organizational Behavior and Human Decision Processes*, 50: 179–211.

Ajzen, I (2002) Perceived behavioral control, self-efficacy, locus of control, and the theory of planned behavior. *Journal of Applied Social Psychology*, 32: 665–683.

American Psychiatric Association (1994) *Diagnostic and Statistical Manual of Psychiatric Disorders*, 4th edition, revised. Washington DC: American Psychiatric Association.

American Psychiatric Association (2000) *Diagnostic and Statistical Manual of Mental disorders*, 4th edition, text revision. Washington, DC: American Psychiatric Association.

Ames, C (1992) Classrooms: Goals, structures, and student motivation. *Journal of Educational Psychology*, 84: 261–271.

Andersen, MB and Williams, JM (1998) A model of stress and athletic injury: Prediction and prevention. *Journal of Sport and Exercise Psychology*, 10: 294–306.

Anderson, AG, White, A and McKay, J (2004) Athletes' emotional responses to injury, in Lavallee, D, Thatcher, J and Jones, M (eds) *Coping and Emotion in Sport*. New York: Nova Science, pp. 207–221.

Anderson, ES, Wojcik, JR, Winett, RA and Williams, DM (2006) Social–cognitive determinants of physical activity: The influence of social support, self-efficacy, outcome expectations, and self-regulation among participants in a church-based health promotion study. *Health Psychology*, 25: 510–520.

Anderson, ES, Winet, RA, Wojcik, JR and Williams, DM (2010) Social cognitive mediators of change in a group randomized nutrition and physical activity intervention: Social support, self-efficacy, outcome expectations and self-regulation in the guide-to-health trial. *Journal of Health Psychology*, 15: 21–32.

Annesi, JJ (2006) Relations of physical self-concept and self-efficacy with frequency of voluntary physical activity in preadolescents: Implications for after-school care programming. *Journal of Psychosomatic Research*, 61: 515–520.

Ansorge, CJ, Sheer, JK, Laub, J and Howard, HJ (1978) Bias in judging in women's gymnastics induced by expectations of within team order. *Research Quarterly*, 49: 399–405.

Armitage, CJ and Connor, M (2001) Efficacy of the theory of planned behaviour: A meta-analytical review. *British Journal of Social Psychology*, 40: 471–499.

Aşçi, FH, Kosar, S and Isler, A (2001) The relationship of self-concept and perceived athletic competence to physical activity level and gender among Turkish early adolescents. *Adolescence*, 36: 499–502.

Aşçi, FH, Tüzün, M and Koka C (2006) An examination of eating attitudes and physical activity levels of Turkish University students with regard to self-presentational concern. *Eating Behaviors*, 7: 362–367.

Ashford, S, Edmunds, J and French, DP (2010) What is the best way to change self-efficacy to promote lifestyle and recreational physical activity? A systematic review with meta-analysis. *British Journal of Health Psychology*, 15: 265–288.

Atienza, FL, Balaguer, I and Garcia Merita, ML (1998) Video modeling and imaging training on performance of tennis serve of 9 to 12 year old children. *Perceptual and Motor Skills*, 87: 191–215.

Backhouse, SH, Ekkekakis, P, Biddle, SJH, Foskett, A and Williams, C (2007) Exercise makes people feel better but people are inactive: Paradox or artifact? *Journal of Sport and Exercise Psychology*, 29: 498–517.

Ball, K (2006) People, places . . . and other people? Integrating understanding of intrapersonal, social and environmental determinants of physical activity. *Journal of Science and Medicine in Sport*, 9: 367–370.

Bamber, D, Cockerill, IM, Rodgers, S and Carroll, D (2000a) 'It's exercise or nothing': A qualitative analysis of exercise dependence. *British Journal of Sports Medicine*, 34: 423–430.

Bamber, D, Cockerill, IM and Carroll, D (2000b) The pathological status of exercise dependence. *British Journal of Sports Medicine*, 34: 125–132.

Bamber, DJ, Cockerill, IM, Rodgers, S and Carroll, D (2003) Diagnostic criteria for exercise dependence in women. *British Journal of Sports Medicine*, 37: 393–400.

Bandura, A (1977) Self-efficacy: Toward a unifying theory of behavioural change. *Psychological Review*, 84: 191–215.

Bandura, A (1986) *Social Foundations of Thought and Action: A Social Cognitive Theory*. Englewood Cliffs, NJ: Prentice-Hall.

Bandura, A (1997) *Self-Efficacy: The Exercise of Control*. New York: WH Freeman.

Bandura, A (2004) Health promotion by social cognitive means. *Health Education and Behaviour*, 31: 143–164.

Baumeister, RF (1984) Choking under pressure: Self-consciousness and paradoxical effects of incentives on skilful performance. *Journal of Personality and Social Psychology*, 46: 610–620.

Baumeister, RF and Showers, CJ (1986) A review of paradoxical performance effects: Choking under pressure in sports and mental tests. *European Journal of Social Psychology*, 16: 361–383.

Bawden, M and Maynard, I (2001) Towards an understanding of the personal experience of the yips in cricket. *Journal of Sports Sciences*, 19: 937–953.

Becker, AJ and Solomon, GB (2005) Expectancy information and coach effectiveness in intercollegiate basketball. *The Sport Psychologist*, 19: 251–266.

Berger, BG, Pargman, D and Weinberg, RS (2007) *Foundations of Exercise Psychology*, 2nd edition. Morgantown, WV: Fitness Information Technology, pp. 301–303.

Bize, R, Johnson, JA and Plotnikoff, RC (2007) Physical activity level and health-related quality of life in the general adult population: A systematic review. *Preventive Medicine*, 45: 401–405.

Blakeslee, M and Goff, DM (2007) The effects of a mental skills training package on equestrians. *The Sport Psychologist*, 21: 288–301.

Blanchard, CM, Rodgers, WM, Spence, JC and Courneya, KS (2001) Feeling state responses to acute exercise of high and low intensity. *Journal of Science and Medicine in Sport*, 4: 30–38.

Boen, F, Vanden Auweele, Y, Claes, E, Feys, J and De Cuyper, B (2006) The impact of open feedback on conformity among judges in rope skipping. *Psychology of Sport and Exercise*, 7: 577–590.

Boen, F, Van Hoye, K, Auweele, YV, Feys, J and Smits, T (2008) Open feedback in gymnastic judging causes conformity bias based on informational influencing. *Journal of Sports Sciences*, 26: 621–628.

Blissmer, B and McAuley, E (2002) Testing the requirements of stages of physical activity among adults: The comparative effectiveness of stage-matched, mismatched, standard care, and control interventions. *Annals of Behavioral Medicine*, 24: 181–189.

Booth, ML, Bauman, A, Owen, N and Gore, CJ (1997) Physical activity preferences, preferred sources of assistance and perceived barriers to increased activity amongst physically inactive Australians. *Preventive Medicine*, 26: 131–137.

Boutcher, SH, McAuley, E and Courneya, KS (1997) Positive and negative affective response of trained and untrained subjects during and after aerobic exercise. *Australian Journal of Psychology*, 49: 28–32.

Boyce, BA, Gano-Overway, LA and Campbell, A (2009) The perceived motivational climate's influence on goal orientations, perceived competence, and practice strategies across the competitive athletic season. *Journal of Applied Sport Psychology*, 21: 381–394.

Brophy, JE and Good, T (1970) Teachers' communication of differential expectations for children's classroom performance: Some behavioural data. *Journal of Educational Psychology*, 61: 365–374.

Brown, DW, Balluz, LS, Heath, GW, Moriarty, DG, Ford, ES and Giles, WH *et al.* (2004) Associations between recommended levels of physical activity and health-related quality of life. Findings from the 2001 Behavioral Risk Factor Surveillance System (BRFSS) survey. *Preventive Medicine*, 37: 520–528.

Bull, SJ, Shambrook, CJ, James, W and Brooks, JE (2005) Towards an understanding of mental toughness in elite English cricket. *Journal of Applied Sport Psychology*, 17: 209–227.

Burgess, G, Grogan, S and Burwitz, L (2006) Effects of a 6-week aerobic dance intervention on body image and physical self-perceptions in adolescent girls. *Body Image*, 3: 27–66.

Burton, D (1989) Winning isn't everything: Examining the impact of performance goals on collegiate swimmers' cognitions and performance. *The Sport Psychologist*, 3: 105–132.

Burton, D, Naylor, S and Holliday, B (2001) Goal setting in sport: Investigating the goal effectiveness paradox, in Singer, RN, Hausenblas, HA and Janelle, CM (eds) *Handbook of Sport Psychology*, 2nd edition. New York: John Wiley & Sons, pp. 497–528.

Burton, D, Pickering, M, Weinberg, R, Yukelson, D and Weigand, D (2010) The competitive goal effectiveness paradox revisited: Examining the goal practices of prospective Olympic athletes. *Journal of Applied Sport Psychology*, 22: 72–86.

Butler, JL and Baumeister, RF (1998) The trouble with friendly faces: Skilled performance with a supportive audience. *Journal of Personality and Social Psychology*, 75: 1213–1230.

Buunk, BP and Nauta, A (2000) Why intraindividual needs are not enough: Human motivation is primarily social. *Psychological Inquiry*, 11: 279–283.

Camiré, M, Trudel, P and Forneris, T (2009) High school athletes' perspectives on support, communication, negotiation and life skill development. *Qualitative Research in Sport and Exercise*, 1: 72–88.

Carnethon, MR, Gidding, SS, Nehgme, R, Sidney, S, Jacobs, DR and Liu, K (2003) Cardiorespiratory fitness in young adulthood and the development of cardiovascular disease risk factors. *Journal of the American Medical Association*, 290: 3092–3100.

Cash, TF (2002) A 'negative body image': Evaluating epidemiological evidence, in Cash, TF and Pruzinsky, T (eds) *Body Image: A handbook of theory, research, and clinical practice*. New York: Guilford, pp. 269–276.

Chatzisarantis, N, Hagger, M, Biddle, S, Smith, B and Phoenix, C (2005) On the stability of the attitude-intention relationship and the roles of autonomy and past behaviour in understanding change. *Journal of Sports Sciences*, 23: 49–61.

Chell, B, Graydon, J, Crowley, P and Child, M (2003) Manipulated stress and dispositional reinvestment in a wall-volley task: An investigation into controlled processing. *Perceptual and Motor Skills*, 97: 435–448.

Christakou, A, Zervas, Y, and Lavallee, D (2007) The adjunctive role of imagery on the functional rehabilitation of a grade II ankle sprain. *Human Movement Science*, 26: 141–154.

Clay, D, Vignoles, VL and Dittmar, H (2005) Body image and self-esteem among adolescent girls: Testing the influence of sociocultural factors. *Journal of Research on Adolescents*, 15: 451–477.

Clifton, RT and Gill, DL (1994) Gender differences in self-confidence on a feminine-typed task. *Journal of Sport and Exercise Psychology*, 16: 150–162.

Clough, P, Earle, K and Sewell, D (2002). Mental toughness: The concept and its measurement, in Cockerill, I (ed.) *Solutions in Sport Psychology*. London: Thomson, pp. 32–43.

Coakley, JA (1992) Burnout among adolescent athletes: A personal failure or social problem. *Sociology of Sport Journal*, 9: 271–285.

Cohn, P (1990) An exploratory study on sources of stress and athlete burnout in youth golf. *Sport Psychologist*, 4: 95–106.

Connaughton, D, Hanton, S and Jones, G (2010) The development and maintenance of mental toughness in the World's best performers. *The Sport Psychologist*, 24: 168–193.

Connelly, D and Rotella, RJ (1991) The social psychology of assertive communication: Issues in teaching assertiveness skills to athletes. *The Sport Psychologist*, 5: 73–87.

Conwell, LS, Trost, SG, Spence, L, Brown, WJ and Batch, JA (2010) The feasibility of a home-based moderate-intensity physical activity intervention in obese children and adolescents. *British Journal of Sports Medicine*, 44: 250–255.

Cook, BJ and Hausenblas, HA (2008) The role of exercise dependence for the relationship between exercise behavior and eating pathology: Mediator or moderator? *Journal of Health Psychology*, 13: 495–502.

Cornelissen, VA and Fagard, RH (2005) Effects of endurance training on blood pressure, blood pressure-regulating mechanisms, and cardiovascular risk factors. *Hypertension*, 46: 667–675.

Cresswell, SL and Eklund, RC (2006) The nature of athlete burnout: Key characteristics and attributions. *Journal of Applied Sport Psychology*, 18: 219–239.

Cresswell, SL and Eklund, RC (2007). Athlete burnout: A longitudinal qualitative study. *The Sport Psychologist*, 21: 1–20.

Csikszentmihalyi, M (1975) *Beyond Boredom and Anxiety*. San Francisco: Jossey-Bass.

Csikszentmihalyi, M (1985) Emergent motivation and the evolution of the self, in Kleiber, DA and Maehr, M (eds) *Advances in Motivation and Achievement*, Vol. 4. Greenwich, CT: JAI Press, pp. 93–119.

Daley, AJ and Maynard, IW (2003) Preferred exercise mode and affective responses in physically active adults. *Psychology of Sport and Exercise*, 4: 347–356.

Daley, LK, Fish, AF, Frid DJ and Mitchell, GL (2009) Stage-specific education/counseling intervention in women with elevated blood pressure. *Progress in Cardiovascular Nursing*, 24: 45–52.

Dalle Grave, R, Calugi, S and Marchesini, G (2008) Compulsive exercise to control shape or weight in eating disorders: Prevalence, associated features, and treatment outcome. *Comprehensive Psychiatry*, 49: 346–352.

Davis, C and Claridge, G (1998) The eating disorders as addiction: A psychobiological perspective. *Addictive Behaviors*, 23: 463–475.

Davis, C and Kaptein, S (2006) Anorexia nervosa with excessive exercise: A phenotype with close links to obsessive-compulsive disorder. *Psychiatry Research*, 142: 209–217.

Davis, C, Kaptein, S, Kaplan, AS, Olmsted, P and Woodside, DB (1998) Obsessionality in anorexia nervosa: The moderating influence of exercise. *Psychosomatic Medicine*, 60: 192–197.

Davis, C, Blackmore, E, Katzman, DK and Fox, J (2005) Female adolescents with anorexia nervosa and their parents: A case-control study of exercise attitudes and behaviours. *Psychological Medicine*, 35: 377–386.

Day, MC, Thatcher, J, Greenlees, I and Woods, B (2006) The causes of and psychological responses to lost move syndrome in national level trampolinists. *Journal of Applied Sport Psychology*, 18: 151–166.

Decety, J and Jeannerod, M (1996) Mentally stimulated movements in virtual reality. Does Fitt's law hold in virtual reality? *Behavioural Brain Research*, 72: 127–134.

Deci, EL and Ryan, RM (1985) *Intrinsic Motivation and Self-determination in Human Behavior*. New York: Plenum.

Deci, EL and Ryan, RM (2000) The 'what' and 'why' of goal pursuits: Human needs and the self-determination of behavior. *Psychological Inquiry*, 11: 227–268.

Deci, EL and Ryan, RM (2002) An overview of self-determination theory: An organismic-dialectical perspective, in Deci, EL and Ryan, RM (eds) *Handbook of Self-determination Research*. Rochester, NY: University of Rochester Press, pp. 3–33.

Deci, EL, Koestner, R and Ryan, RM (1999) A meta-analytic review of experiments examining the effects of extrinsic rewards on intrinsic motivation. *Psychological Bulletin*, 125: 627–700.

Demaree, SR, Powers, SK and Lawlor, JM (2001) Fundamentals of exercise metabolism, in *The American College of Sports Medicine Resource Manual for Guidelines for Exercise Testing and Prescription*, 4th edition. Philadelphia: Lippincott, Williams and Wilkins, pp. 133–140.

De Moor, MHM, Beem, AL, Stubbe, JH, Boomsma, DI and De Geus, EJC (2006) Regular exercise, anxiety, depression and personality: A population-based study. *Preventive Medicine*, 42: 273–279.

Department for Culture, Media and Sport (2002) *Game Plan: A Strategy for Delivering Government's Sport and Physical Activity Objectives*. London: Department for Media, Culture and Sport.

Department for Culture, Media and Sport (2010) *Taking Part: The national survey of culture, media and sport – rolling estimates*. London: Department for Media, Culture and Sport.

Department for Work and Pensions (2005) *Department of Health, Health and Safety Executive: Health, Work and Well-being – Caring for our Future*. Crown Copyright. Accessed 18 January 2011 from www.dwp.gov.uk/docs/health-and-wellbeing.pdf

Diener, E (1984) Subjective well-being. *Psychological Bulletin*, 95: 542–575.

Dishman, RK, Hales, DP, Pfeiffer, KA, Felton, GA, Saunders, R, Ward, DS *et al.* (2006) Physical self-concept and self-esteem mediate cross-sectional relations of physical activity and sport participation with depression symptoms among adolescent girls. *Health Psychology*, 25: 396–407.

Dishman, RK, Vandenberg, RJ, Motl, RW, Wilson, MG and DeJoy, DM (2009) Dose relations between goal setting, theory-based correlates of goal setting and increases in physical activity during a workplace trial. *Health Education Research*, 25: 620–631.

Dugdale, JR, Eklund, RC and Gordon, S (2002) Expected and unexpected stressors in major international competition: Appraisal, coping, and performance. *The Sport Psychologist*, 16: 20–33.

Dunton, GF, Schneider, M, Graham, DJ and Cooper, DM (2006) Physical activity, fitness, and physical self-concept in adolescent females. *Pediatric Exercise Science*, 18: 240–251.

Dunn, AL, Trivedi, MH and O'Neal, HA (2001) Physical activity dose-response effects on outcomes of depression and anxiety. *Medicine and Science in Sports and Exercise*, 33: S587–S597.

Dunn, AL, Triverdi, MH, Kampert, JB, Clark, CG and Chambliss, HO (2005) Exercise treatment for depression: Efficacy and dose response. *American Journal of Preventative Medicine*, 28: 1–8.

Durand-Bush, N and Salmela, JH (2002) The development and maintenance of expert athletic performance: Perceptions of world and Olympic champions. *Journal of Applied Sport Psychology*, 14: 154–171.

Edmunds, J, Ntoumanis, N and Duda, JLD (2006) A test of self-determination theory in the exercise domain. *Journal of Applied Social Psychology*, 36: 2240–2265.

Edmunds, J, Ntoumanis, N and Duda, JL (2007) Adherence and well-being in overweight and obese patients referred to an exercise on prescription scheme: A self determination theory perspective. *Psychology of Sport and Exercise*, 8: 722–740.

Ekeland, E, Heian, F and Hagen, KB (2005) Can exercise improve self-esteem in children and young people? A systematic review of randomised controlled trials. *Journal of Sports Medicine*, 39: 792–798.

Eubank, MR, Collins, DJ and Smith, N (2000) The influence of anxiety direction on processing bias. *Journal of Sport and Exercise Psychology*, 22: 292–306.

European Food Information Council (2003) Physical activity and health: Taking a closer look at the other side of the energy balance. EUFIC Review No. 2. www.eufic.org/article/en/page/RARCHIVE/expid/review-physical-activity-health/

Eysenck, MW (1992) *Anxiety: The cognitive perspective*. Hove, UK: Lawrence Erlbaum Associates Ltd.

Fagard, RH (2001) Exercise characteristics and blood pressure response to dynamic physical training. *Medicine and Science in Sports and Exercise*, 33: S484–S492.

Feltz, DL and Lirgg, CD (2001) Self-efficacy beliefs of athletes, teams and coaches, in Singer, RN, Hausenblas, HA and Janelle, CM (eds) *Handbook of Sport Psychology*, 2nd edition. New York: John Wiley & Sons, pp. 304–361.

Fenigstein, A, Scheier, MF and Buss, AH (1975) Public and private self-consciousness: Assessment and theory. *Journal of Consulting and Clinical Psychology*, 42: 522–527.

Fiedler, K (1996) Processing social information for judgements and decisions, in Hewstone, M, Stroebe, W and Stephenson, GM (eds) *Introduction to Social Psychology*, 2nd edition. Cambridge: Blackwell, pp. 135–166.

Findlay, LC and Ste-Marie, DM (2004) A reputation bias in figure skating judging. *Journal of Sport and Exercise Psychology*, 26: 154–166.

Fishbein, M and Ajzen, I (1975) *Belief, Attitude, Intention and Behavior*. Don Mills, New York: Addison-Wiley.

Fitts, PM and Posner, MI (1967) *Human Performance*. Belmont, CA: Brooks/Cole.

Fox, KR (1997) *The Physical Self: From motivation to well-being*. Champaign, IL: Human Kinetics.

Fox, KR (2000). Self-esteem, self-perceptions, and exercise. *International Journal of Sport and Exercise Psychology*, 31: 228–240.

Fox, KR and Corbin, CB (1989) The Physical Self-Perception Profile: Development and preliminary validation. *Journal of Sport and Exercise Psychology*, 11: 408–430.

Franzoi, SL and Shields, SA (1984) The Body Esteem Scale: Multidimensional structure and sex differences in a college population. *Journal of Personality Assessment*, 48: 173–178.

Frazier, PA, Tix, AP and Barron, KE (2004) Testing moderator and mediator effects in research. *Counseling Psychology*, 51: 115–134.

Fredrickson, BL and Roberts, T-A (1997) Objectification theory: Toward understanding women's lived experiences and mental health risks. *Psychology of Women Quarterly*, 21: 207–226.

Galambos, SA, Terry, PC, Moyle, GM and Locke, SA (2005) Psychological predictors of injury among elite athletes. *British Journal of Sports Medicine*, 39: 351–354.

Gammage, KL, Hall, CR and Martin Ginis, KA (2004a) Self-presentation in exercise contexts: Differences between high and low frequency exercisers. *Journal of Applied Social Psychology*, 34: 1638–1641.

Gammage, KL, Martin Ginis, KA and Hall, CR (2004b) Self-presentational efficacy: Its influence on social anxiety in an exercise context. *Journal of Sport and Exercise Psychology*, 26: 179–190.

Gardner, FL and Moore, Z (2006) *Clinical Sport Psychology*. Leeds: Human Kinetics.

Gardner, RM (2001) Assessment of body image disturbance in children and adolescents, in Thompson, JK and Smolak, L (eds) *Body Image, Eating Disorders and Obesity in Youth: Assessment, prevention and treatment*. Washington, DC: American Psychological Association, pp. 193–213.

Gijsbers van Wijk, CMT, Kolk, AM, van den Bosch, WJHM and van den Hoogen, HJM (1995) Male and female health problems in general practice: The differential impact of social position and social roles. *Social Science and Medicine*, 40: 597–611.

Giles-Corti, B and Donovan, RJ (2002) The relative influence of individual, social and physical environment determinants of physical activity. *Social Science and Medicine*, 54: 1793–1812.

Gleeson-Krieg, JM (2006) Self-monitoring of physical activity: Effects on self-efficacy and behavior in people with type 2 diabetes. *The Diabetes Educator*, 32: 69–77.

Godin, G and Kok, G (1996) The Theory of Planned Behavior: A review of its applications to health-related behaviors. *American Journal of Health Promotion*, 11: 87–98.

Golby, J and Sheard, M (2004) Mental toughness and hardiness at different levels of rugby league. *Personality and Individual Differences*, 37: 933–942.

Gould, D and Maynard, I (2009) Psychological preparation for the Olympic Games. *Journal of Sports Sciences*, 27: 1393–1408.

Gould, D, Dieffenbach, K and Moffett, A (2002) Psychological characteristics and their development in Olympic champions. *Journal of Applied Sport Psychology*, 14: 172–204.

Gould, D, Hodge, K, Peterson, K and Petlichkoff, L (1987) Psychological foundations of coaching: Similarities and differences among intercollegiate wrestling coaches. *The Sport Psychologist*, 1: 293–308.

Gould, D, Udry, E, Tuffey, S and Loehr, J (1996) Burnout in competitive junior tennis players: I. A quantitative psychological assessment. *The Sport Psychologist*, 10: 322–340.

Gould, D, Guinan, D, Greenleaf, C, Medbery, R and Paterson, K (1999) Factors affecting Olympic performance: Perceptions of athletes and coaches from more and less successful teams. *The Sport Psychologist*, 13, 371–394.

Greenlees, I, Buscombe, R, Thelwell, R, Holder, T and Rimmer, M (2005) Impact of opponents' clothing and body language on impression formation and outcome expectations. *Journal of Sport and Exercise Psychology*, 27: 39–52.

Greenspan, MJ and Feltz, DL (1989) Psychological interventions with athletes in competitive situations: A review. *The Sport Psychologist*, 3: 219–236.

Grieve, FG (2007) A conceptual model of factors contributing to the development of muscle dysmorphia. *Eating Disorders*, 15: 63–80.

Grogan, S (1999) *Body Image: Understanding body dissatisfaction in men, women and children*. London and New York: Routledge.

Gucciardi, DF and Gordon, S (2009) Development and preliminary validation of the Cricket Mental Toughness Inventory (CMTI). *Journal of Sports Sciences*, 27: 1293–1310.

Gucciardi, DF, Gordon, S and Dimmock, JA (2009a) Development and preliminary validation of a mental toughness inventory for Australian football. *Psychology of Sport and Exercise*, 10: 201–209.

Gucciardi, DF, Gordon, S and Dimmock JA (2009b) Evaluation of a mental toughness training program for youth-aged Australian footballers: II. A qualitative analysis. *Journal of Applied Sport Psychology*, 21: 324–339.

Gustafsson, H, Hassmén, P, Kenttä, G and Johansson, M (2008) A qualitative analysis of burnout in elite Swedish athletes. *Psychology of Sport and Exercise*, 9: 800–816.

Haddad, K and Tremayne, P (2009) The effects of centering on the free-throw shooting performance of young athletes. *The Sport Psychologist*, 23: 118–136.

Hagger, M, Chatzisarantis, NLD and Biddle, SJH (2002) A meta-analytic review of the theories of reasoned action and planned behavior in physical activity: Predictive validity and the contribution of additional variables. *Journal of Sport and Exercise Psychology*, 24: 1–12.

Hale, B, Seiser, L, McGuire, E and Weinrich, E (2005) Mental imagery, in Taylor, J and Wilson, G (eds) *Applying Sport Psychology: Four perspectives*. Champaign, IL: Human Kinetics, pp. 117–135.

Hamer, M and Karageorghis, CI (2007) Psychobiological mechanisms of exercise dependence. *Sports Medicine*, 37: 477–484.

Hanton, S and Jones, G (1999) The effects of a multimodal intervention program on performers. II: Training the butterflies to fly in formation. *The Sport Psychologist*, 13: 22–41.

Hardman, CA, Horne, PJ and Lowe, CF (2009) A home-based intervention to increase physical activity in girls: The fit 'n' fun dudes program. *Journal of Exercise Science and Fitness*, 7: 1–8.

Hardy, CJ and Rejeski, WJ (1989) Not what, but how one feels: The measurement of affect during exercise. *Journal of Sport and Exercise Psychology*, 11: 304–317.

Hardy, J, Hall, CR, Gibbs, C and Greenslade, C (2005) Self-talk and gross motor skill performance. *Athletic Insight: The Online Journal of Sport Psychology*. Available: www.athleticinsight.com/V017Iss2/SelfTalkPerformance.htm

Hardy, L (1996) Testing the predictions of the cusp catastrophe model of anxiety and performance. *The Sport Psychologist*, 10: 140–156.

Hardy, L and Fazey, J (1987) The inverted-U hypothesis: A catastrophe for sport psychology? Communication to the Annual Conference of the North American Society for the Psychology of Sport and Physical Activity, Vancouver, BC, Canada, June.

Hare, R, Evans, L and Callow, N (2008) Imagery use during rehabilitation from injury: A case study of an elite athlete. *The Sport Psychologist*, 22: 405–422.

Hargie, O and Dickson, D (2004) *Skilled Interpersonal Communication*. East Sussex: Routledge.

Harrison, M, Burns, CF, McGuinness, M, Heslin, J and Murphy, NM (2006) Influence of a health education intervention on physical activity and screen time in primary school children: 'Switch Off-Get Active.' *Journal of Science and Medicine in Sport*, 9: 388–394.

Hart, EA, Leary, MR and Rejeski, WJ (1989) The measurement of social physique anxiety. *Journal of Sport and Exercise Psychology*, 11: 94–104.

Harter, S (1993) Causes and consequences of low self-esteem in children and adolescents, in Baumeister, RF (ed.) *Self-esteem: The puzzle of low self-regard*. New York: Plenum Press, pp. 87–116.

Harvey, DT, Van Raalte, J and Brewer, BW (2002) Relationship between self-talk and golf performance. *International Sports Journal*, 6: 84–91.

Harwood, C (2005) Goals: More than just the score, in Murphy, S (ed.) *The Sport Psych Handbook*. Leeds: Human Kinetics.

Haselwood, DM, Joyner, A, Burke, KL, Geyerman, CB, Czech, DR, Munkasy, BA and Zwald, AD (2005) Female athletes' perceptions of head coaches' communication competence. *Journal of Sport Behavior*, 28: 216–230.

Hatzigeorgiadis, A, Zourbanos, N, Goltsios, C and Theodorakis, Y (2008) Investigating the functions of self-talk: The effects of motivational self-talk on self-efficacy and performance in young tennis players. *The Sport Psychologist*, 22: 458–471.

Hausenblas, HA and Symons Downs, D (2002) Exercise dependence: A systematic review. *Psychology of Sport and Exercise*, 3: 89–123.

Hayley, S, Merali, Z and Anisman, H (2003) Stress and cytokine-elicited neuroendocrine and neurotransmitter sensitization: Implications for depressive illness. *Stress*, 6: 19–32.

Hays, K, Thomas, O, Butt, J and Maynard, I (2010) The role of confidence profiling in cognitive-behavioral interventions in sport. *The Sport Psychologist*, 24: 393–414.

Hays, K, Thomas, O, Maynard, I and Bawden, M (2009) The role of confidence in world class sport performance. *Journal of Sports Sciences*, 27: 1185–1199.

Hellström, J (2009) Psychological hallmarks of skilled golfers. *Sports Medicine*, 39: 845–855.

Herring, MP, O'Connor, PJ and Dishman, RK (2010) The effect of exercise training on anxiety symptoms among patients: A systematic review. *Archives of Internal Medicine*, 170: 321–331.

Highlen, PS and Bennett, BB (1979) Psychological characteristics of successful and nonsuccessful elite wrestlers: An exploratory study. *Journal of Sport Psychology*, 1: 123–137.

Hillsdon, M, Cavill, N, Nanchahal, K, Diamond, A and White IR (2001) National level promotion of physical activity: Results from England's ACTIVE for LIFE campaign. *Journal of Epidemiology and Community Health*, 55: 755–761.

Holland, MJG, Woodcock, C, Cumming, J and Duda, JL (2010) Mental qualities and employed mental techniques of young elite team sport athletes. *Journal of Clinical Sport Psychology*, 4: 19–38.

Holme-Denoma, JM, Scaringi, V, Gordon, KH, Van Orden, KA and Joiner, TE (2009) Eating disorder symptoms among undergraduate varsity athletes, club athletes, independent exercisers, and nonexercisers. *International Journal of Eating Disorders*, 42: 47–53.

Holmes, PS and Collins, DJ (2001). The PETTLEP approach to motor imagery: A functional equivalence model for sport psychologists. *Journal of Applied Sport Psychology*, 13: 60–83.

Horn, TS and Weiss, MR (1991) A developmental analysis of children's perceptions of their physical competence, in Weiss, MR and Gould, D (eds) *Children and Youth in Sport: A biopsychosocial perspective*. Dubuque, IA: Times Mirror, pp. 309–329.

Horn, TS, Lox, C and Labrador, F (2001) The self-fulfilling prophecy theory: When coaches' expectations become reality, in Williams, J (ed.) *Applied Sport Psychology: Personal growth to peak performance*. Mountain View, CA: Mayfield, pp. 68–81.

Horsburgh, V, Schermer, J, Veselka, L and Vernon, P (2009) A behavioural genetic study of mental toughness and personality. *Personality and Individual Differences*, 46: 100–105.

Huhman, M, Potter, LD, Wong, FL, Banspach, SW and Johnston, S (2008) Effects of a mass media campaign to increase physical activity among children: Year-1 results of the VERB campaign. *Pediatrics*, 116: 277–284.

Jackson, SA and Csikszentmihalyi, M (1999) *Flow in Sports*. Leeds: Human Kinetics.

Jacobson, E (1938) *Progressive Relaxation*. Chicago: University of Chicago Press.

Janis, IL and Mann, L (1977) *Decision Making: A psychological analysis of conflict, choice, and commitment*. New York: Free Press.

Jeannerod, M (1995) Mental imagery in the motor cortex. *Neuropsychologia*, 33: 1419–1432.

Jewson, E, Spittle, M and Casey, M (2008) A preliminary analysis of barriers, intentions, and attitudes towards moderate physical activity in women who are overweight. *Journal of Science and Medicine in Sport*, 11: 558–561.

Jonas, BS and Lando, JF (2000) Negative affect as a prospective risk factor for hypertension. *Psychosomatic Medicine*, 62: 188–196.

Jones, G, Hanton, S and Connaughton, D (2002) What is this thing called Mental Toughness? An investigation with elite performers. *Journal of Applied Sport Psychology*, 14: 211–224.

Jones, MV, Paull, GC and Erskine, J (2002) The impact of a team's aggressive reputation on the decisions of association football referees. *Journal of Sports Sciences*, 20: 991–1000.

Jowett, S (2003) When the 'honeymoon' is over: A case study of a coach-athlete dyad in crisis. *The Sport Psychologist*, 17: 444–460.

Keller, C, Steensberg, A, Pilegaard, H, Osada, T, Saltin, B, Pedersen, BK *et al.* (2001) Transcriptional activation of the IL-6 gene in human contracting skeletal muscle: Influence of muscle glycogen content. *Federation of American Societies for Experimental Biology Journal*, 15: 2748–2750.

Kelley, BC, Eklund, RC and Ritter-Taylor, M (1999) Stress and burnout among collegiate tennis coaches. *Journal of Sport and Exercise Psychology*, 21: 113–130.

Kelley, GA and Kelley, KS (2000) Progressive resistance exercise and resting blood pressure: A meta-analysis of randomised controlled trials. *Hypertension*, 35: 838–843.

Kelley, GA, Kelley, KS and Tran, ZV (2001) Walking and resting blood pressure in adults: A meta-analysis. *Preventive Medicine*, 33: 120–127.

Kerr, JH and Grange, P (2009) Athlete-to-athlete verbal aggression: A case study of interpersonal communication among elite Australian footballers. *International Journal of Sport Communication*, 2: 360–372.

Kiefer, F and Wiedemann, K (2004) Neuroendocrine pathways of addictive behaviour. *Addictive Biology*, 9: 205–212.

Kilpatrick, M, Kraemer, R, Bartholomew, J, Acevedo, E and Jarreau, D (2007) Affective responses to exercise are dependent on intensity rather than total work. *Medicine and Science in Sports and Exercise*, 39: 1417–1422.

King, AC, Marcus, B, Ahn, D, Rejeski, WJ, Coday, M, Sallis, JMF and Dunn, AL (2006) Identifying subgroups that succeed or fail with three levels of physical activity intervention: The activity counselling trial. *Health Psychology*, 25: 336–347.

Kingston, K and Hardy, L (1997) Effects of different types of goals on processes that support performance. *The Sport Psychologist*, 11: 277–293.

Klein, H and Shiffman, KS (2006) Messages about physical attractiveness in animated cartoons. *Body Image*, 3: 353–363.

Kobasa, SC (1979) Stressful life events, personality, and health: An inquiry into hardiness. *Journal of Personality and Social Psychology*, 37: 1–11.

Koestner, R and Losier, GF (2002) Distinguishing three ways of being internally motivated: A closer look at introjection, identification and intrinsic motivation, in Deci, EL and Ryan, RM (eds) *Handbook of Self-determination Research*. New York: University of Rochester Press, pp. 101–122.

Koezuka, N, Koo, M, Allison, KR, Adlaf, EM, Dwyer, JJM, Faulkner, G *et al.* (2006) The relationship between sedentary activities and physical inactivity among adolescents: Results from the Canadian community health survey. *Journal of Adolescent Health*, 39: 515–522.

Krane, V and Williams, JM (2006) Psychological characteristics of peak performance, in Williams, JM (ed.) *Applied Sport Psychology: Personal growth to peak performance*, 5th edition. New York: McGraw-Hill, pp. 207–227.

Krane, V, Greenleaf, CA and Snow, J (1997) Reaching for gold and the price of glory: A motivational case study of an elite gymnast. *The Sport Psychologist*, 11: 53–71.

Kremer, J and Moran, AP (2008) *Pure Sport: Practical sport psychology*. London: Routledge.

Kruisselbrink, LD, Dodge, AM, Swanburg, SL and MacLeod, AL (2004) Influence of same-sex and mixed-sex exercise settings on the social physique anxiety and exercise intentions of males and females. *Journal of Sport and Exercise Psychology*, 26: 616–622.

Kübler-Ross, E (1969) *On Death and Dying*. London: Macmillan.

Lacy, AC and Martin, DL (1994) Analysis of starter/nonstarter motor-skill engagement and coaching behaviors in collegiate women's volleyball. *Journal of Teaching in Physical Education*, 13: 95–107.

Lang, PJ, Kozak, MJ, Miller, GA, Levin, DA and McLean, A (1980) Emotional imagery: Conceptual structure and pattern of somato-visceral response. *Psychophysiology*, 17: 179–192.

Latham, GP and Locke, EA (1991) Self-regulation through goal setting. *Organizational Behavior and Decision Making Processes*, 50: 212–247.

Lawlor, DA and Hopker, SW (2001) The effectiveness of exercise as an intervention in the management of depression: Systematic review and meta-regression analysis of randomised controlled trials. *British Medical Journal*, 322: 1–8.

Lawton, R, McEachan, R, Jackson, C and Conner, M (2009) Increasing physical activity: Designing and testing a workplace intervention: Final research report. Institute of Psychological Sciences, University of Leeds.

Lazarus, R (1999) *Stress and Emotion: A new synthesis*. New York: Springer.

Lee, IM and Skerrett, PJ (2001) Physical activity and all-cause mortality: What is the dose-response relation? *Medicine and Science in Sports and Exercise*, 33 (suppl 6): 459–471.

Lee, IM, Rexrode, KM, Cook, NR, Manson, JE and Buring, JE (2001) Physical activity and coronary heart disease in women: is 'no pain, no gain' passé? *Journal of American Medical Association*, 285: 1447–1454.

Lejoyeaux, M, Avril, M, Richoux, C, Embouazza, H and Nivoli, F (2008) Prevalence of exercise dependence and other behavioral addictions among clients of a Parisian fitness room. *Comprehensive Psychiatry*, 49: 353–358.

Lemyre, P-N, Hall, HK and Roberts, GC (2008) A social cognitive approach to burnout in elite athletes. *Scandanavian Journal of Medicine and Science in Sports*, 18: 221–234.

Leone, JE, Sedory, EJ and Gray, KA (2005) Recognition and treatment of muscle dysmorphia and related body image disorders. *Journal of Athletic Training*, 40: 352–359.

Leslie, E, Fotheringham, MJ, Owen, N and Bauman, A (2001) Age related differences in physical activity levels of young adults. *Medicine and Science in Sports and Exercise*, 33: 255–258.

Lester, OP (1932) Mental set in relation to retroactive inhibition. *Journal of Experimental Psychology*, 15: 681–699.

Lewington, S, Clarke, R, Qizilbash, N, Peto, R and Collins, R (2002) Age-specific relevance of usual blood pressure to vascular mortality: A meta-analysis of individual data for one million adults in 61 prospective studies. *Lancet*, 360: 1903–1913.

Lewis, BP and Linder, DE (1997) Thinking about choking? Attentional processes and paradoxical performance. *Personality and Social Psychology Bulletin*, 23: 937–944.

Liao, CM and Masters, RSW (2002) Self-focused attention and performance failure under psychological stress. *Journal of Sport and Exercise Psychology*, 24: 289–305.

Lidor, R, Blumenstein, B and Tenenbaum, G (2007) Periodisation and planning of psychological preparation in individual and team sports, in Blumenstein, B, Lidor, R and Tenenbaum, G (eds) *Perspectives on Sport and Exercise Psychology*, Vol. 2: *Psychology of sport training*. Oxford, UK: Meyer & Meyer Sport, pp. 137–161.

Lindwall, M and Lindgren, E (2005) The effects of a 6-month exercise intervention programme on physical self-perceptions and social physique anxiety in non-physically active adolescent Swedish girls. *Psychology of Sport and Exercise*, 6: 643–658.

Linstead, KD, Tonstad, S and Kuzma, JW (1991) Self-report of physical activity and patterns of mortality in Seventh-Day Adventist men. *Journal of Clinical Epidemiology*, 44: 355–364.

Lirgg, CC (1991) Gender differences in self-confidence in physical activity: A meta-analysis of recent studies. *Journal of Sport and Exercise Psychology*, 13: 294–310.

Locke, EA and Latham, GP (2002) Building a practically useful theory of goal setting and task motivation: A 35-year odyssey. *American Psychologist*, 57: 705–717.

Locke, EA and Latham, GP (2006) New directions in goal-setting theory. *Current Directions in Psychological Science*, 15: 265–268.

Loehr, JE (1995) *The New Toughness Training for Sports*. New York: Plume.

MacNamara, A, Button, A and Collins, D (2010a) The role of psychological characteristics in facilitating the pathway to elite performance part 1: Identifying mental skills and behaviours. *The Sport Psychologist*, 24: 52–73.

MacNamara, A, Button, A and Collins, D (2010b) The role of psychological characteristics in facilitating the pathway to elite performance. Part 2: Examining environmental and stage related differences in skills and behaviours. *The Sport Psychologist*, 24: 74–96.

Mahoney, MJ and Avener, M (1977) Psychology of the elite: An exploratory study. *Cognitive Therapy and Research*, 1: 135–141.

Maiorana, A, O'Driscoll, G, Cheetham, C, Dembo, L, Stanton, K, Goodman, C *et al.* (2001) The effect of combined aerobic and resistance exercise training on vascular function in type 2 diabetes. *Journal of American College of Cardiology*, 38: 860–866.

Maltby, J and Day, L (2001) The relationship between exercise motives and psychological well-being. *Journal of Psychology*, 135: 651–660.

Manley, AJ, Greenlees, I, Graydon, J, Thelwell, R, Filby, WCD and Smith, MJ (2008) Athletes' perceived use of information sources when forming initial impressions and expectancies of a coach: An exploratory study. *The Sport Psychologist*, 22: 73–89.

Markland, D (1999) Self-determination moderates the effects of perceived competence on intrinsic motivation in an exercise setting. *Journal of Sport and Exercise Psychology*, 21: 351–361.

Marsh, HW and Perry, C (2005) Does a positive self-concept contribute to winning gold medals in elite swimming? The causal ordering of elite athlete self-concept and championship performances. *Journal of Sport and Exercise Psychology*, 27: 71–91.

Marsh, HW, Richards, GE, Johnson, S, Roche, L and Tremayne, P (1994) Physical Self-Description Questionnaire: Psychometric properties and a multitrait-multimethod analysis of relations to existing instruments. *Journal of Sport and Exercise Psychology*, 16: 270–305.

Marshall, SJ and Biddle, SJ (2001) The transtheoretical model of behavior change: A meta-analysis of applications to physical activity and exercise. *Annals of Behavioral Medicine*, 23: 229–246.

Martens, R (1987) *Coaches Guide to Sport Psychology*, Champaign IL: Human Kinetics.

Martin, JJ, Kliber, A, Kulinna, PH and Fahlman, M (2006) Social physique anxiety and muscularity and appearance cognitions in college men. *Sex Roles*, 55: 151–158.

Martin, JL, Martens, MP, Serrao, HF and Rocha, TL (2008) Alcohol use and exercise dependence: Co-occurring behaviors among college students? *Journal of Clinical Sports Psychology*, 2: 381–392.

Martin, KA and Fox, LD (2001) Group and leadership effects on social anxiety experienced during an exercise class. *Journal of Applied Social Psychology*, 31: 1000–1016.

Martin, KA, Moritz, SE and Hall, CR (1999) Imagery use in sport: A literature review and applied model. *The Sport Psychologist*, 13: 245–268.

Martin Ginis, KA, Burke, SM and Gauvin, L (2007) Exercising with others exacerbates the negative effects of mirrored environments on sedentary women's feeling states. *Psychology and Health*, 22: 945–962.

Martin Ginis, KA, Prapavessis, H and Haase, AM (2008) The effects of physique-salient and physique non-salient exercise videos on women's body image, self-presentational concerns, and exercise motivation. *Body Image*, 5: 164–172.

Martinez-Gonzales, MA, Varo, JJ, Santos, JL, De Irala, J, Gibney, M *et al.* (2001) Prevalence of physical activity during leisure time in the European Union. *Medicine and Science in Sports and Exercise*, 33: 1142–1146.

Masters, KS and Ogles, BM (1998) Associative and dissociative cognitive strategies in exercise and running: 20 years later, what do we know? *The Sport Psychologist*, 12: 253–270.

Masters, RSW (1992) Knowledge, knerves and knowhow: The role of explicit versus implicit knowledge in the breakdown of a complex motor skill under pressure. *British Journal of Psychology*, 83: 343–358.

Masters, RSW, Polman, RCJ and Hammond, NV (1993) Reinvestment: A dimension of personality implicated in skill breakdown under pressure. *Personality and Individual Differences*, 14: 655–666.

Maynard, I (2010) Debate: At an elite level the role of a sport psychologist is entirely about performance enhancement. *Sport and Exercise Psychology Review*, 6: 59–66.

McAuley, E, Bane, SM and Mihalko, SM (1995) Exercise in middle-aged adults: Self-efficacy and self-presentational outcomes. *Preventive Medicine*, 24: 319–328.

McAuley, E, Talbot, H-M and Martinez, S (1999) Manipulating self-efficacy in the exercise environment in women: Influences on affective responses. *Health Psychology*, 18: 288–294.

McAuley, E, Blissmer, B, Katula, J, Duncan, TE and Mihalko, S (2000) Physical activity, self-esteem and self-efficacy relationships in older adults: A randomised control trial. *Annals of Behavioral Medicine*, 22: 131–139.

McAuley, E, Morris, KS, Motl, RW, Hu, L, Konopack, JF and Elavsky, S (2007) Long term follow-up of physical activity behaviour in older adults. *Health Psychology*, 26: 375–380.

McCabe, MP and James, T (2009) Strategies to change body shape among men and women who attend fitness centers. *Asia-Pacific Journal of Public Health*, 21: 268–278.

McCabe, MP and Ricciardelli, LA (2004) Body image dissatisfaction among males across the lifespan: A review of past literature. *Journal of Psychosomatic Research,* 56: 675–685.

McCarthy, PJ, Jones, MV, Harwood, CG and Davenport, L (2010a) Using goal setting to enhance positive affect among junior multievent athletes. *Journal of Clinical Sport Psychology*, 4: 53–68.

McCarthy, PJ, Jones, MV, Harwood, CG and Olivier, S (2010b) What do young athletes implicitly understand about psychological skills? *Journal of Clinical Sport Psychology*, 4: 158–172.

McDonald, DG and Hodgdon, JA (1991) *Psychological Effects of Aerobic Fitness Training*. New York: Springer.

McKenzie, AD and Howe, BL (1997) The effect of imagery on self-efficacy for a motor skill. *International Journal of Sport Psychology*, 28: 196–210.

McNeill, LJ, Kreuter, MW and Subramanian, SV (2006) Social environment and physical activity: A review of concepts and evidence. *Social Science and Medicine*, 63: 1011–1022.

Mellalieu, SD, Hanton, S and Fletcher, D (2006) An anxiety review, in Hanton, S and Mellalieu, SD (eds) *Literature Reviews in Sport Psychology*. Hauppauge, NY: Nova Science, pp. 1–45.

Mesagno, C, Marchant, D and Morris, T (2008) A pre-performance routine to alleviate choking in 'choking-susceptible' athletes. *The Sport Psychologist*, 22: 439–457.

Mesagno, C, Marchant, D and Morris, T (2009) Alleviating choking: The sounds of distraction. *Journal of Applied Sport Psychology*, 21: 131–148.

Mullen, R and Hardy, L (2000) State anxiety and motor performance: Testing the conscious processing hypothesis. *Journal of Sports Sciences*, 18: 785–799.

Mutrie, N (2000) The relationship between physical activity and clinically defined depression, in Biddle,

SJH, Fox, KR and Boutcher, SH (eds) *Physical Activity and Psychological Well-being*. London: Routledge, pp. 46–62.

National Audit Office (2001) *Tackling Obesity in England*. National Audit Office. London: The Stationery Office.

National Health Service (2010) Statistics on obesity, physical activity and diet, England 2010. The Health and Social Care Information Centre. Accessed 5 January 2010 from www.ic.nhs.uk/webfiles/publications/opad10/Statistics_on_Obesity_Physical_Activity_and_Diet_England_2010.pdf

Nesti, M (2004) *Existential Psychology and Sport: Implications for research and practice*. London: Routledge.

Neumark-Sztainer, D, Paxton, SJ, Hannan, PJ, Stat, M, Haines, J and Story, M (2006) Does body satisfaction matter? Five-year longitudinal associations between body satisfaction and health behaviors in adolescent females and males. *Journal of Adolescent Health*, 39: 244–251.

Nevill, AM, Balmer, NJ and Williams, M (2002) The influence of crowd noise and experience upon refereeing decisions in football. *Psychology of Sport and Exercise*, 3: 261–272.

NHS Information Centre for Health and Social Care (2007) Adult psychiatric morbidity in England, 2007: Results of a household survey. The NHS Information Centre for Health and Social Care. Accessed 5 January 2010 from www.ic.nhs.uk/pubs/psychiatricmorbidity07

NICE (National Institute for Clinical Excellence) (2006) Promotion of physical activity among adults; evidence into practice briefing. National Institute for Clinical Excellence. Accessed 10 January 2011 from www.nice.org.uk/niceMedia/pdf/physical_activity_eip_v3.pdf

Nicholas, CW, Nuttall, FE and Williams, C (2000) The Loughborough Intermittent Shuttle Test: A field test that simulates the activity pattern of soccer. *Journal of Sports Sciences*, 18: 97–104.

Nicholls, JG (1984) Achievement motivation: Conceptions of ability, subjective experience, task choice, and performance. *Psychological Review*, 49: 529–538.

Nicholls, A, Polman, R, Levy, A and Backhouse, S (2008) Mental toughness, optimism and coping among athletes. *Personality and Individual Differences*, 44: 1182–1192.

Nideffer, RM (1976) Test of attentional and interpersonal style. *Journal of Personality and Social Psychology*, 34: 394–404.

Nideffer, RM (1993) Attention control training, in Singer, RN, Murphey, M and Tennant, LK (eds) *Handbook of Research on Sport Psychology*. New York: Macmillan, pp. 542–556.

Nigg, CR, Karly, GS, Motl, RW, Horwath, CC, Wertin, KW and Dishman, RK (2010) A research agenda to examine the efficacy and relevance of the Transtheoretical Model for physical activity behaviour. *Psychology of Sport and Exercise*, 12: 7–12.

Nordin, SM and Cumming, J (2008) Types and functions of athletes' imagery: Testing predictions from the applied model of imagery use by examining effectiveness. *International Journal of Sport and Exercise Psychology*, 6: 189–206.

O'Brien, M, Mellalieu, SD and Hanton, S (2009) Goal setting effects in elite and non-elite boxers. *Journal of Applied Sport Psychology*, 21: 293–306.

Olivardia, R (2007) Muscle dysmorphia: Characteristics, assessment and treatment, in Thompson, JK and Cafri, G (eds) *The Muscular Ideal: Psychological, social and medical perspectives*. Washington, DC: American Psychological Association, pp. 123–140.

Olivardia, R, Pope, HG Jr and Hudson, JI (2000) Muscle dysmorphia in male weightlifters: A case-control study. *American Journal of Psychiatry,* 157: 1291–1296.

Olusoga, P, Butt, J, Hays, K and Maynard, I (2009) Stress in elite sports coaching: Identifying stressors. *Journal of Applied Sport Psychology*, 21: 442–459.

Orlick, T (2000) *In Pursuit of Excellence: How to win in sport and life through mental training.* Leeds: Human Kinetics.

Paffenbarger, RS, Hyde, RT, Wing, AL, Lee, IM, Jung, DL and Kampert, JD (1993) The association of changes in physical activity level and other lifestyle characteristics with mortality among men. *New England Journal of Medicine*, 328: 538–545.

Parfitt, G and Gledhill, C (2004) The effect of choice of exercise mode on psychological responses. *Psychology of Sport and Exercise*, 5: 111–117.

Park, J (2003) Adolescent self-concept and health into adulthood. *Health Reports*, 14(suppl): 41–52.

Partington, S, Partington, E and Olivier, S (2009) The dark side of flow: A qualitative study of dependence in big wave surfing. *The Sport Psychologist*, 23, 170–185.

Pates, J, Cummings, A and Maynard, I (2002) The effects of hypnosis on flow states and three point shooting performance in basketball players. *The Sport Psychologist*, 16: 1–15.

Patrick, TD and Hrycaiko, DW (1998) Effects of a mental training package on endurance performance. *The Sport Psychologist*, 12: 283–299.

Pedersen, BK and Saltin, B (2006) Evidence for prescribing exercise as therapy in chronic disease. *Scandinavian Journal of Medicine and Science in Sports*, 16 (suppl 1): 3–63.

Pelletier, LG, Fortier, MS, Vallerand, RJ and Brière, NM (2001) Associations between perceived autonomy support, forms of self regulation and persistence: A prospective study. *Motivation and Emotion*, 25: 279–306.

Pescatello, LS, Franklin, BA, Fagard, R, Farquhar, WB, Kelley, GA and Ray, CA (2004) American College of Sports Medicine position stand. Exercise and hypertension. *Medicine and Science in Sports and Exercise*, 36: 533–553.

Petersen, AM and Pedersen, BK (2005) The anti-inflammatory effect of exercise. *Journal of Applied Physiology*, 98: 1154–1162.

Petitpas, AJ, Danish, SJ and Giges, B (1999) The sport psychologist-athlete relationship: Implications for training. *The Sport Psychologist*, 13: 344–357.

Pickett, TC, Lewis, RJ and Cash, TF (2005) Men, muscles, and body image: Comparisons of competitive bodybuilders, weight trainers, and athletically active controls. *British Journal of Sports Medicine*, 39: 217–222.

Plessner, H (1999) Expectation biases in gymnastics judging. *Journal of Sport and Exercise Psychology*, 21: 131–144.

Plessner, H and Betsch, T (2001) Sequential effects in important referee decisions: The case of penalties in soccer. *Journal of Sport and Exercise Psychology*, 23: 254–259.

Plotnikoff, RC, Mayhew, A, Birkett, N, Loucaides, CA and Fodor, G (2004) Age, gender, and urban–rural differences in the correlates of physical activity. *Preventive Medicine*, 39: 1115–1125.

Pope, HG, Gruber, AJ, Choi, P, Olivardia, R and Phillips, KA (1997) Muscle dysmorphia: An underrecognized form of body dysmorphic disorder. *Psychosomatics*, 38: 548–557.

Pope, HG Jr, Phillips, KA and Olivardia, R (2000) *The Adonis Complex: The secret crisis of male body obsession.* New York: Free Press.

Prichard, I and Tiggeman, M (2008) Relations among exercise type, self objectification, and body image in the fitness centre environment: The role of reasons for exercise. *Psychology of Sport and Exercise*, 9: 855–866.

Prochaska, JO and DiClemente, CC (1983) Stages and processes of self-change of smoking: Toward an integrative model of change. *Journal of Consulting and Clinical Psychology*, 51: 390–395.

Prochaska, JO and DiClemente, CC (1986) Toward a comprehensive model of change, in Miller, WR and Heather, N (eds) *Treating Addictive Behaviors: Processes of change*. New York: Plenum, pp. 3–27.

Prochaska, JO and Velicer, WF (1997) The transtheoretical model of health behavior change. *American Journal of Health Promotion*, 12: 38–48.

Prochaska, JO, Velicer, WF, Rossi, JS, Goldstein, MG, Marcus, BH, Rakowski, W *et al.* (1994) Stages of change and decisional balance for 12 problem behaviours. *Health Psychology*, 13: 39–46.

Raedeke, T (1997) Is athlete burnout more than just stress? A sport commitment perspective. *Journal of Sport and Exercise Psychology*, 19: 396–417.

Raedeke, TD and Smith, AL (2001) Development and preliminary validation of an athlete burnout measure. *Journal of Sport and Exercise Psychology*, 23: 281–306.

Raedeke, TD, Lunney, K and Venables, K (2002) Understanding athlete burnout: Coach perspectives. *Journal of Sport Behavior*, 25: 181–206.

Raedeke, TD, Focht, BC and Donna Scales, D (2008) Social environmental factors and psychological responses to acute exercise for socially physique anxious females. *Psychology of Sport and Exercise*, 8: 463–476.

Ram, N, Riggs, SM, Skaling, S, Landers, DM and McCullagh, P (2007) A comparison of modelling and imagery in the acquisition and retention of motor skills. *Journal of Sports Sciences*, 25: 587–597.

Rees, T and Freeman, P (2007) The effects of perceived and received support on self-confidence. *Journal of Sports Sciences*, 25: 1057–1065.

Reichenberg, A, Yirmiya, R, Schuld, A, Kraus, T, Haack, M, Morag, A *et al.* (2001) Cytokine-associated emotional and cognitive disturbances in humans. *Archives of General Psychology*, 58: 445–452.

Reis, HT, Sheldon, KM, Gable, SL, Roscoe, J and Ryan, RM (2000) Daily well-being: The role of autonomy, competence, and relatedness. *Personality and Social Psychology Bulletin*, 26: 419–435.

Rhodes, RE, Macdonald, HM and McKay, HA (2006) Predicting physical activity intention and behaviour among children in a longitudinal sample. *Social Science and Medicine*, 62: 3146–3156.

Robbins, LB, Pender, NJ and Kazanis, AS (2003) Barriers to physical activity perceived by adolescent girls. *Midwifery and Women's Health*, 48: 206–212.

Robbins, LB, Pis, MB, Pender, NJ and Kazanis, AS (2004) Exercise self-efficacy, enjoyment, and feeling states among adolescents. *Western Journal of Nursing Research*, 26: 699–715.

Robson, PJ (2003) Elucidating the unexplained underperformance syndrome in endurance athletes: The interleukin-6 hypothesis. *Sports Medicine*, 33: 771–781.

Rose, EA and Parfitt, G (2007) A quantitative analysis and qualitative explanation of the individual differences in affective responses to prescribed and self-selected exercise intensities. *Journal of Sport and Exercise Psychology*, 29: 281–309.

Rosenthal, R (1974) *On the Social Psychology of the Self-Fulfilling Prophecy: Further evidence for Pygmalion effects and their mediating mechanisms*. New York: MSS Modular Publishing.

Rosenthal, R and Jacobson, L (1968) *Pygmalion in the Classroom*. New York: Holt, Rinehart & Winston.

Rowe, DA, Benson, J and Baumgartner, TA (1999) Development of the Body Self-Image Questionnaire. *Measurement in Physical Education and Exercise Science*, 3: 223–248.

Russell, JA (1980) A circumplex model of affect. *Journal of Personality and Social Psychology*, 39: 1161–1178.

Ryan, RM and Deci, EL (2000) Intrinsic and extrinsic motivations: Classic definitions and new directions. *Contemporary Educational Psychology*, 25: 54–67.

Salmon, J, Owen, N, Crawford, D, Bauman, A and Sallis, JF (2003) Physical activity and sedentary behavior: A population-based study of barriers, enjoyment, and preference. *Health Psychology*, 22: 179–188.

Sanctuary, C, Smith, A and Thombs, B (2010) Towards a theory of the interactive factors implicated in successful individual performance in cricket. *International Journal of Sports Science and Coaching*, 5: 321–338.

Sarrazin, P, Boiché, J and Pelletier, LG (2007) A self-determination theory approach to drop-out in athletes, in Hagger, MS and Chatzisarantis, NLD (eds) *Intrinsic Motivation and Self-Determination in Exercise and Sport*. Champaign, IL: Human Kinetics, pp. 229–242.

Scheer, JK, Ansorge, CJ and Howard, HJ (1983) Judging bias induced by viewing contrived videotapes: A function of selected psychological variables. *Journal of Sport Psychology*, 5: 427–437.

Schmalz, DL, Deane, GD, Birch, LL and Krahnstoever Davison, K (2007) A longitudinal assessment of the links between physical activity and self-esteem in early adolescent non-Hispanic females. *Journal of Adolescent Health*, 41: 559–565.

Schmidt, AM and De Shon, RP (2009) Prior performance and goal progress as moderators of the relationship between self-efficacy and performance. *Human Performance*, 22: 191–203.

Schmidt, GW and Stein, GL (1991) A commitment model of burnout. *Journal of Applied Sport Psychology*, 8: 323–345.

Schneider, M, Dunton, GF and Cooper, DM (2008) Physical activity and physical self-concept among sedentary adolescent females: An intervention study. *Psychology of Sport and Exercise*, 9: 1–14.

Schneider, ML and Graham, DJ (2009) Personality, physical fitness, and affective response to exercise among adolescents. *Medicine and Science in Sports and Exercise*, 41: 947–955.

Schücker, L, Hagemann, N, Strauss, B and Völker, K (2009) The effect of attentional focus on running economy. *Journal of Sports Sciences*, 27: 1241–1248.

Secord, PF and Jourard, SM (1953) The appraisal of body-cathexis: Body cathexis and the self. *Journal of Consulting Psychology*, 17: 343–347.

Senécal, J, Loughead, TM and Bloom, A (2008) A season-long team-building intervention: Examining the effect of team goal setting on cohesion. *Journal of Sport and Exercise Psychology*, 30: 186–199.

Shambrook, CJ and Bull, SJ (1996). The use of a single-case research design to investigate the efficacy of imagery training. *Journal of Applied Sport Psychology*, 8: 27–43.

Shavelson, RJ, Hubner, JJ and Stanton, GC (1976) Validation of construct interpretations. *Review of Educational Research*, 46: 407–441.

Sheard, M, Golby, J and Van Wersch, A (2009) Progress towards construct validation of the Sports Mental Toughness Questionnaire (SMTQ). *European Journal of Psychological Assessment*, 25: 186–193.

Shilts, MK, Horowitz, M and Townsend, MS (2004) Goal setting as a strategy for dietary and physical activity behavior change: A review of the literature. *American Journal of Health Promotion*, 19: 81–83.

Short, SE, Monsma, EV and Short, M (2004) Is what you see really what you get? Athletes' perceptions of imagery's functions. *The Sport Psychologist*, 18: 341–349.

Silva, MN, Markland, D, Minderico, CS, Vieira, PN, Castro, MM, Coutinho, SR *et al.* (2008) A randomized controlled trial to evaluate self-determination theory for exercise adherence and weight control: Rationale and intervention description. *BMC Public Health*, 8: 234–247.

Sin, M, Sanderson, B, Weaver, M, Giger, J, Pemberton, J and Klapow, J (2004) Personal characteristics, health status, physical activity and quality of life in cardiac rehabilitation participants. *International Journal of Nursing Studies*, 41: 173–181.

Skinner, BF (1953) *Science and Human Behaviour*. New York: Macmillan.

Slentz, CA, Duscha, BD, Johnson, JL, Ketchum, K, Aiken, LB and Samsa, GP *et al.* (2004) Effects of the amount of exercise on body weight, body composition, and measures of central obesity: STRRIDE-a randomised controlled study. *Archives of Internal Medicine*, 164: 31–39.

Sluijs, EMF, McMinn, AM and Griffin, SJ (2007) Effectiveness of interventions to promote physical activity in children and adolescents: Systematic review of controlled trials. *British Medical Journal*, 335: 703–706.

Smith, D and Holmes, P (2004) The effect of imagery modality on golf putting performance. *Journal of Sport and Exercise Psychology*, 26: 385–395.

Smith, D, Wright, C, Allsopp, A and Westhead, H (2007) It's all in the mind: PETTLEP-based imagery and sports performance. *Journal of Applied Sport Psychology*, 19: 80–92.

Smith, RE (1986) Toward a cognitive-affective model of athletic burnout. *Journal of Sport Psychology*, 8: 36–50.

Sniehotta, FF, Scholz, U and Schwarzer, R (2005) Bridging the intention behaviour gap: Planning, self-efficacy, and action control in the adoption and maintenance of physical exercise. *Psychology and Health*, 20: 143–160.

Snyder, M, Tanke, ED and Berscheid, E (1977) Social perception and interpersonal behavior: On the self-fulfilling nature of social stereotypes. *Journal of Personality and Social Psychology*, 35: 656–666.

Solomon, GB (2001) Performance and personality impression cues as predictors of athletic performance: An extension of expectancy theory. *International Journal of Sport Psychology*, 32: 88–100.

Solomon, GB (2003) Solomon Expectancy Sources Scale. Unpublished paper. California State University, Sacramento, California.

Solomon, GB, DiMarco, AM, Ohlson, CJ and Reece, SD (1998) Expectations and coaching experience: Is more better? *Journal of Sport Behavior*, 21: 444–455.

Sparks, P, Shepherd, R, Wieringa, N and Zimmermans, N (1995) Perceived behavioural control, unrealistic optimism and dietary change: An exploratory study. *Appetite*, 24: 243–255.

Späth-Schwalbe, K, Hansen, K, Schmidt, F, Schrezenmeier, H, Marshall, L, Burger, K *et al.* (1998) Acute effects of recombinant interleukin-6 on endocrine and central nervous sleep functions in healthy men. *Journal of Clinical Endocrinology and Metabolism*, 83: 1573–1579.

Spence, JC, McGannon, KR and Poon, P (2005) The effect of exercise on global self-esteem: A quantitative review. *Journal of Sport and Exercise Psychology*, 27: 311–334.

Sport England (2009) Active people survey 3. Accessed 11 June 2010 from www.sportengland.org/research/active_people_survey/active_people_survey_3.aspx

Sporting Equals (2007) Briefing paper – ethnic minorities and physical activity. Birmingham: Sporting Equals.

Stafford, M, Cummins, S, Ellaway, A, Sacker, A, Wiggins, RD and Macintyre, S (2007) Pathways to obesity: Identifying local, modifiable determinants of physical activity and diet. *Social Science and Medicine*, 65: 1882–1897.

Standage, M, Duda, JL and Ntoumanis, N (2003) A model of contextual motivation in physical education: Using constructs from self-determination and achievement goal theories to predict physical activity intentions. *Journal of Educational Psychology*, 95: 97–110.

Steffen, K, Pensgaard, AM and Bahr, R (2009) Self-reported psychological characteristics as risk factors for injuries in female youth football. *Scandanavian Journal of Medicine and Science in Sports*, 19: 442–451.

Stice, E, Mazotti, L, Weibel, D and Agras, SW (2000) Dissonance prevention program decreases thin-ideal internalization, body dissatisfaction, dieting, negative affect, and bulimic symptoms: A preliminary experiment. *International Journal of Eating Disorders*, 27: 206–217.

Strachan, L, Côté, J and Deakin, J (2009) An evaluation of personal and contextual factors in competitive youth sport. *Journal of Applied Sport Psychology*, 21: 340–355.

Strauss, RS, Rodzilsky, D, Burack, G and Colin, M (2001) Psychosocial correlates of physical activity in healthy children. *Archives of Pediatrics and Adolescent Medicine*, 155: 897–902.

Strelan, P and Hargreaves, D (2005) Reasons for exercise and body esteem: Men's responses to self-objectification. *Sex Roles*, 53, 495–503.

Strelan, P, Mehaffey, SJ and Tiggemann, M (2003) Self-objectification and esteem in young women: The mediating role of reasons for exercise. *Sex Roles*, 48: 89–95.

Subramanian, U, Hopp, F, Mitchinson, A and Lowery, J (2008) Impact of provider self-management education, patient self-efficacy, and health status on patient adherence in heart failure in a veterans administration population. *Congestive Heart Failure*, 14: 6–11.

Sustrans (2008) Active travel in the workplace, case studies. Accessed online 23 February 2011 from www.sustrans.org.uk/assets/files/AT/Active%20Travel%20Cymru%20Toolkit/casestudies_ENG.pdf

Sutton, S (2000) Interpreting cross-sectional data on stages of change. *Psychology and Health*, 15: 163–171.

Svebak, S and Murgatroyd, S (1985) Metamotivational dominance: A multimethod validation of reversal theory constructs. *Journal of Personality and Social Psychology*, 48: 107–116.

Swain, A and Jones, G (1995) Effects of goal-setting interventions on selected basketball skills: A single-subject design. *Research Quarterly for Exercise and Sport*, 66: 51–63.

Taylor, AH (2000) Physical activity, anxiety, and stress, in Biddle, SJH, Fox, KR and Boutcher, SH (eds) *Physical Activity and Psychological Well-being*. London: Routledge, pp. 10–45.

Taylor, AH and Fox, KR (2005) Effectiveness of a primary care exercise referral intervention for changing physical self-perceptions over 9 months. *Health Psychology*, 24: 11–21.

Taylor, SE (1999) *Health Psychology*, 4th edition. Boston, MA: McGraw-Hill.

Tenenbaum, G (2001) A social-cognitive perspective of perceived exertion and exertion tolerance, in Singer, RN, Hausenblas, HA and Janelle, CM (eds) *Handbook of Sport Psychology*, 2nd edition. New York: John Wiley & Sons, pp. 810–820.

Tessier, S, Vuillemin, A, Bertrais, S, Boini, S, Le Bihan, E, Oppert, J *et al.* (2007) Association between leisure-time physical activity and health-related quality of life changes over time. *Preventive Medicine*, 44: 202–208.

Thelwell, R, Weston, N and Greenlees, I (2005) Defining and understanding mental toughness within soccer. *Journal of Applied Sport Psychology*, 17: 326–332.

Thelwell, RC, Greenlees, IA and Weston, NJV (2006) Using psychological skills training to develop soccer performance. *Journal of Applied Sport Psychology*, 18: 254–270.

Thelwell, RC, Such, BA, Weston, NJV, Such, JD and Greenlees, IA (2010a) Developing mental toughness: Perceptions of elite female gymnasts. *International Journal of Sport and Exercise Psychology*, 8: 170–188.

Thelwell, RC, Greenlees, IA and Weston, NJV (2010b) Examining the use of psychological skills throughout soccer performance. *Journal of Sport Behavior*, 33: 109–127.

Thøgersen-Ntoumani, C and Ntoumanis, N (2006) The role of self-determined motivation to the understanding of exercise-related behaviours, cognitions and physical self-evaluations. *Journal of Sports Sciences*, 24: 393–404.

Thøgersen-Ntoumani, C and Ntoumanis, N (2007) A self-determination theory approach to the study of body image concerns, self-presentation and self-perceptions in a sample of aerobic instructors. *Journal of Health Psychology*, 12: 301–315.

Thøgersen-Ntoumani, C, Fox, KR and Ntoumanis N (2005) Relationships between exercise and three components of mental well-being in corporate employees. *Psychology of Sport and Exercise,* 6: 609–627.

Thompson, MA, Vernacchia, RA and Moore, WE (1998) *Case Studies in Applied Sport Psychology*. Iowa: Kendal/Hunt.

Tiggeman, M and Williamson, S (2000) The effect of exercise on body satisfaction and self-esteem as a function of gender and age. *Sex Roles*, 43: 119–127.

Tilg, H, Dinarello, CA and Mier, JW (1997) IL-6 and APPs: Anti-inflammatory and immunosuppressive mediators. *Immunology Today*, 18, 428–432.

Tiryaki, MS (2005) Assessing whether black uniforms affect the decisions of Turkish soccer referees: Is the finding of Frank and Gilovich's study valid for Turkish culture? *Perceptual and Motor Skills*, 100: 51–57.

Torres, R and Fernandez, F (1995) Self-esteem and the value of health as determinants of adolescent health behaviour. *Journal of Adolescent Health Care*, 16: 60–63.

Trautwein, U, Gerlach, E and Lüdtke, O (2008) Athletic classmates, physical self-concept, and free-time physical activity: A longitudinal study of frame of reference effects. *Journal of Educational Psychology*, 100: 988–1001.

Trenholm, S and Jensen, A (1996) *Interpersonal Communication*, 3rd edition. Belmont, CA: Wadsworth Publishing Company.

Trost, SG, Owen, N, Bauman, A, Sallis, J and Brown, W (2002). Correlates of adults' participation in physical activity: Review and update. *Medicine and Science in Sports and Exercise*, 34: 1996–2001.

Tucker, P and Gilliland, J (2007) The effect of season and weather on physical activity: A systematic review. *Public Health*, 121: 909–922.

Vallerand, RJ (2000) Deci and Ryan's Self-Determination Theory: A view from the hierarchical model of intrinsic and extrinsic motivation. *Psychological Inquiry*, 11: 312–318.

Van Amelsvoort, LGPM, Spigt, MG, Swaen, GMH and Kant, I (2006) Leisure time physical activity and sickness absenteeism: A prospective study. *Occupational Medicine*, 56: 210–212.

Van der Bij, AK, Laurant, MG and Wensing, M (2002) Effectiveness of physical activity interventions for older adults: A review. *American Journal of Preventive Medicine*, 22: 120–133.

Van de Vliet, P, Knapen, J, Onghena, P, Fox, KR, David, A, Morres, I *et al.* (2002) Relationships between self-perceptions and negative affect in adult Flemish psychiatric in-patients suffering from mood disorders. *Psychology of Sport and Exercise*, 3: 309–322.

Van Quaquebeke, N and Giessner, SR (2010) How embodied cognitions affect judgements: Height-related attribution bias in football foul calls. *Journal of Sport and Exercise Psychology*, 32: 3–22.

Vargas-Tonsing, TM, Myers, ND and Feltz, DL (2004) Coaches' and athletes' perceptions of efficacy enhancing techniques. *The Sport Psychologist*, 18: 397–414.

Veale, D (1995) Does primary exercise dependence really exist? in Annett, J, Cripps, B and Steinberg, H (eds) *Proceedings of Warwick University workshop: Exercise addiction: Motivation for participation in sport and exercise*. Leicester: British Psychological Society, pp. 1–5.

Vealey, RS (1986) Conceptualization of sport-confidence and competitive orientation: Preliminary investigation and instrument development. *Journal of Sport Psychology*, 8: 221–246.

Vealey, RS (1988) Sport-confidence and competitive orientation: An addendum on scoring procedures and gender differences. *Journal of Sport and Exercise Psychology*, 10: 471–478.

Vealey, RS (2001) Understanding and enhancing self-confidence in athletes, in Singer, RN, Hausenblas, HA and Janelle, CM (eds) *Handbook of Sport Psychology*, 2nd edition. New York: John Wiley & Sons, Inc., pp. 550–565.

Vealey, RS, Hayashi, SW, Garner-Holman, M and Giacobbi, P (1998) Sources of sport-confidence: Conceptualisation and instrument development. *Journal of Sport and Exercise Psychology*, 20: 54–80.

von Guenthner, S, Hammermeister, J, Burton, D and Keller, L (2010) Smoke and mirrors or wave of the future? Evaluating a mental skills training program for elite cross country skiers. *Journal of Sport Behavior*, 33: 3–24.

Walker, NC, Thatcher, J, Lavallee, DE and Golby, J (2004) The emotional response to injury: Re-injury anxiety, in Lavallee, D, Thatcher, J and Jones, M (eds) *Coping and Emotion in Sport*. New York: Nova Science Publishers, pp. 87–99.

Walker, N, Thatcher, J and Lavallee, D (2007) Psychological responses to injury in competitive sport: A critical review. *Journal of the Royal Society for the Promotion of Health*, 127: 174–180.

Wallace, HM, Baumeister, RF and Vohs, KD (2005) Audience support and choking under pressure: A home disadvantage? *Journal of Sports Sciences*, 23: 429–438.

Wang, J and Ramsey, J (1997) Interpersonal communication-overcoming barriers and improving coach and athlete relationships. *Journal of the International Council for Health, Physical Education, Recreation, Sport, and Dance*, 34: 35–37.

Wankel, LM, Yardley, JK and Graham, J (1985) The effects of motivational interventions upon the exercise adherence of high and low self-motivated adults. *Canadian Journal of Applied Sport Science*, 10: 147–155.

Wanlin, CM, Hrycaiko, DW, Martin, GL and Mahon, M (1997) The effects of a goal setting package on the performance of speed skaters. *Journal of Applied Sport Psychology*, 9: 212–228.

Warr, PB and Knapper, C (1968) *The Perception of People and Events*. Chichester: Wiley.

Wegner, DM (1989) *White Bears and Other Unwanted Thoughts: Suppression, obsession, and the psychology of mental control*. New York: Viking/Penguin.

Weinberg, RS, Burke, KL and Jackson, A (1997) Coaches' and players' perceptions of goal setting in junior tennis: An exploratory investigation. *The Sport Psychologist*, 11: 426–439.

Weinberg, RS, Burton, D, Yukelson, D and Weigand, D (2000) Perceived goal setting practices of Olympic athletes: An exploratory investigation. *The Sport Psychologist*, 14: 279–295.

Weinberg, RS, Butt, J and Knight, J (2001a) High school coaches' perceptions of the process of goal setting: A qualitative investigation. *The Sport Psychologist*, 15: 20–47.

Weinberg, RS, Burton, D, Yukelson, D and Weigand, D (2001b) Perceived goal setting practices of Olympic athletes: An exploratory investigation. *The Sport Psychologist*, 14: 279–295.

Weinberg, RS, Butt, J, Knight, B, Burke, KL and Jackson, A (2003) The relationship between the use and effectiveness of imagery: An exploratory investigation. *Journal of Applied Sport Psychology*, 15: 26–40.

Weiss, WM and Weiss, MR (2003) Attraction- and entrapment-based commitment among competitive female gymnasts. *Journal of Sport and Exercise Psychology*, 25: 229–247.

Weiss, WM and Weiss, MR (2006) A longitudinal analysis of commitment among competitive female gymnasts. *Psychology of Sport and Exercise*, 7: 309–323.

Wells, CL (1999) Physical activity and cancer prevention. Focus on breast cancer. *ACSM's Health Fitness Journal*, 3: 13–18.

Welsh Assembly Government (2010) *Creating an Active Wales*. Cardiff: Welsh Assembly Government.

Wiese-Bjornstal, DM, Smith, AM, Shaffer, SM and Morrey, MA (1998) An integrated model of response to sport injury: Psychological and social dynamics. *Journal of Applied Sport Psychology*, 10: 46–69.

Wilcox, S, Castro, C, King, AC, Housemann, R and Brownson, RC (2000) Determinants of leisure time physical activity in rural compared with urban older and ethnically diverse women in the United States. *Journal of Epidemiology and Community Health*, 54: 667–672.

Williams, AM and Elliot, D (1999) Anxiety, expertise and visual search strategy in karate. *Journal of Sport and Exercise Psychology*, 21: 362–375.

Williams, DM, Anderson, ES and Winett, RA (2005) A review of the outcome expectancy construct in physical activity research. *Annals of Behavioural Medicine*, 29: 70–79.

Williams, DM, Lewis, BA, Dunsiger, S, Whiteley, JA, Papandonatos GD, Napolitano, MA *et al.* (2008) Comparing psychosocial predictors of physical activity adoption and maintenance. *Annals of Behavioural Medicine*, 36: 186–194.

Williams, JM and Andersen, MB (1998) A model of stress and athletic injury: Prediction and prevention. *Journal of Applied Sport Psychology*, 10: 5–25.

Williams, JM and Krane, V (1993) Psychological characteristics of peak performance, in Williams, JM (ed.) *Applied Sport Psychology*. Mountain View, CA: Mayfield, pp. 137–147.

Woodman, T and Hardy, L (2003) The relative impact of cognitive anxiety and self-confidence upon sport performance: A meta-analysis. *Journal of Sports Sciences*, 21: 443–457.

Wyer, SJ, Earll, L, Joseph, S and Harrison, J (2001) Deciding whether to attend a cardiac rehabilitation programme: An interpretative phenomenological analysis. *Coronary Health Care*, 5: 178–188.

Yager, Z and O'Dea, J (2009) Body image, dieting and disordered eating and activity practices among teacher trainees: Implications for school-based health education and obesity prevention programs. *Health Education Research*, 24: 472–482.

Index